PASSING
THE BATON

SPORT AND SOCIETY

Series Editors
Aram Goudsouzian
Jaime Schultz

Founding Editors
Benjamin G. Rader
Randy Roberts

A list of books in the series appears at the end of this book.

PASSING THE BATON

BLACK WOMEN TRACK STARS AND AMERICAN IDENTITY

CAT M. ARIAIL

UNIVERSITY OF ILLINOIS PRESS
Urbana, Chicago, and Springfield

Library of Congress Cataloging-in-Publication Data
Names: Ariail, Cat M., 1987– author.
Title: Passing the baton : black women track stars and
    American identity / Cat M. Ariail.
Other titles: Sprints of citizenship.
Description: Urbana : University of Illinois Press,
    [2020] | Series: Sport and society | Revision of
    author's thesis (doctoral)—University of Miami,
    2018, titled Sprints of citizenship : black women
    track stars and the making of modern citizenship
    in the United States and Jamaica, 1946–1964. |
    Includes bibliographical references and index.
Identifiers: LCCN 2020023704 (print) | LCCN
    2020023705 (ebook) | ISBN 9780252043482
    (hardcover) | ISBN 9780252085383 (paperback) |
    ISBN 9780252052361 (ebook)
Subjects: LCSH: African American women track and
    field athletes—History—20th century. | African
    American women track and field athletes—Social
    conditions. | African American women—Race
    identity. | African American women—Social
    conditions. | Track and field for women—United
    States—History—20th century. | Discrimination
    in sports—United States—History—20th century.
    | United States—Race relations—History—20th
    century.
Classification: LCC GV1060.6 .A82 2020 (print) | LCC
    GV1060.6 (ebook) | DDC 796.42082—dc23
LC record available at https://lccn.loc.gov/2020023704
LC ebook record available at https://lccn.loc.gov/
    2020023705

For Ace and Ed

CONTENTS

Acknowledgments   ix

Introduction   1

1   Raising the Bar: Alice Coachman and the Boundaries
    of Postwar American Identity, 1946–1948   12

2   Sprints of Citizenship: Identity Politics and
    Black Women's Athleticism, 1951–1952   46

3   Passing the Baton toward Belonging: Mae Faggs
    and the Making of the Americanness of Black
    American Track Women, 1954–1956   81

4   Winning as American Women: The Heteronormativity
    of Black Women Athletic Heroines, 1958–1960   115

5   "Olympian Quintessence": Wilma Rudolph, Athletic
    Femininity, and American Iconicity, 1960–1962   139

    Conclusion. The Precarity of the Baton Pass: Race, Gender,
    and the Enduring Barriers to American Belonging   165

    Notes   175

    Bibliography   209

    Index   223

ACKNOWLEDGMENTS

A relay race metaphor serves as an apt metaphor for a book project. Although one person breaks the tape to triumph, the result is the product of a collective effort. The list of those who deserve credit for this victory begins with Dr. Don Spivey. When I entered the PhD program at the University of Miami in the fall of 2013, there was no way that I could imagine how fortunate I would be to work under Dr. Spivey. He was the epitome of an excellent adviser, or coach, offering wise and insightful guidance yet always insisting that I make the final decisions.

This book project built on the paper produced in a two-semester research and writing seminar with Dr. Kate Ramsey. Kate then remained the kindest critic, asking conscientious, careful questions. Much appreciation also to Drs. Robin Bachin and Marvin Dawkins, who made time in their already too-busy schedules to also offer commentary on my research. And, of course, a huge shout out to Drew and Stephanie, our unconventional little cohort. I miss our powwows about writing, research, teaching, and our love-hate relationship with South Florida. From Miami, I was fortunate to find support for this project from the folks at the University of Illinois Press. Danny Nasset, as well as the Sport and Society series editors, Jaime Schultz and Aram Goudsouzian, have helped make the book writing process painless, even enjoyable. I am also grateful for the thoughtful commentary provided by my readers, especially the incredibly detailed suggestions and questions from Dr. Katherine Mooney.

ACKNOWLEDGMENTS

Finally, much love to those who, to continue the relay race metaphor, watched from the stands. Thanks to Carol, who intuitively provided the best form of sisterly support—a sense of humor. And, most of all, Eddy and Ace. The true origin of this project lies in y'all's willingness to encourage your sports-obsessed daughter to be just that—all about sports. Yes, somehow, allowing me to want to be a combination of Michael Jordan, Mia Hamm, Cynthia Cooper, and Allen Iverson resulted in a critical deconstruction of the identity of the American woman athlete. Eddy, thank you for never hesitating to have me tag along to Georgia football games, the golf course, or any and all other sporting events, before later driving around the Southeast to watch me play soccer. Ace, thanks for the unending, ever-optimistic support you provided by playing so many roles—my gardening assistant, card-playing partner, personal chef, fellow Hawks analyst, and, of course, Coach Mom.

PASSING
THE BATON

INTRODUCTION

In Palo Alto, California, in late July 1962, with the second largest crowd in the history of US track and field watching, Wilma Rudolph waited. The young woman who had captured the hearts of Americans by sprinting to three gold medals at the 1960 Olympic Games in Rome stood still, at least temporarily. Then, she readied herself to run.

To her side, Mariya Itkina and Galina Popova successfully exchanged their baton, seemingly situating the Soviet Union to win the women's 400-meter relay at the fifth annual dual track and field meet between the United States and Soviet Union, held in front of more than 153,000 at Stanford Stadium. Mere seconds later, Vivian Brown passed the baton to Rudolph. Rudolph took the stick. And then took off with a burst. She eliminated almost immediately the deficit and anchored another American victory. The relay win, scored in one of the most symbolically significant battles of the sporting Cold War, appeared to affirm Rudolph's exceptionality. As *Sports Illustrated* enthused, "But in action or repose, red or red-white-and-blue, black or white, male or female, no one in Palo Alto could match the incomparable Wilma Rudolph Ward for effortless grace and poise."[1]

Nonetheless, for all Rudolph's self-evident athletic excellence, it is necessary to critically consider how and why Rudolph could be so lauded as the exemplar of Americanness. How and why was this great and graceful young black woman considered an uncontested icon of the United States? And why was it Rudolph, in particular, who would attain this cultural status? How and

FIGURE 1. Wilma Rudolph and her Soviet competitor, Mariya Itkina, wait for start of the 400-meter relay at the 1962 US-USSR dual track and field meet at Stanford Stadium in Palo Alto, California.
Courtesy of Stanford University Libraries, Stanford athletics photograph collection, 1929–1973

why could she appear to overcome long-entrenched ideologies of race, gender, and sexuality to represent ideal Americanness?

BLACK AMERICAN TRACK WOMEN AND THE BOUNDARIES OF BELONGING

The 1962 relay victory not only serves as an apt window into the rise of Wilma Rudolph but also introduces how black American women track stars index the boundaries of belonging. On the track in Stanford Stadium, it may have appeared that the singular sprinting superiority of Rudolph secured the American victory. Yet the steady efforts of Willye White, Edith McGuire, and Vivian Brown situated Rudolph to claim the comeback win.

Similarly, a lineage of overlooked and underappreciated black American women track stars paved the way for Rudolph's celebrated iconization. Beginning when Alice Coachman became the first black women to win an Olympic gold medal with her victory in the high jump at the 1948 Olympic Games in London, black women track stars have repeatedly asserted themselves as American athletes and, in turn, raised questions about the raced and gendered boundaries of American belonging. Throughout the 1950s, a small, select group of young black women, highlighted by Jean Patton, Catherine Hardy, Mae Faggs, Barbara Jones, and Mildred McDaniel, achieved successes in international track and field competitions, thereby requiring that mainstream and black American sports cultures recognize, and reckon with, black women's athleticism. The influence of their achievements would be augmented by their image, as the culture of black women's track and field demanded that young black women athletes always and expertly adhere to conventional, conservative gender norms, presenting themselves as appropriate and unimpeachable young women. Nonetheless, the reckonings that black women track stars increasingly inspired did not result in their uncontested acceptance as athletes, American athletes, or Americans. Because of the intersection of ideologies of race, gender, and sexuality, their status never was secure. The path to the recognition of Wilma Rudolph's "grace and poise" thus remained ever uncertain.

BLACK WOMEN'S ATHLETICISM AND THE PRECARITY AND POSSIBILITY OF AMERICANNESS

Uncertainty also is characteristic of the sport of track and field, especially a relay race. A relay requires precision and perfection. A runner must run with great speed but also with careful composure. She must strategically calibrate her pace in order to precisely pass the baton to her teammate. The next runner must quickly but conscientiously grab the baton, safely securing it before unleashing her speed. During the 1962 US–Soviet Union women's 400-meter relay, the foursome of young black women did this. White, McGuire, and Brown exactly executed, allowing Rudolph to prevail.

The year prior, things did not go as planned. The women's 400-meter relay at the 1961 US–Soviet Union dual in Moscow was contested tightly as the teams entered the critical, final stretch. With Rudolph slated to run the anchor leg, the Americans could feel rather confident. Yet, this sense of assurance soon would evaporate. Vivian Brown and Rudolph fumbled their handoff. As the baton tumbled to the track, the Soviet Union's Tatyana Shchelkanova took a commanding lead. Temporarily stunned by the mistake, Rudolph slowly picked up the stick before she began fully to appreciate her seemingly impossible situation. Nonetheless, she began to chase down her competition. After steadily closing the gap through fifty yards, she then found another gear. In a dominating display of her special speed, Rudolph caught and cleared her Soviet opponent, scoring a new world record as she broke the tape.[2] The dropped baton appeared to doom the American squad in 1961, only for the moment of tragedy to become one of triumph. Precarity became possibility.

Rudolph appeared to possess a preternatural ability to turn precarity into possibility. The twentieth of twenty-two children in a poor, rural black family in Clarksville, Tennessee, Rudolph suffered from polio and other illnesses as a child. Although she would not run until age twelve, she would make her first Olympic team at fifteen in 1956. Four years later, after giving birth to a daughter and struggling to balance motherhood with her athletic and academic obligations at Tennessee State University (TSU), she would ascend to the apex of international sport, winning three gold medals on the track in Rome. But while Rudolph was exceptional, she was not unique. Creating possibility from precarity defined the experience and influence of the black American women track stars of the postwar period. In her analysis of the writings of black women intellectuals, race and gender studies scholar Brittney Cooper insists on "a commitment to seeing the Black female body as a form of possibility not a burden," understanding their "intersecting identities—primarily of race and gender, but also of class and nation—as a point of possibility."[3] This perspective must also apply to black American track women, as their experiences negotiating their intersecting identities in spaces of sport can critically illuminate the "point[s] of possibility" and progress that have been fulfilled, as well as have remained unfulfilled, in the postwar United States.

Buoyed by victory in World War II, the United States aimed to establish itself as an undisputed superpower and exemplar of democracy. However, the realities of the emergent civil rights movement often did not cohere with the increasingly pressing priorities of the Cold War, complicating the United States' democratic claims. The symbolism of sport allowed the nation to attempt to address its contradictions, codifying and communicating an idealized American citizenry. Sport also allowed black America to insert the African American experience into the definition of Americanness, with the successes of black male athletes in incrementally integrating sports seen as signaling black Americans' fitness for citizenship.[4] Black American track women, however, disrupted these imagined paradigms.

Due to the cultural prerogatives of Cold War America, few young white women competed in the sport of track and field. While the supposedly masculine connotations of the sport always had made it understood as less than appropriate, the need for social stability during the uncertainty of the 1950s required a stricter adherence to traditional gender expectations. As such, white women who participated in a "masculinizing" sport were seen has having forsworn the privileges of white womanhood.[5] White women's abandonment of the sport opened a space for black women. Yet, black women were not simply beneficiaries of white women's absence. They claimed the sport. Because black America possessed an alternative understanding of womanhood, more willing to recognize the compatibility between femininity and activity, young black women faced less community opprobrium for their competitive inclinations. Nevertheless, their athletic pursuits rarely found enthusiastic approval, especially since the performance of normative white gender roles was central to the black middle class's quest for citizenship. Black male athletes were celebrated while black women athletes were tolerated.[6] Women's track and field thus was consigned to the farthest margins of American sport culture, bound to irrelevancy due to ideologies and realities of race and gender—except that black women track athletes would make themselves relevant.

Although they almost daily encountered discriminations of race, gender, sex, and class, these young black women consistently chose to compete in a much-maligned sport. And as they competed they improved. And as they improved they succeeded. Since track and field was featured in the Olympic Games and other international competitions, young black track women had the opportunity to represent the United States. At such events, they were not simply present; rather, they had presence, both on and off the track. They not only performed athletically on the track, challenging expectations of who could be an elite athlete, but they also performed identity off the track, carefully negotiating expectations about race, gender, and sexuality to present themselves as uncontroversial young American women.

Yet, although ostensibly uncontroversial, their comportment in fact was quite controversial. Conditions of time and place made them so. As appropriately feminine young black women participating in elite track and field, they not only defied often-negative assumptions about women athletes and black women, but they also complicated the respective postwar visions of ideal-ized Americanness held by mainstream and black American cultures. They problematized the priorities of Cold War American culture, which, despite declarations of democracy, privileged heteronormative whiteness as most indicative of Americanness. The athletic agency of these young black women also did not accord with the masculine prerogatives of the movement for civil rights, which imagined men as most proving the Americanness of black Americans. In exercising their bodies on the stages of international sport, all while wearing the uniform of the United States, black American women track stars exercised ideological impact. They demonstrated the capacities of black-ness and femaleness to sporting, social, and political cultures often resistant to both. Their achievements thus altered ideas about the relationship between sport, race, gender, and nation.

As an indication of the impact of these young black women athletes, the institutions of white and black American sport interpreted and reinterpreted their successes, seeking to reconcile the meaning of black women's athleticism with their idealized visions for postwar America. The efforts of young black women athletes were ignored, accommodated, criticized, or celebrated accord-ing to the perceived demands of the historical moment. While the priorities of the Cold War and the pressures of the civil rights movement influenced their access to opportunity and acclaim, black American women track stars also influenced understandings of American identity during the time of Cold War and civil rights. The ideological machinations they inspired serve as evidence of their influence. Their efforts repeatedly begged the question: when, where, and how should, or could, blackness and femaleness represent Americanness?

Wilma Rudolph, ostensibly, provided the answer to this question. Yet, the praise she would receive for her apparent Americanness was the product of a process. Her predecessors passed her the baton. Through individual efforts, they made collective impact, consistently pressing against the boundaries of American belonging so that, eventually, a young black woman athlete could be celebrated for belonging to America. Of course, although Rudolph represented the nation's possibilities, she rarely lived them. She struggled to make a secure life for herself, encountering barriers and biases of race and gender. Ideological impact did not alter material realities, thus raising questions about the real power of black American women track stars. Rudolph, however, was not sim-ply a pawn, offering a falsely satisfying image of a "democratic" America. It is important to recognize and emphasize that the institutions of American sport, society, and state did not seek black women athletes as symbols. By converting precarity into possibility, black American women stars forced themselves to be considered symbols of American possibility. They actively inserted themselves into the meaning of American identity in the postwar United States.

THE ATHLETIC AGENCY OF BLACK AMERICAN TRACK WOMEN

In her study of black women's political power in North Carolina at the turn of the twentieth century, Glenda Gilmore undertakes a "revisioning" of southern politics, centering the actions of black women in order to offer an alternative historical narrative of the Jim Crow South.[7] This book likewise encourages a "revisioning," emphasizing the agentic influence of black American women athletes. Brittney Cooper, in her aforementioned study, further argues that scholarship has "not yet engaged with the content of what Black women intellectuals actually *said*, even as we celebrate all the they *did*."[8] The scholarship on black women track and field athletes can be described similarly. Although their achievements have been recognized and analyzed, the actions and decisions that produced their achievements have not been appreciated. The agency of black American women track stars deserves to be taken seriously. While the combination of their racial and gender identities seemingly consigned them to a life of precarity, both in American sport and American society, they nonetheless created possibilities for themselves and, in doing so, articulated alternative possibilities for American identity, proving blackness and femaleness to be constitutive to Americanness. They thus contributed to the conversation about the content and extent of American identity that characterized the postwar United States. As the propagandistic priorities of the Cold War collided with the aspirations of the civil rights movement to unsettle the imagined foundation American identity, young black women who competed for the United States in track and field authored their own representation of Americanness. As they passed the baton—or cleared the bar or broke the tape—they pressed against the boundaries of American belonging. From precarity, they created possibility and, in turn, power.

This story of precarity, possibility, and power primarily was written at the Olympic Games and other major, international sport events. In incremental, chronological spurts, black women track stars progressively, albeit often unevenly, proved that they and, in turn, people that looked and lived like them, were American. This process began with Alice Coachman. Chapter 1 chronicles the international athletic experiences of Coachman, the first black woman to win an Olympic gold medal, examining how her successes, especially at the 1948 Olympic Games in London, challenged the image of ideal American athleticism and, in turn, ideal American identity. The relative invisibility of Coachman in the mainstream sporting press indicates that black women's athleticism raised uncomfortable questions about race, gender, and American belonging. The interracial homecoming held in her hometown of Albany, Georgia, and a visit to the Oval Office further expose the ways in which Coachman's gold medal required white America to rethink the racial and gendered boundaries of Americanness. Black sport culture, in contrast, lauded Coachman. Yet, when doing so, they always presented her as figure of black womanhood, highlighting how black Americans aimed to attain cultural belonging through careful commitment to conventional gender roles. That Coachman remained invisible to dominant, white-defined culture, in spite of her apparently appropriate gendering, underscores the racialization of gender, as her blackness overwhelmed her femaleness, thereby denying her Americanness.

Chapter 2 examines how the performances of black American track women at the 1951 Pan-American Games in Buenos Aires and 1952 Olympic Games in Helsinki made it impossible for the institutions of mainstream American sport to articulate an uncontested, universal American identity. With the escalation of the Cold War, the United States Olympic Committee (USOC) and Amateur Athletic Union (AAU) became more committed to using American male athletes, both white and black, to advertise the superiority of American democracy. Black women track stars, however, disrupted this project, doubly raising anxieties for the institutions of American sport because they inserted both blackness and femaleness into the image of Americanness. As bearers of the double burden of race and gender, they pressed too far the preferred boundaries of American identity. Highlighted by the accomplishments of Jean Patton at the Pan-American Games and the effort of Catherine Hardy at the Olympic Games, black American track women contested the dominant vision of Americanness for international observers and domestic audiences, both white and black. In doing so, they also demonstrated that sport, despite its conservative, traditional connotations, served as a rare cultural space in which black American women could display their capacity and autonomy.

Chapter 3 analyzes how the colliding demands of the Cold War and civil rights movement began to endow black women track athletes with propagandistic purpose, as the interpretations of them at the 1955 Pan-American

INTRODUCTION

Games in Mexico City and 1956 Olympic Games in Melbourne demonstrate. By highlighting the extreme incompleteness of American racial equality, the direct-action nonviolent civil rights movement placed more pressure on the United States to prove its democratic bona fides. The intensification of the Cold War, including the Soviet Union's increasing criticisms of American racial discrimination, required that the United States better perform democracy. The sporting Cold War presented a possible solution, with black women athletes enlisted as evidence of the nation's progress toward racial equality. For mainstream, white-controlled American culture, the double burden of blackness and femaleness, which previously had placed black women track stars outside the boundaries of idealized American identity, now made them powerful symbols of the promise of American democracy. This attitudinal shift also is a testament to the subtle effectiveness of these young women athletes' repeated performances of gendered respectability, as their careful gender calculus had altered understandings. In turn, black American sport culture more enthusiastically embraced them as race women, active contributors to the effort for black rights. Yet, this changed cultural standing would not have been possible without the achievements and abilities of the athletes themselves, especially Mae Faggs. As a three-time member of the US Women's Olympic Track and Field Team and captain of the TSU Tigerbelles, Faggs modeled an independent yet cooperative brand of black women's athleticism, demonstrating the often-overlooked agency that young black women athletes both possessed and expressed.

Chapter 4 explores how black women track stars emerged as exemplars of American identity, particularly after their performance at the inaugural US–Soviet Union dual track and field meet in Moscow in 1958. However, it was not their athletic ability but their almost perfect adherence to normative, white-defined gender expectations that allowed black American track women to assume this symbolic status. Because they always embodied conventional gender norms, black American track women, especially the sprinters and jumpers of TSU, protected, rather than contested, the traditional racial and gender order of American society. No longer a threat to normative boundaries of American belonging, they were constitutive to a conservative vision of America. The emergence of Wilma Rudolph as the leading black women's athletic star ahead of the 1960 Olympic Games further highlights the central role of heteronormativity in determining the boundaries of belonging in modern America. Rudolph, with her normative femininity, exemplified and

9

advertised a conservative, assimilationist, and thus comfortable vision of American equality. ·

Chapter 5 further deconstructs the cultural and social meanings ascribed to Wilma Rudolph, following the 1960 Olympic Games in Rome and continuing through the 1961 and 1962 US–Soviet Union dual track and field meets in Moscow and Palo Alto. As a black woman widely admired for her athletic greatness and feminine gracefulness, Rudolph offered a new image of American women's athleticism and black American womanhood. She seemed to transcend the traditional barriers to national belonging. However, while the popular image of Rudolph advertised a more inclusive American identity, understandings of her in fact inscribed a disciplinary, exclusive model of Americanness. The interpretations imposed on her by mainstream and black American sport cultures illustrate that even as black women track stars challenged ideas about sport, race, gender, and nation, they did not change these ideas in ways that reduced their relevance. Rather, sport culture marshaled these ideologies to contain the more radical possibilities represented by black women's athleticism and preserve a more conservative model of American belonging.

The conclusion considers the implications of Wilma Rudolph's iconicity. By introducing the possibility of a feminine American woman athlete, Rudolph opened a space for white women to earn acclamation as athletes. Yet, at the same time, she established an almost impossible standard for the acceptance and acclamation of black American women athletes. Black American women athletes not only need to perform normative, white-defined Americanness perfectly but also need to satisfy sociopolitical priorities. As bearers of the double burden, black American women athletes only enter the popular consciousness when needed to meet the particular political and social demands of the historical moment, inspiringly expressing the promises of their nation. Black American women athletes must bolster, not threaten, the racialized and gendered foundations of America's believed democracy. As such, Wyomia Tyus, a heroine at the 1964 Olympic Games in Tokyo and 1968 Games in Mexico, received little attention. However, her invisibility, as much as Rudolph's visibility, suggests much about the relationship between race, gender, and national identity, confirming that black American women athletes offer a penetrating perspective of the construction and reconstruction of the boundaries of national belonging.

From the late 1940s through early 1960s, young black women consistently competed in track and field, increasingly dominating the sport at the national and international levels. While they oftentimes remained relegated to the margins of the sporting world, at certain, unexpected moments they made their presence known. And their presence had power. Often, "troubling" power. They embodied cultural studies scholar Nicole Fleetwood's conception of a "troubling vision." Fleetwood asserts, "Blackness troubles vision in western discourse. And the troubling effect of blackness becomes heightened when located on certain bodies marked as such."[9] Because black American women track stars embodied the exclusions that defined idealized American identity, their presence in the center of sport repeatedly raised provocative questions about race, gender, and American identity. Yet, their power ultimately would be contained. In both mainstream and black American cultures, ideologies would be reorganized to make black American track women safer representations of an Americanness that reinforced, rather than reconceived, what it meant to be an American. Black American women challenged but did not change the raced and gendered boundaries of American belonging. Nonetheless, their experiences, as well as those of prominent black women athletes who have competed in track and field and other sports since the 1960s, critically expose the incompleteness of Americanness, indexing how American belonging has been imagined and reimagined in ways that render the Americanness of those marked by race, gender, and other minority identities seemingly accessible but ever-unfulfilled.

1

RAISING THE BAR

ALICE COACHMAN AND THE BOUNDARIES
OF POSTWAR AMERICAN IDENTITY, 1946–1948

Alice Coachman grabbed the baton, safely securing it as she began to sprint. She soon caught and cleared her competitor, breaking the tape in record time. For Coachman, the effort was rather unremarkable. Since the early 1940s, she had proved herself the top US women's track talent, succeeding in the sprints, relay, and especially the high jump, her specialty. Recently, Stella Walsh, the Polish American sprinting sensation, even had deemed Coachman "the toughest opponent I've ever met."[1] However, the setting of her accomplishment made her anchor-leg relay run rather remarkable. It was the summer of 1946, and Coachman was competing in Canada, representing the United States in a dual track and field meet in Molson Stadium at McGill University in Montreal. The record that Coachman secured was a Canadian national record. And she set it with a trio of white American track women, Kay Geary, Eleanor Millheiser, and Nancy Cowperthwaite.[2] Coachman also was the only black woman athlete competing for either team. Her participation in the event marked the first time a black woman had represented the United States abroad since the 1936 Olympic Games. Her presence and performance, therefore, raised questions about the identity of an American athlete, and in turn, the identity of an American.

That same summer another black American athlete made his mark in Montreal, presenting similar questions about American identity. Throughout the summer of 1946, Jackie Robinson played for the Montreal Royals, the prelude to his historic reintegration of Major League Baseball the following season. When Robinson took the field as the second baseman for the Brooklyn Dodgers, the so-called national pastime appeared to enact the progress imagined for the nation, modeling the making of the more equal, more democratic America promised by the Allied victory in World War II. He was an embodied extension of the Double V campaign, thus occupying a central place in narratives of sport and national identity.[3]

Yet, the carefully managed desegregation process experienced by Robinson does not adequately capture the dynamic remaking of national belonging that unfolded in the postwar United States.[4] Expectations and assumptions of race, gender, and sex were changing and colliding, destabilizing the definition of normative Americanness.[5] As a longtime racially integrated sport that featured athletes of both sexes, track and field brought to the fore the politics of identity. At competitions, especially the Olympic Games and other international events, the nation's track stars problematized the traditional associations of American athleticism and, in turn, American identity. Marked by race and gender, black American women who competed for the United States embodied and epitomized such destabilization and problemization.

Because of the organizational character of track and field, as a national and international sport that featured black and white athletes of both genders, the experiences of Alice Coachman, rather than those of Jackie Robinson, better illuminate the complicated meanings of Americanness. From competitions in Canada to the Olympic Games in London to the streets of her hometown of Albany, Georgia, Coachman's presence raised questions about American identity. The efforts and achievements of Coachman and her fellow young black track women not only contested the designs and desires of the official institutions of American sport, namely the AAU and USOC, that sought to contain the significance of black American track women, but they also complicated the preferences and priorities of black American sport culture, which privileged black American male athletes as exemplars of black citizenship.

But Coachman and her compatriots would not be contained; they introduced and inaugurated how black American women track stars would contest and complicate conceptions of Americanness throughout the postwar period. The experiences and interpretations of Coachman before, during, and after the 1948 London Games offer an insightful window into the negotiation and renegotiation of the boundaries of national belonging. She made vivid America's enduring dilemmas. She was the first young black woman to pick up and then pass the baton.

THE ATHLETIC ARRIVAL OF ALICE COACHMAN

Yet, rather than passing the baton, Coachman would be best known for clearing the bar. Although she participated in any and all sports as a young girl growing up on the outskirts of Albany, Georgia, she fell in love with track and field. Especially jumping. Despite the protestations of her pious mother and patriarchal father, who both believed athletic activity inappropriate for young women, Coachman created competitive opportunities for herself. She frequently fashioned a high jump bar in her backyard, tying together sticks with rags so she repeatedly could jump, barefoot, over the homemade obstacle, resulting in the unique high jumping style she would use throughout her career. She also frequently challenged neighborhood boys to jumping contests, almost always exceeding their best efforts. When she reached Albany's Madison High School, she joined the girls' track team and, finally, had the opportunity to test her talents in formal competition.

In 1939, the Madison track squad traveled to the Tuskegee Relays, where Coachman unleashed a 5 foot, 4 inch leap that not only helped Madison win the meet's junior title but also broke the meet's record for both the junior and senior divisions. Coachman's performance attracted the interest of Tuskegee Institute's athletic director, Cleveland Abbott, who soon traveled to Albany to recruit Coachman, convincing her parents to permit her to compete for the Tigerettes' junior squad. After Coachman won the National AAU Junior Championships in the high jump in the summers of 1939 and 1940, Abbott then encouraged her to transfer to Tuskegee's high school.[6] Attending high school at Tuskegee not only allowed her to improve her athletic ability, but training year-round with the Tigerettes also inculcated her into the tradition of black women's athleticism established by Abbott. Foremost, the Tuskegee athletic director required Tigerettes to abide by the expectations of appearance imposed on most black middle-class women. Describing the strict beauty standards of the black middle class, sociologist Maxine Craig argues, "The body, bodily practices, and representations of the body became sites for the construction of community and thus place specific demands on women, whose bodies are generally more subject to symbolic usage and public scrutiny."[7] She further explains, "A woman who put time and money into her appearance was dignified, and her dignity spoke well of the race. Grooming was a weapon in the battle to defeat racist depictions."[8] "A well-behaved, attractive, young black lady with neat pressed hair was an asset to her race," she summarizes.[9]

Tuskegee Tigerettes were far from exempt from these representational obligations; in fact, participation in athletics placed additional pressure on their public identity. To ensure that Tuskegee's young women athletes contributed to the school's mission of demonstrating the character and capacity of black Americans in a way that appealed to and assured white America, Abbott, in the words of historian Martha Verbrugge, "created a nuanced model of femininity, athleticism, and black identity." As Verbrugge explicates, "Laying claim to femininity, the Institute granted black girls a measure of respectability usually reserved for white Americans. Tuskegee's ideal diverged from white middle-class norms, though, by affirming physical challenges and vigor as womanly and expanding students' opportunities during and after their time at school." Through lessons in manners and attention to appearance, Tuskegee's young track women became "refined" and "polished" "bronze Dianas," refuting any assumptions about the uncouthness of black women athletes.[10] This image of black athletic womanhood would enhance the power of Alice Coachman's presence when she later entered the center of international sport as a representative of the United States. The coalescence of her careful performance of femininity and her demonstration of athletic excellence would complicate conventional expectations of race and gender, raising provocative questions about American identity.[11]

In 1943, the same year she graduated from Tuskegee's high school and enrolled in the Institute, Coachman earned three spots on the AAU All-American women's track team, testifying to her elite ability in the high jump and sprints. If not for the cancellation of the 1944 Olympic Games due to World War II, Coachman likely would have been preparing to make her international athletic debut and test her talents against Europe's top women athletes. Instead, she continued to compete domestically, sparking a rivalry with one of the best European-born women athletes, the Polish sprint star Stella Walsh. A resident of Cleveland, Walsh competed for Poland in the 1932 and 1936 Olympic Games, capturing the 100-meter gold in Los Angeles in world record time but finishing second to American Helen Stephens in Berlin. Although the combination of her evident ability and nonfeminine appearance resulted in the continued questioning of her womanhood, Walsh was undeterred. Remaining in the

United States after the 1936 Games, she continued to compete in, and dominate, AAU meets.[12] At the 1944 National AAU Championships in Harrisburg, Pennsylvania, Coachman would battle Walsh for national athletic supremacy.

They faced off in the 100-meter dash, with Walsh winning by a mere foot. Nonetheless, Coachman nearly stole the individual national championship crown, tallying twenty-eight points to Walsh's thirty. As put by *Afro-American* sportswriter Sam Lacy, "Miss Walsh, odds-on favorite to cop the individual title, was forced to her greatest single day of triumphs in order to nose out the brilliant Miss Coachman."[13] As mentioned, Walsh offered profuse praise for Coachman, naming her "the toughest opponent I have ever met." She explained, "That isn't the hardest question I've had to answer for newspaper men during my career, though my answer may not be what is expected. I think Alice Coachman is the finest runner I've ever raced against." Walsh continued, "I also know that it was quite fortunate for me that I was at my peak whenever I faced Alice. Everything considered, I think she is the toughest opponent I've ever met."[14]

Although they likely did not reach an audience outside the small world of women's sport, Walsh's words are significant in multiple ways. First, they reflect the unquestioned interracialism of the sport. Although all teams remained segregated, black and white young women frequently and peaceably competed against each other. While men's track and field included integrated teams and competitions, racial difference remained determinative. Male athletic champions, especially in an international sport such as track and field, were understood as representatives of idealized American masculinity.[15] Thus, the racial identity of male track stars was significant, leading to tensions based on racial differences. Women's track and field, in contrast, held no such symbolic significance. The supposedly masculine connotations of the sport had always made it understood as less than appropriate for young white women.[16] In a postwar United States seeking social stability, the emphasis on the strict adherence to conventional gender expectations was intensified.[17] White women who competed in track and field seemingly forswore the privileges of white womanhood. Black and white track women thus together competed, cooperatively and copacetically, on the margins of American sport culture, seemingly irrelevant and summarily ignored.

However, the rumored revival of the Olympic Games potentially could change this calculus. The Olympic Games would provide women an opportunity to move from the margins to the center, or near the center, of national and international sport. Based on the words of Stella Walsh, it thus was imaginable that Alice Coachman could be more than just a young black woman track star; she could be an American athlete. Recognizing Coachman soon could earn wider acclaim, Sam Lacy took care to present her in a certain way. Writing in the *Afro-American*, a leading tribune of the black American middle class, he insisted, "These dames are all right, and this Coachman is a real patootie. She's got everything," before further asserting, "No, she's definitely effeminate. Coachman's got charm, personality, and dimples, and she cuts a nice figure—running, walking, or standing."[18] Lacy emphasized that Coachman was an exemplar of black womanhood. He worked to reassure any black middle-class readers who remained skeptical of women's athletic pursuits, especially due to fears of the supposedly masculinizing effects of competitive sport. This understanding of Coachman would prevail throughout the American sporting press. Her appropriate, heterosexual black womanhood, as much as her excellent athletic ability, would define her and, in turn, define American women's athleticism. Nonetheless, this confluence of blackness, femaleness, feminineness, and Americanness was not uncontroversial. Black and mainstream American sport cultures would wrestle with the meanings of black women's athleticism, seeking to control what Coachman, as well as the other young black women who soon would compete for the United States, communicated about race, gender, and American identity.

The contested participation of black women at the previous two Olympiads introduces the severe discomfort their status as prospective American athletes caused. Ahead of the 1932 Games in Los Angeles, Tidye Pickett and Louise Stokes, respective products of the public recreation programs in Chicago and Malden, Massachusetts, became the first black women to qualify for the US Women's Olympic Track and Field team, with both slated to run in the 400-meter relay. However, the presence of the two black women appeared to make their white teammates and coaches uncomfortable. The explicit and subtle racism they encountered throughout their Olympic experience culminated with two white athletes replacing them in the relay at the last minute. Despite this humiliation, the two again attempted to represent their nation at the 1936 Games in Berlin. While Pickett did compete in the 80-meter hurdles, Stokes, who qualified as a member of the 400-meter relay squad, was, once again, replaced by a white athlete.[19] The discrimination experienced by Stokes and Pickett highlights the ingrained uncertainty raised by black women track athletes, an uncertainty more acute than that inspired by much-maligned white women athletes who competed in the "mannish" sport of track. Because their racial and gender identities diverged from that of the imagined ideal American athlete, which was a white heterosexual man, black women athletes were cast ostensibly illegitimate American athletic representatives.

However, the 1948 Olympic Games, which the International Olympic Committee (IOC) announced would be held in London, represented a potential moment of change. In the wake of World War II, declarations of democracy emanated from institutions of American politics, society, and culture, including sport. For instance, the AAU situated itself alongside other organizations, such as the United Nations, that used the language of democracy to assert authority in the postwar world. Former AAU and current USOC president Avery Brundage, a documented racist and sexist, even offered idealistic rhetoric about sport, especially track and field, effusing, "It is a most democratic and characteristically American sport where each athlete depends solely on his ability and wealth or politics or creed or color does not count."[20] Although Brundage rather blithely ignored enduring inequities of race, class, and gender (inequities that he and the leading organizations of American sport often perpetuated and, in turn, implicitly approved of), the language of democracy did impose demands, especially since the United States envisioned itself as the rightful and righteous leader of the postwar world. Because this world included populations captivated by promises of democratization and decolonization, the nation's sport culture needed to perform, or at least better perform, inclusivity.[21]

Alice Coachman would test the nation's democratic self-definition. Her ability outpaced that of her black predecessors, as well as her white contemporaries, making her right to represent the US Women's Olympic Track and Field team undeniable. Her evident talent, in combination with her appropriate comportment, positioned her to insert black American track women into the image of American athletic identity.

ALICE COACHMAN AND THE REARTICULATION OF AMERICAN IDENTITY

At the aforementioned US-Canada track and field dual in Montreal in the summer of 1946, Coachman first expanded the boundaries of American belonging, becoming the first black woman to represent the nation in an international athletic competition in a decade. Although a seemingly insignificant event in the spectrum of American sport history, the attitudes and actions of black and mainstream American sport culture indicate its importance. Black American sport culture appreciated Coachman's opportunity. "One of the classiest fields to line up for a track meet here in several seasons, will be on deck at Molson Stadium," anticipated the *Afro-American*, celebrating Coachman as the "only non-white member" on "a smart entry of women track stars."[22] The paper also noted her expected off-track experiences, reporting, "A special Pullman car will be attached to the Montreal train leaving New York City Thursday, August 1. Friday, August 2, will be devoted to sight-seeing. The meet will take place Saturday afternoon, August 3, and will be followed by a banquet."[23] This attention to travel, tourism, and other events reveals a recognition of sport's more than symbolic significance; it also conferred material power, providing access to opportunities often restricted for black Americans, especially black American women.

Nonetheless, it was Coachman's mere presence that carried greater ramifications. The composition of the US women's team indicates as much. AAU secretary-treasurer Daniel J. Ferris, in consultation with Catherine Meyer, chairwoman of the AAU's national women's track and field committee, selected the team.[24] While standards for selection were not disclosed, recent performances at national meets suggest other young black women deserved also to make the squad. For example, at the 1946 National AAU Indoor Championship in Cleveland in late March, Lillian Young, a competitor for the Chicago Bureau of Recreation, finished ahead of Eleanor Millheiser in the 50-yard dash. Yet, the white Millheiser was selected for the team, while Young was not. Several of Coachman's Tuskegee teammates also seemed to have been snubbed. Despite finishing second to Stella Walsh in the 220-yard race, Juanita Watson would not receive an invitation. Neither would Lillie Purifoy, even though she claimed the 50-yard hurdles title over Nancy Cowperthwaite, who was named to the team. Young and Purifoy also were members of the 1945 AAU All-American team. Of the white women selected, only Cowperthwaite had earned All-American honors.[25] Moreover, at the 1946 National AAU Outdoor Championships, which were held in Buffalo, New York, the weekend after the dual meet in Montreal, Tuskegee captured their tenth national title, a further confirmation of the talent of black track women and an indication that, if sending the most talented cohort of American track women to Canada had been the goal, the United States team should have included additional Tigerettes.[26] Announcements for the members of the men's squad noted the recent titles scored by the named athletes, suggesting performance most determined their selections.[27]

Yet for track women, other considerations appeared to assume priority. The composition of the women's team was strategic, an effort to communicate a certain, contained image of American identity. As discussed, ideologies of gender caused uncertainty about women athletically representing the nation. Black women heightened this uncertainty. Both their gender and race countered the identity of the ideal white American male athlete. However, in the postwar climate where the nation proudly preached the promises of democracy, black women athletes could not be so explicitly excluded. The participation of only Coachman was an effort to navigate this conundrum. Coachman, as the lone black female representative and the meet's most outstanding woman athlete, could be understood as exceptional, a uniquely talented young black woman. Her rather petite stature and careful feminine comportment also made her an "appropriate" example of black American women's athleticism. Nonetheless, Coachman still complicated the assumptions of gender, race, and Americanness that officials of American sport attempted to contain through her singular selection. In easily winning the high jump, she attracted the attention of the American track world. While other athletes executed a "western roll" or "scissors" jump, Coachman combined the two styles, resulting in her appearing to effortlessly sail over the high jump bar. The *New York Times's* leading track writer, Joseph Sheehan, took note, sharing significant praise for her. He compared Coachman to Elmore Harris, the black American male star who also captured three victories: "By taking the high jump as well as the century, Miss Coachman, a student at Tuskegee Institute, excelled in her field on a level comparable to Harris."[28]

Sheehan's comparison introduces the symbolic power of men and women athletes, black and white, competing in the same space. Such circumstances had the potential to destabilize traditional associations and arrangements of race, gender, and athleticism. First, sex integration heightened gender distinction, presumably proving the femininity of women athletes. Yet, men athletes also legitimated women athletes as athletes. Just like their male counterparts, women athletes applied techniques and strategies in order to achieve victory. The conditions of the meet, therefore, simultaneously validated women athletes as both feminine women and able athletes, two designations that society resisted granting young women, especially young women of color, who participated in sport. Coachman, by wearing the jersey of the United States as she easily won three titles, showed the ideological power inherent in black women representing the nation athletically. Her presence and performance exposed the fallacies of gender and race that organized American identity. Despite the seeming insignificance of the small international meet in Montreal, the influence of her imagery is evident in the increased anxiety and uncertainty with which mainstream and black American sport cultures would approach and interpret black women's athleticism. Coachman raised the bar in Canada, requiring American sport culture to adjust.

ALICE COACHMAN AND THE UNCERTAINTIES OF BLACK AMERICAN WOMEN'S ATHLETICISM

Although the black sports press expressed enthusiasm about Alice Coachman, such enthusiasm did not obviate a sense of uncertainty about black women's athleticism. As noted, young black track women were expected to demonstrate the normative womanhood of black women more broadly. But nothing more. The black sport community did not desire to envision young black women athletes as agents in the quest for black citizenship.

For instance, the 1947 National AAU Outdoor Championship was slated for San Antonio, Texas. The previous year, San Antonio served as the site for men's title meet, a decision that rallied the racial pride of the black American track community. Since 1910, the AAU held National Track and Field Championships in nonsegregated cities in the North and Midwest. The unjustified and unexplained return to the segregated South inspired Joe Yancey, coach of the interracial Harlem-based track club, the New York Pioneers, to threaten to lead a boycott. Yancey's call initiated an active conversation among the leaders of black American sport. While some interpreted the decision as a direct insult to the manhood of black track stars, insisting that they boycott, others opposed a boycott, as the absence of black contenders guaranteed only white champions. This vigorous debate raged until late June of 1946 when AAU secretary-treasurer Daniel Ferris arranged for a separate, interracial train car to transport black track stars to San Antonio, protecting these men from the ignominies of segregated travel in order to encourage their participation.[29] Yancey, as a matter of principle, still prohibited his Pioneers, both black and white, from participating.[30]

However, the AAU awarding the segregated city of San Antonio the women's national championship did not inspire the ire of the black sport community. The prospect of black women athletes bearing the burdens of Jim Crow sport was not understood as a problem worth protesting. The realities of women's track, where not only were the majority of teams were segregated but the majority of black teams also were located in the segregated South, best explain why the meet location did not emerge as an issue. Black women's track programs regularly accommodated the realities of segregation, developing the necessary strategies to ensure safe travel and housing. Burdened by racism and sexism, black women athletes also did not possess the leverage needed to demand racial equality. But as revealed by the men's boycott threat, the leading voices of black American sport culture did have such power. Seemingly, insisting upon integrated transportation and accommodation for all black women competitors could have contributed to the broader effort against segregation. Yet no campaign emerged.

The fight for racial rights in sport, as in other spheres of society, was gendered. Black citizenship and black masculinity were understood as coterminous, a belief strengthened by World War II, where returning black servicemen motivated the emerging movement for civil rights.[31] While black male athletes unquestionably stood as race men whose athletic opportunities and achievements complemented wider efforts for equality, black women athletes were not considered race women whose performances punctured white supremacy, in San Antonio or other southern spaces. They were understood only as examples of black womanhood. In short, the male leaders of black American sport, while willing to praise the feminine performance of Alice Coachman, resisted recognizing the possibilities for progress presented by the wider population of aspiring black women athletes.

Nonetheless, black women's athletic autonomy clearly was on display in San Antonio. The 1947 title meet featured the most competitors ever to participate, with 165 women athletes striving for championships in the midsummer heat of southwestern Texas. But neither the increased number of challengers nor the extreme heat was enough to deter Alice Coachman. Having graduated from Tuskegee, she now represented Albany State College, where she was pursuing a graduate degree in physical education, as a one-woman team, successfully defending her 50-meter dash and high jump crowns.[32] The meet's most exciting event, however, was an unexpected duel between the stalwart Stella Walsh and the emergent Audrey Patterson, who preferred to be called by her nickname, "Mickey." The lone representative for Texas's Wiley College, Patterson gave Walsh quite the scare in the 200 meters. According to the *Atlanta Daily World*, "Miss Walsh, away like a bullet, led Miss Patterson most of the way, but, 20 yards from the finish, Lady Patterson pulled abreast, and the two ran stride for stride until almost to the tape, when Walsh 'kicked' away to win by 30 inches."[33] In spite her advanced age and injury struggles, Walsh still served as a barometer of elite women's track ability. By threatening Walsh, Patterson, a native of New Orleans, established herself as a future contender, while also indicating the undiscovered depth of black women's athletic talent.

However, soon after the meet an article in the *New York Times* bemoaned, "Officials of the Amateur Athletic Union were gloomy today over prospects of the United States winning the women's track and field championship of the 1948 Olympic games." The paper then quoted AAU secretary-treasurer Ferris, who reported, "There has been a big fall-off in interest in women's track. We do not have enough big, rugged girls to expect to win the Olympics. The other countries have them."[34] These comments indicate an unease with the meanings and implications of women's athleticism. For, while Ferris correctly recognized that the performances of American track women did not approach those of the best European track women, his contention about "a big fall-off in interest" ignores the fact that the 1947 title meet included the most contestants in the event's history. Along with denying this reality, Ferris's statements also failed to recognize the role of the AAU in producing ostensibly inadequate women's track talent. The white male officials of the AAU largely ignored the pleadings of the AAU women's track and field committee, refusing to provide the material support needed to host the number of meets required to develop a deeper well of women's track talent. Instead, his suggestion that the United States lacked "big rugged girls" proffered a stereotypical image of unfeminine and mannish women athletes, thus perpetuating false perceptions about the sport's masculinizing effects in order to justify the underinvestment.

But most of all, his statement also evinces an enduring inability to accept black women athletes as American athletes. Ferris notably did not mention that Alice Coachman achieved heights in the high jump that met Olympic standards.[35] His silence intimates at the central role of racial difference in making the white male-controlled institutions of American sport resistant to women's athleticism. Ferris frequently demonstrated an insensitivity to racial discrimination in the world of men's track. Such racialist thinking intersected with sexist sentiments to skew Ferris's and his fellow officials' views of women's track and field.[36] Dolores Boeckman, former chairwoman of the US women's Olympic committee, echoed the estimations of Ferris, suggesting that "this country would probably be beaten by the women athletes of China and India, and also those of Europe." She noted that the nation's "best strength would come from the Tuskegee (Negro) college girls," lamenting that "American girls from California, the Northwest and the Southwest were not represented at our national championships." She insisted, "It's high time for Miss America to wake up to her deplorable weakness in track and field pastimes."[37] Boeckman's statement reveals a believed distinction between (presumably white) "American girls from California, the Northwest, and the Southwest" and young black women. While the athletic talent of black women was recognized, they were not understood as potential "Miss Americas" of sport. Nonetheless, American women's athleticism increasingly was black American women's athleticism. In reaction, Ferris preemptively predicted the inadequacy of US track women, seeking to script their shortcomings in order to avoid reckoning with the ideological implications of their abilities.

The second edition of the US-Canada dual track meet, held again in Montreal in the late summer of 1947, further confirms the uncomfortability caused by black women athletes. Despite other deserving talents, especially the promising Mickey Patterson, Alice Coachman would be the only young black woman athlete named to the team. The composition of the squad again resulted in an image of American women's athletes that misrepresented the reality of the sport.[38] Albeit a bit contradictorily, these attitudes and actions reveal the influence of black women track athletes. Young black women had claimed the sport of women's track and field and, by doing so, situated themselves to assert their blackness, femaleness, and Americanness on more significant sporting stages. They were, in fact, "Miss Americas." They were ready to make real the declarations of democracy that the institutions of American sport readily proclaimed but often failed to practice. And, in doing so, they also threatened to trouble the gendered ideology of middle-class black America. Thus, making this democracy real would be difficult.

THE IMAGINED AND REAL ANXIETIES ABOUT AMERICAN WOMEN'S ATHLETICISM

"Women athletes who aspire to places on the U.S. Olympic women's track and field team must run faster and jump and throw farther than in 1947, to make the squad," advertised a USOC press release.[39] Such standards for selecting Olympians should be expected and, thus, uncontroversial. Except that the USOC only imposed these demands on women's track and field. According to Catherine Meyer, chairwoman of the women's track and field committee, who also would serve as the women's track and field team manager in London, "It was not anticipated that women's track and field would be the only sport to adhere strictly to the rule regarding minimum standards." Yet, Meyer determined that this was the case, noting of athletes in other sports, "It is questionable whether they would have qualified had standards been set."[40] In context with the commentary following the 1947 National AAU Championship, the standards appear not as an effort to guarantee the quality of the women's track team but as a covert way to limit the quantity of women's track athletes "eligible" to go to London. It was a policy designed to fulfill the dire prediction of Daniel Ferris, where lack defined women's track.

Meyer further suggested that fundraising capacity, rather than athletic ability, dictated the number of athletes to be sent to London for most sports. Meyer criticized the USOC's lack of consistency, asking, "Are we to have representation only in the 'monied' sports, are we to select a team only of athletes who meet standards of performance, or are we to be represented in all sports?"[41] Yet, such an inconsistent policy proved suitably malleable for the white male officials who controlled the USOC, permitting them to privilege certain sports while burdening others. As the least favored of sports, women's track and field faced qualification standards in addition to funding demands. Although the USOC would reallocate funds raised by the men's track and field and men's basketball committees to finance the women's track and field team's travel to London, it is important to recognize that they imposed the funding requirements with the knowledge that women's track and field likely could not raise the requisite amount. "Fund raising for women's track and field has been a problem since its inception on the Olympic program and will continued to be so until greater interest is shown by more AAU associations and more women are encouraged to participate," asserted Meyer.[42] Her statement indicated that the inability of women's track to raise money was the product of the longstanding lack of investment in the sport by the AAU and USOC. The funding demands exploited and perpetuated these inequalities. They also communicated the believed illegitimacy of the women's track team, subtly signaling that track women were not considered full members of the US Olympic Team.

It also is worth considering further the role of race in inspiring this USOC-sanctioned effort to limit, or even eliminate, women's track representation in London. The sexism and racism of the authoritative USOC president Avery Brundage, in concert with the USOC's history of discrimination against black

women track athletes, justifies such a presumption. Through the funding demands and qualification standards inequitably imposed on women's track and
field, Brundage and his ilk aimed to prevent blackness and femaleness representing Americanness. Red tape was designed to do ideological work, evading the
demands of democracy that mainstream American sport, at least rhetorically,
advocated. Nonetheless, the USOC's policies did not discourage approximately
sixty young women, black and white, from striving to claim an Olympic team
berth at the tryouts held at Brown University in July 1948. Expectedly, Alice
Coachman exceeded the high jump standard, establishing a new American record
of 5 feet, 4¾ inches.[43] Past her prime speed, she did not attempt to qualify in the
sprint races. However, a collection of black women sprinters showed themselves
ready to join Coachman on the voyage to London. Mabel Walker, of Tuskegee,
punched her ticket with a 12.3-second 100-meter effort, with Mickey Patterson,
who had transferred from Wiley College to TSU, chasing her across the line to
finish second in the standard-meeting time of 12.4 seconds.[44] Patterson also
qualified in the 200 meters, capturing the race in 25.3 seconds, well under the
26-second qualifying standard. Nell Jackson, also of Tuskegee, finished second
to Patterson in the 200 meters, likewise bettering the qualifying mark. Mae
Faggs, a sixteen-year-old sprinter from Bayside, New York, who had developed
her skills running for the Police Athletic League (PAL), also met the 200-meter
standard. Emma Reed, a student at TSU, claimed a spot in the long jump.[45]

Despite this array of elite-level performances from black women athletes,
accompanied by several strong performances from white women athletes in
the field events, the narrative emerging from the trials inaccurately affirmed
Ferris's prediction. The *New York Times* reported that "the performances in
some of the other final tryouts were so disappointing that Mrs. Catherine
Donovan Meyer and her Olympic women's track and field committee had to go
into a three-hour session before they could select the make-up of the team."[46]
This contention over-dramatized the process. Several athletes almost met the
arbitrary qualifying standards, suggesting their selection should not have
required much deliberation. Eventually, the women's track and field committee named twelve young women, nine black and three white, to the Olympic
team. So, for all the USOC's machinations, athletic merit ultimately trumped
any ideological prejudice, as a squad of majority black young women would
define American women's athleticism in London.

Their accomplishments inspired an alternative narrative in the black sporting press, which celebrated their combination of athletic ability and girlish

appeal. A correspondent for the Associated Negro Press (ANP) deemed Patterson the favored "pet" of the crowd, a designation that recognized her exciting athleticism, albeit in a rather infantilizing manner. The ANP report noted that "the popular Miss drew a round of applause from the spectators each time she passed the stands." Mabel Walker received recognition for her display of drive and desire during her 100-meter win. "So overcome with happiness at her win, she broke down and cried right in the middle of the track."[47] Her emotion assumedly affirmed her appropriate gender identity. But black American sport culture resisted fully recognizing the athletic autonomy of black women athletes. In particular, the black sporting press promoted young black track women's use of peanut oil. According to Russ Cowans, sports correspondent for the National Negro Press Association. "One of the by-products developed by Dr. [George Washington] Carver from the peanut is an oil which has been used extensively as a rubbing liniment by athletes, particularly those attending Tuskegee Institute. That the girls had benefitted from the oil can be attested by the success they've had as individuals and as a team in National AAU competition. The gals have been unbeatable." Harry Hainsworth, equipment manager of the US Olympic Team, told Cowans, "Miss Coachman and the girls from Tuskegee have talked so much about the benefits they've derived from the oil that all the girls want to use it."[48] Whether the athletes themselves used the oil to massage their muscles or merely moisturize their skin, attention to the believed athletic benefits of the peanut oil detracted from the athletic ability of the young women, instead crediting their successes to something invented by a black man. Publicizing the young black women's apparent obsession with the peanut oil also worked to underscore their feminineness, tapping into the believed association between women, cosmetic products, and consumption. Rather than trained athletes, they were young women who enjoyed indulging in oils, creams, and other beauty remedies.[49] The believed dependency of the quartet of Tuskegee Olympians on the peanut oil thus preserved the preferred gender order of black America.

As an additional example of the emphasized gendering of black track Olympians, the *Chicago Defender* published a photo of the entire women's track and field squad on board the *S.S. America* as they prepared to sail to London. The twelve women wore stylish dresses, skirts, and blouses, with their hair expertly coiffed, presenting the womanliness of women athletes, both black and white.[50] Black American sport culture chose to present black American track women in ways that complemented their highly gendered perspective of black citizenship. Upon arriving in London, the nine young black American track women—Alice Coachman, Mickey Patterson, Nell Jackson, Mabel Walker, Theresa Manuel, Bernice Robinson, Emma Reed, Lillian Young, and Mae Faggs—would introduce this image to the international athletic world. The Olympic stage, however, also would allow black women athletes to complicate the limited identities imposed on them.

THE POMP, CIRCUMSTANCE, AND IDENTITY POLITICS OF INTERNATIONAL SPORT

Coachman and the eight other black American women track athletes embodied what the proponents of the Olympic Movement conveniently elided when they proclaimed that amateur sport, in the words of Avery Brundage, provided opportunity "without regard for race, creed, or color."[51] For differences of race, creed, and color could not be disregarded. Race, color, creed, and, of course, gender were essential not only for determining who was and could be an athlete, but also who was and could be a citizen in the postwar world. Their presence proved that the Olympic Games were a political project. On the most prominent stage of sport, Coachman, in particular, required white and black American sport cultures to rethink the relationship between race, gender, athleticism, autonomy, and national identity. She made impossible an easy, uncontested, and noncontradictory image of Americanness.

The USOC, however, attempted to offer such a vision of ideal, universal Americanness in the opening ceremony parade, held on July 29, 1948, in Wembley Stadium. The nearly 350 parading American athletes were to advertise the "American Way." In her analysis of the propagandistic promotions produced by the United States Information Association (USIA) in the postwar period, historian Laura Belmonte describes the ways in which US information officials struggled to define national identity, seeking to sell "the United States as a nation that valued, freedom, tolerance, and individuality."[52] Nevertheless, varied representations of "an American" all were founded on normative, middle-class whiteness. This also was the image of American identity presented in the opening ceremony parade. The USOC carefully outfitted its athletes, styling athletic bodies to communicate a preferred image of the national body. For women athletes, the supplies and equipment committee "wanted to provide the women members of the party with clothing that would be of style and quality that would present a good appearance and be useful after the Games in

London," outfitting them in a combination that included a "gray flannel skirt, white tropical worsted skirt, nylon stockings, white blouse and blue plastic shoulder bag."[53] As the USOC further described in their official report, "The US colors were worn by an even dozen women ranging from a high school teen-ager to two housewives."[54] The imagined, post-Olympic utility of the outfits, appropriate for either wholesome housewives or studious secretaries, signaled that young women's participation in sport was temporary. The practical yet feminine outfits also guarded against any accusations of mannishness. American women athletes appeared to offer a respectable and relatable image of the nation.

Yet, the USOC could not communicate Americanness through its women athletes so easily. Black women athletes complicated the ideal image of the American Way. Although their blackness obviously disrupted the believed whiteness of Americanness, black women athletes wore parading uniforms that implicitly granted them the imprimatur of dominant, white-defined gender norms. Styling black women athletes as appropriately feminine young women was a progressive, even radical, move, one that complemented the priorities of black American sport culture. Ceremoniously circling the track in front of the international sporting audience, the young black women who composed the majority of the American women's track and field team enacted and experienced their inclusion in the American sporting nation, regardless of the ideological priorities of American sport, state, and society. The parade thus introduces how, in ways subtle but significant, the Olympic experiences of Coachman and her black teammates would press against the preferred boundaries of American belonging.

However, through much of the women's Olympic track and field competition, the Netherlands' Fanny Blankers-Koen defined women's athleticism for the international sporting world. Tall, slim, and blonde, the thirty-year-old Blankers-Koen embodied appropriate Western white European women's athleticism. A mother of two, she earned the moniker the "Flying Dutch Housewife," a nickname that did not simply emphasize the compatibility of her wifehood and motherhood with her athletic womanhood but also positioned her wifehood and motherhood as constitutive to her athletic womanhood. Her seemingly self-evident femininity allowed her to compete in four Olympic events, an aggressive and ambitious athletic program that exceeded that of most male Olympians. The presses from across the Western sporting world thus anticipated witnessing Blankers-Koen display her amenable athleticism.[55]

For example, the *New Yorker's* Mollie Panter-Downes shared his fascination with Blankers-Koen, enthusing, "Mrs. Fanny Blankers-Koen, a veteran of thirty, looks magnificent on the track," while also suggesting that Holland "seems to be turning out a formidable breed of long-legged blond women athletes with a stride like that of a dromedary heading home to supper."[56] In short, Blankers-Koen was white women's athleticism made safe. She made it possible for mainstream American sport culture to imagine a laudable woman athlete, one who resembled and therefore reinforced the image of an ideal American womanhood defined by wifehood and motherhood.[57] Blankers-Koen's performances proved just as admirable as her image. She won the 100 meters in an Olympic record time, then took the gold in the 80-meter hurdles, and next triumphed in the 200-meter sprint. She finished her four-gold feat by anchoring the Netherlands to a win in the 400-meter relay.[58]

Yet, for all of Blankers-Koen's dominance, the image of women's athleticism that she offered was not uncontested. When black women from the United States, as well as Jamaica, lined up to race against her, they made black women's athleticism visible, disrupting the more comfortable image of white athletic womanhood. Mickey Patterson most successfully showed the capacity of blackness and femaleness. After winning her 200-meter qualifying heat, she finished a close second to Blankers-Koen in the semi-final round, good enough to advance to the final. In the final, Patterson faced off against Blankers-Koen and four other white Western women.[59] Patterson thus was hyper-visible. Although the majority of the spectators in Wembley Stadium likely focused their attention on Blankers-Koen, as she was seeking a historic third gold, they also could not help but see Patterson. Considering the pre-Olympic rhetoric about the inadequacy of American track women, the combination of Patterson's racial and national identities made her presence surprising and significant.

When the starting gun fired, Blankers-Koen blazed out of the starting blocks, taking a clear lead by the 50-meter mark to secure her third gold medal in dominating fashion. Just as her triumph "touch[ed] off quite so much excitement" among the thousands assembled in Wembley, Patterson stole a surprising third place from Australia's Shirley Strickland, finishing just one-tenth of a second behind silver medalist Audrey Williamson of Great Britain.[60] With her extra effort, Patterson became the first black woman to win an Olympic medal. However, the mainstream American sporting press refused to recognize, or possibly failed to realize, the historic nature of Patterson's achievement. Considering the sexism and racism of sport and society in the United States, this circumstance was not necessarily surprising, but as a spirit of national pride percolated throughout the Olympic fortnight, the almost total absence of any celebration of Patterson's medal, historic or not, was somewhat curious. For instance, the *Times*'s Allison Danzig, who had expressed no shortage of enthusiasm in accounting the triumphs of both white and black American track men, only briefly remarked on Patterson's bronze, noting that she "surprised in taking third place for the United States, which has had little chance to cheer in women's track and field."[61] Rather than praising Patterson, Danzig's commentary relied on and perpetuated the preexisting belief in the inadequacy of American track women. The *Times* also published a picture of Blankers-Koen, the ostensible embodiment of appropriately feminine athleticism, winning the 200-meter title, with the caption not even mentioning Patterson.[62]

These editorial choices expose the role of racial identity in inspiring mainstream American resistance to women's athleticism. The athletic achievements of women could expose the constructedness of gender ideologies, disproving the supposed superiority of masculinity. However, attention to the womanhood of white women Olympians, such as Blankers-Koen, guarded against such understandings, reasserting traditional gender arrangements. Yet, black women athletes problematized this paradigm. Because of the believed incompatibility between blackness and femininity, exhibitions of black women's athleticism could not be contained by celebrations of their feminineness. Black women athletes demonstrated the capacity of blackness and femaleness and, therefore, doubly defied the white heteropatriarchal privilege that organized politics, society, and culture in the United States. The prospect of black women's athleticism representing the nation thus was a threatening one for mainstream American sport culture. So, the dominant institutions of US sport simply ignored Patterson, making her as invisible as possible in order to quiet the anxieties activated by her success. Blankers-Koen instead was promoted, with her whiteness and feminineness allowing her to be inaugurated as an almost honorary American.

Nonetheless, Patterson would mount the medal rostrum, standing alongside Blankers-Koen and Williamson. Like her fellow white medalists, Patterson smartly arranged her hair and smiled appropriately, presenting an amenable image of black womanhood alongside white femininity. This scene spoke to the power of sport's unscriptedness. Patterson not only identified the United

States with black athletic womanhood, but she also inserted black women into the Western world's definition of feminine athleticism, regardless of the preferences of the officials of American sport and state. In the *Afro-American*, Olympic correspondent Ollie Stewart praised Blankers-Koen and the other white women who secured track medals, suggesting that the "blonde mother of two children" and "these European women are real stars, no doubt about it."[63] Emphasizing both the femininity and ability of white women implied that the black women against whom they competed also possessed these traits. While Patterson threatened white America's vision of sport and citizenship, she fulfilled the imaginings of black America, showing the womanhood of black women.

THE CONTESTED AMERICANNESS AND ATHLETICISM OF ALICE COACHMAN

Alice Coachman would even better express the gendered aspirations of black America, while also further activating the anxieties of race and gender for white America. Although it was the final event on the final day of the Olympic track and field program, the women's high jump competition still inspired a significant degree of interest. The mostly British partisans who filled the seats in Wembley had their eyes on Dorothy Tyler, the last hope for the host country to win a track and field gold medal. The combination of the dreary London weather and the impending threat of darkness created a dramatic setting for Tyler's potential triumph.[64] Yet, the competition itself provided the most drama. A roster of talented women athletes continually matched each other's leaps, including five black women. Along with Coachman, Emma Reed and Bernice Robinson represented the United States, while Carmen Phipps and Vinton Beckett jumped for Jamaica. In addition to this notable number of black women competitors, Coachman's jumping style made black women's athleticism visible. Her unique style, a product of her practicing barefoot on the dirt roads of Albany, Georgia, scripted her history, a physical articulation of the exclusion she, as well as other black women athletes, navigated in order to achieve success. Her unconventionality not only caused thousands of white, primarily European sport fans to notice black women's athleticism but also resulted in them bearing witness to the ingenuity that produced black women's athletic excellence.

Coachman's style also intrigued Tyler and her other competitors, encouraging them to attempt to imitate it. Recognizing this, Coachman executed a sly strategy, moving the starting point of her approach slightly back in order to throw off her competitors. While she made the necessary adjustment to still clear the bar, the altered approach path produced a miss from Tyler.[65] Tyler recovered to clear the bar on her second attempt, but this initial miss would prove consequential. The tactic illuminates Coachman's creativity, as well as her competitiveness, which she often hid below her modest mien. She later recalled, "I didn't want to let my country down, or my family and school. Everyone was pushing me, but they knew how stubborn and mean I was, so it was only so far they could push me."[66]

As the competition approached the three-hour mark, six women remained in contention. With the evening sky darkening and other events having concluded, the more than 60,000 fans still in Wembley intently observed the infield, where two black and four white women athletes engaged in an extended battle. After the elimination of Great Britain's Bertha Crowther, Canada's Doreen Dredge and Jamaica's Vinton Beckett proved unable to match the height attained by France's Micheline Ostermeyer, Tyler, and Coachman. Then, Ostermeyer bowed out, leaving a final, dramatic duel between Tyler and Coachman. British journalist Edwin Roth described the scene:

> Perhaps the tensest moments of all came during the final athletics event of the games, the personal high-jumping battle between America's small, black, sinewy Alice Coachman, highly-strung like a thoroughbred racehorse, and Britain's tall, fair-haired Dorothy Tyler. It was Britain's last chance to get an individual athletic gold medal, and there was so much electricity in the air you could almost feel the shock.[67]

Roth's racialist descriptions convey how the many thousands of Britons in Wembley read the athletes. Coachman was seen as distinct and different from the "fair-haired" Tyler. For white observers, her blackness made her appear animalistic, far beyond the bounds of femininity. But, nonetheless, she was also described as an American, underscoring that she was understood as a representative of the United States. The pair both cleared the bar at 5 feet, 5¼ inches and then 5 feet, 6⅛ inches, a new Olympic record. But 5 feet, 7 inches proved too much, as neither athlete cleanly cleared the bar on their two attempts. These misses, however, gave Coachman the gold. Because she had totaled fewer misses, partially due to the subtly clever strategy she executed earlier in the competition, she earned first place honors. And a place in history—the first black woman athlete to win an Olympic gold medal.

High Jump
Saut en hauteur

1st A. Coachman   U. S. A.
1.68 m. (5 ft. 6 1/2 in.)
Olympic record

FIGURE 2. Alice Coachman glides over the high jump bar on her way to her historic gold medal at the 1948 Olympic Games.

Despite denying the British their hoped-for gold, Coachman received a rousing ovation from the tens of thousands of fans. On the field, Tyler embraced Coachman, kindly congratulating her conqueror. Their hug communicated her acceptance in the international community of women athletes. The enthusiastic response of the Wembley crowd likewise signaled her status as an undisputed international athletic champion. Because Coachman and Tyler technically tied, since Coachman never actually jumped higher than Tyler, her victory could have been contested, rationalized, or even delegitimized. But it was not. The electric emotionalism of the event made Coachman recognized as a citizen of the sporting world. Photos in the European sport press testify to the impression Coachman made on Olympic observers, showing throngs of white fans seeking an autograph from the gold medalist.[68] Coachman herself was moved by her victory, viewing it as a validation of her Americanness. "I saw it on the board 'A. Coachman, U.S.A., Number One,'" she remembered many years later. "I went on, stood up there, and they started playing the national anthem. It was wonderful to hear."[69] In receiving her gold medal from King George VI, Coachman demonstrated that blackness and femaleness were constitutive of Americanness. Her gold medal radically refuted preferred presumptions about the identity of American athleticism, as well as American identity more broadly.

Nonetheless, the racial and gender ideologies that Coachman contested through her victory limited the appreciation of her historic accomplishment in mainstream American sport culture. Her status as an athletic representative of the nation troubled white America. Because the British and European fans who embraced Coachman were removed from the American racial context, they could celebrate her as an athletic heroine without reservation. In contrast, the American reaction to her would have ramifications for the raced and gendered associations of American identity.[70] So, rather than reckoning with Coachman as an American athlete, the white sporting press rendered her a footnote. In the *Times*, Danzig expressed more sympathy for Tyler and her inability to secure a gold for Britain, suggesting that "fate had ordained that Britain shouldn't win a gold."[71] Even the USOC led their report on the women's track and field program with Blankers-Koen, before expressing at least some excitement for Coachman. "Not to be overlooked is the outstanding performance of Miss Alice Coachman, the US high jumper, whose duel for the championship in this event held 65,000 spectators in the seats in Wembley Stadium when all other competition had been completed on the final day of the track and field program," the USOC recounted.[72]

Black American sport culture, in contrast, pedestaled Coachman. "Alice Coachman, a slim and lithe young woman from Albany State," wrote the *Atlanta Daily World*, "won the only women's track and field title [meaning gold medal] scored by the United States."[73] A headline in *Afro-American* declared, "Coachman Is Only Woman Victor for U.S."[74] The *Chicago Defender* likewise trumpeted, "Alice Coachman Only U.S. Girl Winner in Olympic Track Meet."[75] This praise overlooked the historic, and still impressive, achievement of Mickey Patterson. Because Coachman earned a brighter medal, it was understandable that she would receive additional attention and recognition. However, this individualized conception of Coachman also had ideological underpinnings. Black sport culture chose to make cultural space for only a single black woman athlete, thereby protecting and promoting the superiority of black male athletes. The black American male athletes who found much success in London unquestionably were celebrated as race men who advanced the quest for black freedom through their sport success. The black sports press particularly proclaimed Harrison Dillard, who won a surprising gold in the 100 meters, and Mal Whitfield, gold medal winner in the 800 meters. Both men had served in World War II, with the combination of their military and athletic service encouraging the leading voices in the black press to promote them as exemplars of black masculine citizenship.[76]

Although black sport culture supported women's athleticism, it did so in a way that bolstered traditional gender norms. The *Pittsburgh Courier* deemed Coachman "a real Olympic queen" who was "a deserving and real All-American girl."[77] Coverage further positioned her as a singular figure of black athletic womanhood by giving greater attention to her non-athletic interests than her athletic achievement. Writing in the *Afro-American*, society columnist Revella Clay emphasized that Coachman "prefers costume designing, art, sewing and cooking to jumping, sprinting or running." She also shared, "Her personality and physical mien reflect her diametric interests. She is tall and has a lissome lean build of the athlete. Her complexion is a smooth tan. She has dreamy brown eyes and a quick friendly smile that chases away her little-girl shyness."[78] After an interview with the Olympic champion, Rubye Weaver Arnold, social correspondent for the *Daily World*, likewise established, "The Olympic winner is a typical, soft-spoken, starry-eyed, vivacious co-ed, gracious in manners and the possessor of a most charming effervescent smile."[79]

This conception of Coachman governed black Atlanta's honors for her. On September 24, 1948, "Alice Coachman Day" would be celebrated at halftime of Morris Brown College's season-opening football game. The *Atlanta Daily World* anticipated the affair, proclaiming, "All of the frills and trappings that are traditionally associated with a queen whether she represents royalty or sports will feature Miss Coachman's triumphant reception here."[80] The night before the halftime ceremony, black Atlanta's leading ladies held a reception for Coachman, as well as teammates Mabel Walker, Theresa Manuel, and Nell Jackson, at the Butler Street YMCA.[81] The next day Coachman served as the main attraction of the pregame parade, which wound through Atlanta's black communities before concluding at Morris Brown's Herndon Stadium. Coachman and her teammates then put on a track and field exhibition before Morris Brown took the field. At half-time of the game, which Morris Brown would win resoundingly over Alabama State, 30–0, Coachman received a citation from Atlanta mayor William B. Hartsfield.[82]

In total, the festivities presented Coachman as a feminine young black woman. During the reception and parade, Coachman wore a smart suit, with an orchid pinned to her lapel. And while she and her teammates had the opportunity to demonstrate their athletic skill, the light exhibition of women's athleticism contrasted with the subsequent football game and its display of black masculine strength. The celebration reveals black sport culture's navigation of black women's athleticism. The athletic interests of black young women were accommodated, even celebrated, but in ways that strengthened gender distinctions. Soon after the Olympics, Coachman announced her intention to retire from competition, marry, and become a teacher, decisions that underscored her adherence to traditional gender norms.[83] "That was all of it," she simply said.[84] More than an athletic pioneer, Coachman was an icon of black womanhood.

By competing in the Olympic Games, Coachman, as well as her teammates, engaged in a radical act, offering unscripted representations of blackness and femaleness to a world resistant to both. Yet, in different ways, white and black American sport cultures chose to see, or not see, their performances in ways that dulled their potential radicalness. The intersecting racial and gender anxieties raised by black women's athleticism was made more palatable. The agency of young black women track athletes was rendered invisible, obscuring not only the possibilities they represented but also the more quotidian needs and desires that they possessed.

ALICE COACHMAN'S SENTIMENTS OF SPORT AND CITIZENSHIP

Although she remained relatively silent, a smattering of comments from Coachman, both from the period and later, reveal some of her priorities and preferences, which exceeded those imagined by mainstream and black American sport cultures. Coachman emphasized collective support and self-determined ambition. Her version of her story suggests she envisioned possibilities for black American women that recognized and reinforced their opportunities and capacities, a contrast to the limited rights and recognition determined and doled out by the sporting leaders of black America.

Throughout her career, Coachman remained driven by the familial and community disapproval she had received for participating in sport as a young girl. "All the people would say, 'There goes Alice, that crazy fool, playing with them boys.' But I didn't care," she told the *Philadelphia Tribune* almost fifty years later.[85] She stringently ignored social norms of race and gender, although she did suffer the consequences for her stubbornness, receiving a "terrible whipping" from her father for her persistent running and jumping.[86] She recalled, "My father wanted his girls to be dainty, sitting on the front porch."[87] Coachman refused to sit still. As soon as she completed her chores, she jumped the fences that dotted the landscape of rural black Albany, running to playgrounds to race the neighborhood boys. "I was just interested in boys to give me competition. They dared not say anything out of the way or even touch me because I would beat up on them," she later shared.[88]

This self-confidence kept her competing in sport, even after the cancellation of the 1940 and 1944 Olympic Games. She later asserted, "I was one of those who had a lot of determination and I didn't care because it was something I wanted to do."[89] However, her Olympic experience did not begin ideally. Soon after the US Olympic team's voyage aboard the *SS America* began, Coachman suffered from homesickness. Yet she soon found a sense of belonging that boosted her spirits. Midway through the trip, athletes from across the American Olympic team participated in a joyous entertainment ceremony, with Coachman, outfitted in a white leotard, performing a dance routine to "St. Louis Blues."[90] Along with going to the Olympic Games, she was able, at least temporarily, to live out her other dream—becoming a Shirley Temple–like show star.[91] "It was a lovely trip. The moon, the sun, and the beautiful water. We would go from deck to deck, meeting people from all-over the world. We sang, played games, I really hated it to end," she recollected.[92] In short, the Olympic journey conferred a feeling of full Americanness on Coachman. "We were like one big family," she recalled.[93] Unmoored on the Atlantic, the seemingly intractable racial and gender barriers that structured American society sailed away. The ship served as an incubator of the possibility of a more equitable, inclusive America, where all, including black women, enjoyed unfettered access to the privileges of Americanness.

Her gold medal further gave her a greater sense of belonging, while also validating her personal commitment to competitive sport. To put it simply, her historic gold confirmed that she was not "crazy." Rather, she was creative, using her love of sport to make meaning for herself despite the racism and sexism she constantly encountered. "I wanted to win for the country. I wanted to be somebody. I wanted the world to know me, and I was just determined to make something of myself," she proclaimed to the *New York Amsterdam News* two decades after her London triumph.[94] In short, she wanted the rights and privileges of American citizenship. Coachman's reflections reveal a conception of a black women's citizenship premised on opportunity; the opportunity not to obey the limitations imposed because of one's identity categories. Sport provided Coachman with access to a greater semblance of such opportunity, allowing her, however momentarily, to experience rights and privileges almost always denied. Sport also had the power, however momentarily, to encourage an intransigent white America to take pride in Coachman's accomplishments.

THE INFLUENCE OF ALICE COACHMAN IN ALBANY

Even as the mainstream sporting press devoted little coverage to Coachman's triumph, her status as an Olympic champion proved too much for her home state of Georgia to ignore. As the only gold medalist from Georgia, Coachman inspired state pride. At the same time, her accomplishment, specifically the implications of her accomplishment, activated racialized gender anxieties. Georgia's celebration for her thus highlights how she forced a rethinking of the raced and gendered boundaries of belonging. She not only raised questions about the identity of an American athletic hero (or heroine), but the identity of an American.

The combination of excitement and unease that Coachman caused for her home state was evident before she even returned to the States. As the *SS Washington* carried members of the 1948 US Olympic team back from London, two photographers from *Life* magazine stood waiting at New York's Twenty-First Street Pier, anticipating the arrival of Coachman. The photographers' interest in Coachman, however, did not derive from an appreciation of her historic gold medal. Instead, they had heard rumors that white officials from the state of Georgia would be present to welcome Coachman. The prospect of a delegation of white men representing a state devoted to segregation greeting a young black woman understandably piqued the interest of *Life*. The resulting image ostensibly would prove the ability of sport to supersede segregation. Yet, Georgia's representatives, who also were expected to escort Coachman home to Albany, did not show.[95] Exceptional athletic achievement did not erode entrenched racial and gender biases.

However, when she arrived in Atlanta, Coachman did receive a rousing welcome, with black and white Georgians crowding the train station to catch a glimpse of the Olympic champion. Photographers and reporters from *Life* and *Time* solicited quotations and snapped photographs. A motorcade procession then carried Coachman from Atlanta to Albany, where white officials and black civic leaders had planned a citywide celebration. In route, citizens of Georgia, both black and white, lined the streets of Griffin, Macon, Fort Valley, Montezuma, and Americus to cheer the returning champion. By the time the motorcade arrived in Albany, the procession had swelled to more than two hundred, including cars, floats, marching bands, and enthusiastic citizens. Fourteen years before Dr. Martin Luther King Jr. and activists with the Southern Christian Leadership Conference and Student Non-Violent Co-ordinating Committee would lead an ultimately unsuccessful movement for voting rights and the desegregation of public places, Albany welcomed a young black woman as a conquering heroine.[96]

The parade concluded at Albany Municipal Auditorium, where the mayor and approximately twenty other city and county officials greeted Coachman as both black and white citizens watched from the auditorium's seats. Mayor James Smith offered praise, applauding her for maintaining a focus on academics throughout her athletic career. According to the *Atlanta Constitution*, "The Mayor then recalled the long, hard struggle of Alice Coachman to reach the top. He said by reaching that goal that the young woman had not only won honors for herself, but for her family, her school, and her community."[97] By identifying Coachman with "her family, her school, and her community," Smith exposed, intentionally or not, how an awareness of racial difference defined the ostensibly integrated event. While all of Albany was, at least temporarily, celebrating Coachman, she was of only a certain Albany. In other words, white Albany and black Albany remained distinct. The seating arrangements in the auditorium confirmed this sentiment. Although both black and white citizens attended, seating was segregated, with the balcony reserved for white attendees. The seating on the stage likewise was segregated, with Coachman and representatives from Albany State College on one side and the city's white leaders on the other.[98]

Smith's actions, or lack thereof, also revealed the white racial anxieties that percolated through the auditorium. Smith did not look at Coachman as her made his statement. And when he finished speaking, Smith did not shake her hand. As described by *Atlanta Daily World* sports editor Marion E. Jackson, "He was as frigid as a snow-capped mountain and as uncomfortable as an icicle in the summertime."[99] Speaking after Smith was James H. Gray, editor of the *Albany Herald,* who served as the master of ceremonies. He offered a much less anxious, albeit much more inaccurate, statement, announcing, "Alice Coachman's triumph was a personal one, but as we acknowledge that today we also like to feel that in some manner, both tangible and intangible, Albany itself contributed to her success."[100] In contrast to Smith, Gray did not hesitate to claim Coachman's achievements for all of Albany, blithely crediting a city that remained strictly segregated for its unspecified contribution to a young black woman's Olympic achievement. Nonetheless, Dr. Aaron Brown, president of Albany State, positively responded to Smith, Gray, and the city's other white civic leaders, thanking them and the city for showing that, as reported by the *Chicago Defender,* "persons of good will of whatever race can work together to build a better community and a better nation."[101] Coachman did not have the opportunity to speak at her own ceremony.

An Associated Press article published in newspapers across the nation captured the seeming improbableness of the affair, stating, "For the first time in history this south Georgia town is going to have a parade for a Negro—Alice Coachman, Olympic champion."[102] Civic pride appeared to have usurped racial prejudice. Yet, the organization and conduct of the entire ceremony—with a pair of visibly uncomfortable white civic leaders sharing favorable statements in front of an interracial, albeit segregated, audience—symbolized the struggle of white Albany and, in extension, white America to reckon not only with a world champion black woman athlete but also with the ability of women of color to contribute to the nation. White Albany's response to Coachman encapsulates the larger issues she and, by extension, black American women athletes raised for white American sport culture. Who can be an athlete? Who can be an American athlete? Who can be an American?

Somewhat surprisingly, the celebration of Coachman also challenged preconceptions about sport, race, gender, and citizenship for black American sport culture, as it indicated, however imperfectly, that a black woman athlete could advance racial change as much as, or even more than, a black male athlete.

FIGURE 3. Alice Coachman, flanked by her mother and Albany State president Dr. Aaron Brown, sits on the stage during the interracial celebration held for her in her hometown in September 1948.
Courtesy of Albany State University, The James Pendergrast Memorial Library, University Archives, Ben Cohn Hampton Pictorals

Coachman served as a figure through which to evaluate white Georgia's acceptance of black Georgians. She was a barometer of black citizenship. The *Chicago Defender* estimated:

> The whole affair must be put on the credit side of the race relations ledger. Here was evidence of that good impulses were at work and that there was a spark of decency in the leadership. They were afraid to stand up and be true Americans, true lovers of democracy, true Christians but they gave us some reasons to believe the day is going to come when the color line is going to lose its magic in Dixie.[103]

In the *Atlanta Daily World*, Jackson echoed this assessment:

> Georgia had seen Democracy in action. It was not a homecoming for a Negro Olympic star, but a champion of champions. As I watched the faces of thousands

of Georgians from all over the state, it was interesting to note that all of the prejudices, preferences, passions and hates were momentarily swept from their countenance as if a heavy rain storm had drenched a mountainous street.[104]

The leading voices in black American sport culture were forced to see her as an indicator for the possibility of racial equality. In other words, Coachman represented more than just black womanhood; she also embodied black America.

THE INFLUENCE OF ALICE COACHMAN IN THE OVAL OFFICE

The Harry S. Truman administration appeared to understand Coachman as significant of black America. In October 1948, Coachman, along with Mickey Patterson, Nell Jackson, Mabel Walker, Theresa Manuel, and Emma Reed journeyed to Washington, DC, where the sextet of black women Olympians joined 100-meter champion Harrison Dillard for a visit in the Oval Office with President Truman.[105] By posing for photos with the athletes and applauding them for their performances, Truman aimed to prove himself an ally of the black community and, hopefully, earn votes in the upcoming election. Although a staged moment of political glad-handing, the gathering powerfully signaled the Americanness of black women Olympians. This presidential recognition complemented the ways in which the athletes symbolically had contested the dominant racial and gender boundaries of American identity through their athletic strivings. Alice Coachman intuited as much, telling the *Afro-American* that the visit "gave her the greatest thrill," deeming it even more rewarding than her gold medal.[106]

However, the decision to invite one black man and six black women Olympians suggests the Truman administration strategically scripted the image of black Americanness they invited into the White House. It certainly was curious that the relatively unheralded young black track women were extended this honor. It was even more curious that other black American male Olympic heroes, namely double-gold middle-distance man Mal Whitfield and sprinter Barney Ewell, who won two silvers and a gold, were not invited. The Olympic achievements of Dillard, Whitfield, and Ewell followed their service in World War II, with Dillard stationed in the Mediterranean theater, Whitfield, who was still enlisted, flying with the renowned Tuskegee Airmen, and Ewell serving stateside at Virginia's Camp Lee and New Jersey's Camp Kilmer.[107] Their Olympic success and military service seemingly would position them as the most appealing representatives of black America. For Truman himself, it was the brutal racism experienced by black World War II veteran Isaac Woodard, who was beaten and blinded in South Carolina, that finally made him aware of the need for executive civil rights action.[108] Yet, the prospect of multiple, indisputably masculine black athletes receiving the imprimatur of full Americanness from the president proved too provocative. Not only would welcoming a group of black servicemen-turned-Olympians have signaled too directly the president's support for the Double V campaign, the *Pittsburgh Courier*'s call for black servicemen to fight fascism abroad and racism at home, but the image of these men in the Oval Office also would have threatened the nation's racialized gender hierarchy. It would have positioned black male athletes as exemplars of American manhood, a status reserved for white male Olympians, such as sprint hero Mel Patton, who won the 200-meter gold, and the youthful decathlon champion Bob Mathias.[109]

For the Truman administration, Dillard, whose smaller stature belied his athletic ability, Coachman, and the five other black women athletes more safely expressed the belonging of black Americans. Not only did including Dillard as the lone representative of black male athleticism protect the supposed superiority of white masculinity, but the six young black track women also preserved the racialization of ideal American womanhood. Despite Fanny Blankers-Koen's dominance in London, American society still clung to the belief that track and field was inappropriate for white women. In short, it was understood as a sport for black women. Although the prospect of only black women representing the United States in the most prestigious spaces of international sport was discomfiting for the AAU and USOC, the lack of elite white women athletes also was understood as signaling the supposedly superior and sacred femininity of white American women. So even though Coachman, Patterson, Jackson, Walker, Manuel, and Reed dressed in their appropriately feminine Olympic parading uniforms as they stood for photos with the president, the very fact that they were women track athletes signaled the enduring difference between black and white women.

The ways in which black women athletes simultaneously activated racialized gender anxieties and communicated racialized gender distinctions and differences captures how, as individuals marked by race and gender who became visible as representatives of the nation, they sharply illuminated the contradictions of American identity. The contradictoriness suited Truman's political purposes. While he had encouraged some rather significant, substantive civil rights developments, including the President's Committee on Civil Rights and the desegregation of the armed forces, he also was facing a challenge from the

Dixiecrats, a white supremacist third-party bid that threatened his election prospects. A calibrated, circumspect commitment to black rights thus was required. Coachman and her fellow black track women served as safe symbols; they showed the president's support for expanding the rights of citizenship to black Americans without overtly offending white Americans, who mostly believed in a version of racial equality that largely preserved white superiority.[110]

Nevertheless, it was not insignificant that Truman shook hands with the first black woman to win an Olympic gold medal. This symbolic progress was not unreal progress. For all the competing messages of the visit, its symbolism, like that of a black woman athlete on the medal rostrum as the US national anthem played, did challenge the nation's dominant values and norms. In the Oval Office, Coachman and the others made visible the respectable model of black athletic womanhood emphasized by Cleve Abbott at Tuskegee Institute. The visit confirmed the viability of this model, establishing it as an absolute in the culture of black women's track and field. When he assumed head coaching duties at TSU in 1953, Edward S. Temple adopted and perfected this model with his Tigerbelles. At the 1960 Olympic Games in Rome, Ed Temple's most famous charge, Wilma Rudolph, would make black feminine athleticism more visible. And soon thereafter, she also would receive an invitation to the Oval Office, exchanging pleasantries with President John F. Kennedy. She most powerfully would identify Americanness with blackness and femaleness.

Rudolph would not have been possible without Coachman, not only due to the athletic accomplishments she achieved but also because of the ideological adjustments she caused. Coachman introduced black women's athleticism to the nation and the world. A rare, visible example of the agencies and capacities of black womanhood, she demonstrated that black women could serve the nation and, therefore, deserved to belong in the nation. She required the sport cultures of white and black America to question the relationship between sport, gender, race, and nation. Following in the footsteps of Coachman and preparing the path for Rudolph, black American women track stars would continue to exercise subtle but significant influence over the boundaries of American belonging as they repeatedly took to national and international spaces of sport. In other words, the likes of Mae Faggs, Catherine Hardy, and Barbara Jones would receive the baton from Coachman and carry it forth, continuing along a path of precarity and possibility.

2

SPRINTS OF CITIZENSHIP

IDENTITY POLITICS AND BLACK WOMEN'S ATHLETICISM, 1951–1952

Mae Faggs approached Barbara Jones, adjusting her speed in order to successfully pass the baton to her teammate. Running the first leg of the women's 400-meter relay final at the 1952 Olympic Games, Faggs had remained on the heels of her rivals from Australia, Germany, and Great Britain. Now she could only watch as Jones and then Janet Moreau sprinted around the track, staying in contention for the hoped-for podium finish. But suddenly, the precariousness of the baton pass opened a more propitious opportunity. Australia's Marjorie Jackson failed to secure the stick from Winsome Cripps, eliminating the favored Australian foursome from contention. In contrast, Moreau and Catherine Hardy expertly executed their exchange, allowing Hardy immediately to unleash her speed. Faggs, as well as Jones and Moreau, cheered Hardy as she chased Germany's Marga Petersen and Britain's Heather Armitage. Showing no signs of slowing, Hardy broke the tape in the world-record time of 45.9 seconds to capture the gold medal. She soon was mobbed by her teammates. The one white and three black women athletes jumped joyously down the track and into the infield. Locking arms, they skipped and scampered, an inspiring display of the cooperative spirit of Olympism.[1] American sport culture, however, did not know what to make of the fantastic foursome.

In the 1950s, the Cold War increasingly influenced the conduct and import of American sport, both domestically and internationally. The disagreements and distrust that developed between the United States and Soviet Union during World War II intensified through the late 1940s and into the 1950s.[2] The battle between democracy and communism not only governed world affairs but also winded and wormed its ways into social and cultural arenas. In the United States, sport served as means through which to communicate and consolidate American values, cultivating a conformist, anticommunist culture organized around "capitalism, consumerism, absence of manifest class divisions, the 'American Dream' of social mobility, and religion."[3] However, as the Soviet Union readily used evidence of American racial inequality as a cudgel in this ideological battle, sport also served as vehicle for proving American racial progress, with experiences of black athletes highlighted, or hidden, in order to aid the image of the United States.[4] Sport, in short, was a crucial cultural technology, a seemingly apolitical but richly propagandistic tool on which American state and society increasingly relied to construct an amenable, admirable vision of the nation.[5] All the more, with the Soviet Union joining the Olympic Movement in 1952, athletics offered an opportunity to tangibly demonstrate the superiority of democracy, with American athletes' triumphs over their Soviet counterparts understood as ideological victories.

Yet, the institutions and authorities of mainstream American sport deemed black American track women irrelevant to the newly launched sporting Cold War. Marked by race and gender, they doubly diverged from the desired, normative image of an athlete and citizen.[6] Nevertheless, American track women made their presence known and, in turn, made impossible the easy, uncontroversial narratives of democracy that the institutions of American sport aimed to communicate through the Helsinki Games. Faggs, Jones, and Hardy disrupted the dominant idea of the American Way. They instead embodied alternative possibilities, thereby demanding that institutions and authorities rethink, even if only briefly, assumptions of race, gender, and American identity.

Because sport, especially international sport, was (and is) a political space where athletes advertise imagined national identities, black women track athletes were (and are) important political actors.[7] Before Faggs, Jones, and Hardy, aided by Janet Moreau, would problematize their nation's democratic proclamations on the track in Helsinki, Jean Patton, Evelyn Lawler, and Nell Jackson would assert the constitutiveness of blackness and femaleness to Americanness at the 1951 Pan-American Games in Buenos Aires, Argentina. Thus, the exertions and experiences of young black track women before, during, and after the 1951 Pan-American Games and 1952 Olympic Games offer an insightful perspective of the identity politics that organized American society during the early Cold War.

AMERICAN NATIONALISM AND THE PAN-AMERICAN SPORTING STAGE

In the late summer of 1950, the *Afro-American* published an article titled, "Misses May Miss Pan-Olympics." The text read:

> The possibility of colored girls from the United States competing in the coming Pan-American Games in Buenos Aires, Argentina, received a severe blow when the U.S. Olympic Association voted against women track stars being included on the American team. The executive board of the association instead lists women's track among the sports to be included "only if they are able to finance their own expenses."[8]

Following the 1948 Olympic Games, the inaugural Pan-American Games, to be held in Buenos Aires, Argentina, in March 1951, were the next opportunity for black women track athletes to represent the United States on an international sporting stage. However, as the above text from the *Afro-American* indicates, their path to Buenos Aires would be quite ponderous. While appearing to expand the boundaries of American belonging, Alice Coachman's achievement in fact inspired the opposite, highlighting the curious and contradictory, but also real, influence of black women athletes. Coachman's gold medal motivated the institutions of American sport to seek to manage more closely the racial and gender boundaries of the nation's athletic identity, epitomized by the USOC's attempt to absent black women's athleticism from the image of Americanness to be articulated at the Pan-American Games.

The 1951 Pan-American Games represented the long-delayed realization of an event designed to encourage inter-American understanding through athletics. Since before World War II, national sport officials from the United States, Argentina, Cuba, Mexico, Peru, and Colombia had attempted to plan a hemispheric sporting festival.[9] Meeting in London during the 1948 Olympic Games, representatives from the National Olympic Committees (NOCs) of these nations finalized the first edition of the Pan-American Games for Buenos Aires in March 1951. As with the Olympic Games, the event encouraged idealistic proclamations from officials. "Not only will the Pan American Games provide outstanding competition for the athletes involved, but also they will build new and closer bonds between the American democracies," asserted Avery Brundage, who, as president of the USOC, also served as the president of the Pan American Sports Organization.[10] A USOC fundraising message parroted Brundage, describing it as "a sports event designed to build new and close bonds between the American democracies and to provide their amateur athletes with additional international competition equally spaced between each Olympiad."[11]

This statement also hints at how the Pan-American Games served as political project for the United States. As demonstrated by sports studies scholar Toby C. Rider, the "US Government used the Olympic Games as a propaganda platform to promote US foreign policy objectives during the early years of the Cold War."[12] Rider details the wide-ranging "state-private network" that "presented a carefully constructed image of US participation at each Olympic festival, an image that depicted the athletes as paragons of the US 'way of life.'"[13] The Pan-American Games also served as such a propagandistic platform, especially in context with the Cold War–inspired concerns that percolated within the American hemisphere. While Franklin Roosevelt had implemented the Good Neighbor Policy, fostering a cooperative relationship with the United States' southern neighbors, the end of World War II and arrival of the Cold War altered the nation's relations with Latin America, with the United States imposing its priorities more aggressively in order to ensure that democracy remained the hemisphere's dominant political ideology.[14] Sport presented a potent space in which to exercise soft power.

The claim about "bonds between the American democracies" exposes the influence of Cold War–related concerns on the US approach to the Games. They were an opportunity to counteract anti-Americanism and corral the hemisphere to the side of democracy. With the support from state and commercial actors, the USOC subtly executed these political aims. Fundraising letters sent to business leaders suggest an understanding of the broader political possibilities presented by the Games. "These Games are not just [an] Argentine show," the USOC declared in its solicitations. "You can be sure if [the] United States [is] not represented it will be misrepresented," the letters asserted, emphasizing that supporting the American squad would ensure "our presence there will operate as it has in scores [of] other cases to build good will from which your business will benefit."[15] Assistant Secretary of State Edward W. Barrett likewise endorsed the USOC's efforts, writing a letter to Brundage that praised sport for "stimulating friendship and good will," especially for "hav[ing] done much to remove the misapprehensions and antagonisms toward the United States."[16] Although Brundage repeatedly insisted that the Games were "beyond the most powerful political manipulation," these letters suggest otherwise.[17] The athletes who would compete in Buenos Aires were believed to embody the best of American democracy and free enterprise, a representational role seemingly similar to but actually appreciably different from that at the 1948 Olympic Games.

The London Games can be seen as an athletic extension of the Marshall Plan, with the US Olympic contingent intended to exemplify democracy's potential to the ravaged and recovering European continent. The relatively diverse population of US athletes who first marched in the opening parade and then dominated athletic competition ostensibly embodied the inherent rightness of the values that the United States proclaimed. Athletes, through their appearance and ability, demonstrated that the United States deserved to lead the free world. But whereas the United States saw itself as a beacon of possibility in a sporting community of relative equals in London, it viewed itself as unquestionably superior to its Latin American counterparts in the realms of sport, society, and politics. In Buenos Aires, bolstered by the support of political and corporate leaders, the United States expected to establish and exercise its hegemony, the same attitude with which the nation approached Latin America throughout the Cold War.

Because elite white men from the worlds of sport, politics, and business managed the USOC's Pan-American project, maleness and whiteness enjoyed unquestioned status as identifiers of the American superiority they desired to assert. This presumption explains the *Afro-American's* report that "Misses May Miss the Pan-Olympics." Elaborating on the evidence that the USOC sought to prevent women's track and field athletes from participating in the Pan-American Games, the paper suggested, "This action was interpreted by a number of coaches as a 'definite effort' to keep colored girls out, although the Argentine organizing committee had placed women's track and field second on its list of important events."[18] The paper further emphasized that "the Olympic committee is headed by Avery Brundage, often termed 'anti-Negro,'" quoting an unnamed coach who declared, "The chairman is dead set against track and field for women on an international basis."[19]

Although the Truman administration had accessed the symbolic power of Alice Coachman and other black women Olympians for particular political purposes, the USOC's approach to the Pan-American Games involved different political, social, and cultural motivations and calculations. In short, the sporting stage had shifted, and black women athletes did not fit the desired script; the combination of their gender and racial identities cast them as a threat to the American sporting narrative. Black women athletes were presumed to prevent the US Pan-American team from communicating a stabilizing, uncomplicated, and authoritative image of Americanness to their southern neighbors. Their presence, as well as potentially victorious performances, raised uncomfortable questions about raced and gendered boundaries of American identity, both in sport and beyond. Held only a few months before the *Afro-American* would report that "Misses May Miss Pan-Olympics," the May 1950 Los Angeles Coliseum Relays were a rare racially and gender-integrated national track meet that would make evident the ideological disruptiveness of young black women athletes. When welcomed into the center of sport, they challenged the preferred understandings of American athleticism, thus inspiring the discriminatory machinations of the USOC's Pan-American planners.

JEAN PATTON'S JOLT AT THE 1950 LOS ANGELES COLISEUM RELAYS

In the spring of 1950, Horace Owens, a Los Angeles–based writer who graduated from Tuskegee Institute, pressed for the inclusion of members of the Tigerettes at the 1950 Los Angeles Coliseum Relays.[20] Established in 1940, the Coliseum Relays were the West Coast's leading meet and thus one of the nation's most prominent athletic affairs, annually attracting more than 40,000 fans by the end of the decade. In 1949, for the first time, the meet included a women's program, with quadruple gold medalist Fanny Blankers-Koen serving as the women's athletic star. The "Flying Dutch Housewife" thrilled the 50,000 fans in attendance as she romped to victory in the 80-meter sprint and 80-meter hurdles. She then joined a white girls' club team from Glendale, California, to defeat a foursome of Canadian women athletes in the 400-meter relay. Running anchor, Blankers-Koen astounded the tens of thousands of fans when she closed a deficit of more than forty yards to break the tape.

The *New York Times* thus acclaimed, "Speed, muscle and glamour, mixed with record-making performances, marked the ninth annual Coliseum Relays."[21] Their assessment indicates that the importance of Blankers-Koen exceeded her athletic exploits. She advertised an image of women's athleticism organized around whiteness, femininity, and heterosexuality, presumably providing an imitable model for young, white American women. This prospect particularly

pleased the white women leaders of the AAU women's track and field committee. In an April 1949 editorial in *Amateur Athlete*, Catherine Meyer, still
the head coach of the US women's track and field team, assertively argued for
the need for more support for women's track, especially with the 1951 Pan-
American Games and 1952 Olympic Games on the horizon. "We must start
now in the promotions of women's athletics. We must look to broader fields,
to the schools and colleges, playgrounds and industry," she demanded.[22]

Notably, Meyer referenced juvenile delinquency to make her argument
more persuasive. She posited, "Everyone is interested in combating juvenile
delinquency, in doing something for boys, yet with few exceptions, no one does
anything for girls in an athletic way."[23] She further retorted, "If participation
in sports builds character in boys, why shouldn't this hold true for girls?"[24] By
cleverly tapping into the widespread social anxiety that surrounded juvenile
delinquency, a paranoia that primarily percolated in white American society in
the early Cold War era due to concerns about mass consumption, communism,
and black civil rights, Meyer aimed to inject young women's athletic opportunities with purpose. She situated track and field as an activity that made
young white women better citizens in order to make the sport understood
as appropriate for these same young women. Blankers-Koen, pictured in the
New York Times gracefully clearing a hurdle at the Coliseum Relays, embodied
successful, citizenship-ready white women's athleticism.[25]

In 1950, the Coliseum Relays again would advertise this image; Marjorie
Jackson, Australia's rising sprint talent, crossed the Pacific to model athletically excellent yet satisfyingly feminine athleticism.[26] These developments
encouraged Horace Owens to seek entry for Tuskegee's top talents and, in
turn, introduce black athletic womanhood to the West Coast. Along with the
Tuskegee foursome of Gladys Talley, Juanita Watson, Evelyn Lawler, and Nell
Jackson, TSU's Jean Patton received an invitation.[27] Since the retirement of
Alice Coachman, Patton had established herself as the nation's top women's
track talent. At the 1949 National AAU Outdoor Championship in Odessa,
Texas, she won the 100-meter crown.[28] In the winter of 1950, she captured
the indoor counterpart, showing her ability to swiftly navigate the boards of
Madison Square Garden.[29] In early May 1950, she led TSU to a historic victory
at the twenty-first edition of Tuskegee Relays. By winning the 50-meter and
100-meter dashes, Patton positioned her Tigerbelles to defeat the Tigerettes,
the first time the host squad had failed to win the title.[30] Based on this recent
streak of strong performances, the organizers of the Coliseum Relays likely

extended Patton an invitation in hopes that she would provide an exciting challenge to Marjorie Jackson. Yet, Patton did more, stunning the 50,000 fans.

Despite a slow start, Jackson had taken the lead in the nine-woman 80-yard sprint race by the 50-yard mark, seemingly on the way to her expected, easy win. Patton, however, crashed her coronation, unleashing a burst of speed to steal victory in the final ten yards. "The win bowled over the crowd of 50,000 because Miss Jackson had been regarded as an almost certain winner of the event, one of the feature attractions of the track and field festival," exclaimed the *Atlanta Daily World*.[31] The *Pittsburgh Courier* echoed this analysis, enthusing that "Tennessee State's jet-propelled Jean Patton [has been] crowned as the new fastest female human."[32] Patton's hometown paper, Nashville's *The Tennessean*, proclaimed, "Patton Whips Aussie Star in LA Relays."[33]

With this surprising success, Patton made black women's athleticism visible. She disrupted the vision of women's athleticism the meet desired to communicate through Jackson's assumed triumph. The 1950 Coliseum Relays thus displayed the troubling ideological power of black women's athleticism. At a gender- and racially integrated meet, Patton, like Coachman before her, exposed the inconsistent ideas about race and gender that constructed the understanding of ideal American athleticism. Due to the promoted presence of white women athletes, Patton and the Tuskegee quartet could not easily be marked as deviant. For instance, Evelyne Hall, the national AAU women's track and field chairwoman, proclaimed track and field a "lady-like" sport because "there is no body contact." "It is an accepted fact that track and field build up the body in three ways, physically, mentally, and competitively. All these items are an asset to the American way of living," she insisted in a 1950 *Amateur Athlete* editorial.[34] If track and field could make young white women into fine, fit, and feminine American citizens, it arguably did the same for their black challengers. Competing in the Coliseum in front of close to 50,000 fans also situated black women track talents as serious athletes. It is important to emphasize that the Coliseum Relays represented one of the most prestigious US-based track meets to include black women athletes in the history of the sport. The result, in short, was unavoidably significant. The Coliseum Relays confirmed the racial reality of women's track and field, where, despite the designs of Meyer, Hall, and others, black women athletes defined American women's athleticism. And, because of this definitional role, they apparently piqued the anxieties of the white male officials who controlled American sport.

The following year, the Coliseum Relays ended its two-year women's program without explanation, in spite of the excitement injected by women athletes both years. Their decision suggests a real discomfort with black women's athleticism. The USOC similarly sought to extinguish the potential power of black women athletes by constructing blatant barriers to their participation at the Pan-American Games. Jean Patton and her fellow black women athletes not only did not fit the script of American superiority that the USOC aimed to enact in Buenos Aires, but as Patton demonstrated in Los Angeles, they also had the potential to flip the script in ways in which the officials and institutions of white-controlled American sport were unwilling to reckon.

THE CONTESTED VISIONS OF AMERICAN WOMEN'S ATHLETICISM

At a USOC meeting at New York's Leone's Restaurant in January 1951, Lyman J. Bingham, USOC executive director, announced the intent "to send a full team of 112 athletes" to Buenos Aires for March's Pan-American Games, asserting that "full-scale United States participation had the enthusiastic support of the State Department."[35] Yet, a "full team" and "full-scale" effort did not include women's track and field. The demand that American track women self-fund or miss the Games had been made months prior, indicating that Bingham dismissed women's track when making his patriotic proclamations. Even as the USOC collected a surplus of funds, they did not share them with the women's track and field committee.[36] Women track athletes were prohibited from accessing the privileges given to the nation's other athletic representatives. But members of the USOC and AAU women's track and field committees were undeterred by this prejudiced policy. Evelyne Hall, who would serve as the team manager, embraced independent fundraising initiatives with aplomb. In a letter to Avery Brundage, she enthused, "The Women's Track & Field Committee have full steam ahead and we plan difinitely [sic] to raise the funds necessary to send the girls team to the games." She further wrote, likely much to Brundage's disdain, that he should "please be assured that as chairman of the Women's Track & Field committee, I will do all in my power to raise all the money needed for my team. No stone will be left unturned."[37]

Hall's efforts would prove successful. Considering the gender conventionality of 1950s white America, her ardency may seem surprising.[38] But for all the ways in which strict prohibitions against the athletic pursuits of white women defined the 1950s, the decade featured much active discussion about white women's athleticism.[39] Sports studies scholar Jaime Schultz aptly states that "the 1950s marked a time of intense debate about whether and how to invigorate women's sport."[40] For Hall and her compatriots, arguing for the acceptability of track and field assumed priority. It is worth noting that although they envisioned the sport as "ladylike," a term that carries connotations of whiteness, they never excluded black women. In their quest to build the sport, Hall and the other white women who captained the women's committees of the AAU and USOC welcomed, rather than feared, black women athletes, recognizing that they helped facilitate the sport's growth. At the national level, the AAU women's track and field committee worked to produce high-quality title meets open to women athletes of all races and ethnicities. For the 1949 National AAU Indoor Championship in New York, the Coordinating Council of the New York Police Department (NYPD), which directed the meet, arranged for the NYPD's union to provide accommodations for eight Tuskegee Tigerette competitors at the Park-Sheraton Hotel.[41] This gesture was significant, signaling a recognition of the place of black women in the sport. The 1949 AAU National Outdoor Championship in Odessa, Texas, not only provided affordable and integrated accommodations for all athletes, but the Odessa Shrine Club, which organized the meet, also hosted a pre-competition barbecue. Highlighted by a singing and dancing exhibition, the celebration presumably allowed white and black American athletes, as well as Latina athletes from Cuba and Mexico, to socialize freely, creating a scene that contravened the social preferences and practices of western Texas.[42]

Yet this racial inclusivity existed alongside assumptions of racial superiority. The shared fight against sexism reduced the racial biases of the AAU and USOC women's track and field committees, but it did not eliminate them. For the sport's white women leaders, the success of the sport still would be measured by the success of white women athletes. Black women athletes were valued as placeholders, preparing and preserving the sport until the likes of Hall, Meyer, and others could convince more white young women to compete. That the US women's Pan-American track and field team featured a majority of white women athletes reflected their racially inflected priorities. Because of the uncertainty about women's track participation, no formal trials were held; instead, the USOC's women's track and field committee used performances from the 1950 National AAU Outdoor Championship, held in Freeport, Texas, to guide their selections. This process allowed Hall and other members of the committee to shape the squad to their preferences.

Although their choices were not flagrantly biased, they did raise questions. Of the eight women athletes who would compete in Buenos Aires, three of them were black—Jean Patton, Evelyn Lawler, and Nell Jackson. As discussed, Patton, a nineteen-year-old Nashville native in her sophomore year at TSU, recently had established herself as the nation's best women's track talent, winning multiple national sprint titles in the previous two years. Both Lawler and Jackson attended Tuskegee. A junior from Gadsden, Alabama, the twenty-year-old Lawler, whose specialty was the hurdles, was widely considered "the best all-round girl athlete in the college."[43] Jackson, also a twenty-year-old in her junior year, was a native of Athens, Georgia, who, after competing in the 1948 Olympics, had improved her sprinting form, becoming an elite-level 200-meter runner.[44] However, two other black national champions were not named to the team, while two white women athletes who finished second and third in their specialties were selected. Likewise, Tuskegee Institute won the team title, yet only two Tigerettes, Lawler, winner of the 80-meter hurdles, and Jackson, winner of the 200-meter sprint, made the team.[45] As was the case with the Alice Coachman–led AAU teams that competed in Canada, it seems ability was not necessarily the selection committee's top priority. Evidence suggests the committee chose Nancy Cowperthwaite-Phillips, who finished second in the 80-meter hurdles in Freeport, over Mabel Landry and Juanita Watson, the respective long jump and baseball throw champions, because of the image of she presented.[46] The AAU's official organ, *Amateur Athlete*, proudly had promoted Cowperthwaite-Phillips as prospective icon of white American women's athleticism, often publishing photos of her to accompany coverage of women's track and field.[47] In sum, black women athletes had a place, but white women athletes were privileged. The path of the trio of black women athletes to participating in the Pan-American Games illuminates their contested place in the American sporting nation. However, at the inaugural Pan-American Games, Patton, Lawler, and Jackson would have access to a powerful and public platform. Their efforts would encourage a rethinking of American athletic identity.

EXPANDING THE BOUNDARIES OF BELONGING IN BUENOS AIRES

On February 23, 1951, the octet of women athletes arrived in Buenos Aires via Miami, having traveled on one of two specially chartered Pan-American Airlines flights arranged for the almost 120 American athletes.[48] Considering the uncertainty that surrounded their participation, Patton, Lawler, and Jackson probably were relieved to reach South American soil. Their arrival in the women's village likely turned this sense of relief into one of excitement. In contrast to the USOC's continued unease, the Argentine Olympic Committee (AOC) signaled their comfort with and support for women's athleticism.

Like the US government, Argentine president Juan Perón understood the political power of sport. He thus envisioned the inaugural Pan-American Games as an opportunity to contest the hemispheric hegemony of the United States, using the Games as an opportunity to perform Latin American unity, as well as enhance his own authority.[49] The conduct of the Games also countered US priorities in more subtle ways. At the urging of First Lady Eva Perón, the institutions of Argentine sport modeled greater gender equity. So while US officials of sport, state, and commerce may have disapproved of the active involvement of the Peróns in the planning of the Pan-American Games, women athletes likely appreciated the efforts of Eva, who insisted upon equal accommodations and resources for visiting women athletes.[50] Women athletes actually enjoyed superior accommodations, since the women's village was closer to most athletic facilities. This housing situation contrasted with that of the 1948 Olympics, when the American women's track and field delegation was relegated to second-class housing far from training and competition locations.[51] Eva Perón further expressed women's athletic equality by including women athletes in many of the ceremonies surrounding the Games. Most notably, she pressed for a women's representative from each nation to take the Olympic oath alongside the men's representative.[52] The oath taking created a scene that powerfully contested gender conventions. This symbolism, along with the housing conditions, made the Buenos Aires Games a rare safe space of sport for a multiracial collection of young women athletes, many of whom had their athletic pursuits discouraged and disdained by their home countries. The Games modeled an alternative sporting world, organized around uncontested racial integration and greater gender equity.

If the USOC desired to dismiss women track athletes in order to present a supposedly stable vision of the American nation that privileged traditional racial and gender hierarchies, the conditions in Buenos Aires clashed with their effort. Eva Perón and the AOC conferred athletic legitimacy on the three black, as well as five white, track women representing the United States. The circumstances in Buenos Aires situated American women athletes to articulate an alternative vision of the American sporting nation, one that altered assumptions about the raced and gendered boundaries of American belonging. On the track in Buenos Aires, Jean Patton very much would contest these boundaries. Once again, the big stage seemed to have spurred her to unleash more speed. In the 200-meter race, Patton and Nell Jackson engaged in an exciting duel, with Patton besting her teammate by two yards. The 70,000 fans in River Plate Stadium thus saw black women athletes embody American athletic excellence. Patton also inscribed this vision in the register of international sport, as she set a new South American record of 25.3 seconds for the distance. The *New York Times* noted her performance, writing, "The second United States track championship of the day went to Miss Jean Patton, rangy Nashville (Tenn.) girl, who shaded a teammate, Miss Nell Jackson of Alabama's Tuskegee Institute, in the 200-meter run. It was the first track victory for the United States women."[53] This statement captures the partial, still uneasy acceptance of young black track women. By offering a positive assessment of Patton's performance, the *Times* included her in the American sporting nation. However, describing Patton as "rangy," a racially coded term used to convey a body type different from a shapely, and implicitly white, one, racialized her, communicating her difference. In short, while recognized as a black American woman track athlete, she was not celebrated as an unmarked American athlete.

The following day Patton again would complicate ideal American athleticism and, in turn, ideal American identity. Partnering with Nell Jackson, Dolores Dwyer, and Janet Moreau, Patton anchored the American women to a win in the 4x100-meter relay. Although American women's track culture included several interracial club teams, namely New York's PAL and Chicago's Catholic Youth Organization (CYO), the pair of black and white young women athletes cooperating to win a relay gold inserted an image of interracial, equitable American women's athleticism into the center of hemispheric sport. This image collapsed the racialized distinctions between young black and white women that organized American women's athleticism, refuting any notions of "rangy" blackness or protected whiteness.

Patton fell just short of securing a third gold medal, finishing one-tenth of a second behind Peru's Julia Sánchez in the 100 meters.[54] She still was one of only two American athletes, along with the widely admired Mal Whitfield, to win three medals. She thus received a significant degree of recognition for her exploits in the South American sporting press, certifying her status as a recognized representative of the United States. For instance, *El Gráfico*, a

South American sport magazine, published a photo of Patton with the caption, "La negrita norte-americana Jean Patton fué figura saliente en las pruebas de velocidad" (The black North American girl Jean Patton was a prominent figure in the sprints).[55] Patton thus made real a vision that the USOC had sought to avoid. Through her performances, she authored an alternative American sporting narrative, proving that black American women's athleticism was constitutive to American athleticism.

Patton, Jackson, Lawler, and their white teammates also appear to have made a positive impression on their competitors. A spirit of Pan-American goodwill and friendship percolated through the women's village. Evelyne Hall, who served as team manager, later expressed particular appreciation for a bilingual Mexican athlete from El Paso, who, after making friends with some of the American athletes, translated Spanish signs and announcements for the US team.[56] The trio of black American women also could have formed solidarities with black representatives of South American nations, such as Brazil's Wanda dos Santos, the long jump bronze medalist.[57] However, the eight American athletes seemed to have formed the strongest bonds with the all-white Chilean team, who invited the American women to compete in an international meet in Santiago immediately following the Pan-American Games. At the Chilean meet, these young track women further would position themselves as valid representatives of the United States, regardless of official approval.

After the conclusion of the women's track and field program in Buenos Aires, Hall and her team of eight piled into a small plane for Santiago, enjoying a scenic flight over the Andes mountain range.[58] When they arrived, the American contingent, in the words of Hall, "were treated royally."[59] Yet, the thrilling flight and warm welcome did not dampen the competitive drive of the athletes, especially that of Evelyn Lawler. Seemingly spurred by her inability to secure a medal in Buenos Aires, when she stumbled over the first hurdle in the final, Lawler authoritatively asserted her hurdling supremacy.[60] In route to her victory in the 80-meter hurdles, she not only set a new South American record but also bettered the times earned by all hurdling medalists in Buenos Aires. The *New York Times* recognized her achievement, reporting that Lawler "distinguished herself in the 80-meter hurdles, winning in 11.3 seconds, two-tenths of a second better than the South American record held by Argentina's Noemi Simonetto."[61] She also avenged her Pan-American high jump disappointment. Although she had tied for the highest leap, her number of misses relegated her to sixth.[62] In Santiago, she tied for first in the high jump before finishing fourth in the long jump.[63]

The most impressive display of American, specifically black American, women's athleticism occurred in the 100-meter sprint, where Lawler and Jackson pushed Patton to a new South American record for the distance. Patton then paired her 100-meter crown with the 200-meter title, with Jackson again finishing second. The trio of black women track stars also teamed with Dolores Dwyer to triumph in the 400-meter relay, trouncing their competitors with a nearly three second victory. Their time not only proved too much for their challengers but also improved upon that registered in Buenos Aires.[64] Santiago thus became a space defined by black American women's athletic excellence, with the threesome of Lawler, Patton, and Jackson together claiming a total of ten medals. This hardware haul was material evidence of their claim to their Americanness. They far exceeded how the USOC imagined Americanness, associating blackness and femaleness with American athletic identity across the Pan-American athletic world.

JEAN PATTON AND THE GENDER OF BLACK AMERICAN ATHLETICISM

The United Nations seemed to have taken notice of this symbolic power. Soon after the American track women returned to the States, the organization invited Jean Patton to New York to meet with diplomats at their temporary headquarters in Lake Success, New York, and preview their new facility in New York City. The *Chicago Defender* reported, "Wing footed Jean Patton, who is used to traveling 100 yards in less than 12 seconds under her own power, got a first hand view of the slow process of building international accord during a visit to the United Nations Organization here last week. But even the tortuous path of diplomacy is a welcome one when it leads to good will and peace, the Tennessee State college sophomore indicated."[65]

After she "watched openly amazed as the story of what makes the UN tick" unfolded, she met with UN Human Rights Division secretary Edward Lawson, exchanged autographs with the chief of the Caribbean section James Bough, dined with England's attaché Marjorie Campbell, and chatted with Chinese representative Clara Chen and Indian representative Rasil Singh.[66] The *Defender* published photographs of these scenes, making visible Patton's status as a respected citizen of the world. She then traveled to the city to enjoy an exclusive tour of the brand-new building, which would open in 1952.[67] Patton's visit was an exceptional opportunity for a young black woman athlete. She entered a privileged space of international politics as a representative of the nation, appearing progressively to expand the raced and gendered boundaries of American identity.

However, the *Defender's* article on Patton's UN visit did not expound upon its wider importance. Rather, the paper feminized her, reinforcing her gendered respectability. Following the template established with Alice Coachman, Patton was presented as an exemplar of normative black womanhood. The article text focused on her relationship with Elihu Latimer, her longtime boyfriend who was also a student, and basketball star, at TSU. According to the *Defender*, "Getting married is very much in order, but not for at least two years. Both will have to finish college and get settled in a job first. They are not yet certain where they will live after the knot is tied."[68] The paper further probed their relationship, asking, "How does her future mate like the idea of her being a national champion and highly publicized figure, having set two world's records?" "Well all right," replied Patton, leading the paper to clarify, "That is, all right except that he is a man—and most men like the idea of the male being the hero of the family."[69]

In short, the *Defender* used her to envision a respectably gendered version of black American belonging. Her athleticism enhanced her womanhood. For instance, *Afro-American* society columnist Lula Garrett celebrated her as "Queen of the Cinder Path," including her in a column that also recognized other young, feminine black women of accomplishment.[70] Lawler and Jackson received similar praise, with coverage of their achievements in the black sporting press serving to underscore their adherence to gender conventions. For instance, the *Philadelphia Tribune* described Lawler and Jackson as "very good students [who] plan to go on to graduate school upon completion of their work at Tuskegee," while also noting their involvement with the Red Cross.[71] In the *Chicago Defender*, Chuck Davis praised the performances of "Miss L," "La Lawler," and "Little Nellie," infantilizing designations that, while reflecting sexist thinking, also represented an effort to underscore the femininity of the young women.[72] These interpretations indicate the black middle-class belief in gender normativity as the symbolic language of citizenship, a way in which to earn the approval of white America. Historian Thaddeus Russell has analyzed the ways in which "the project of attaining [black] citizenship was constructed upon heterosexuality and in opposition to nonheteronormative behavior," asserting that Dr. Martin Luther King Jr. "understood that the attainment of full citizenship for African Americans required the creation of a heteronormative black culture."[73]

This strategy, of course, was not necessarily misguided; gender normativity did organize 1950s white America.[74] However, by endorsing white-defined gender roles, the black sport community circumscribed the agency and influence of black women track stars. They failed to see them as black athletic activists. Black track men, in contrast, unquestionably were seen as race men, with their athletic involvements and accomplishments read as part of the fight for racial equality. At the Pan-American Games, the black press repeatedly emphasized that Mal Whitfield, who secured the most success of American male track stars, was given a leave of absence from his Air Force assignment in Korea to compete in Buenos Aires.[75] His military and athletic service combined to certify him as an activist who contributed to the effort to make a better black America. Yet, despite a visit to the UN, Patton did not earn the status of race woman. By inviting Patton, the UN appeared to realize the potential of black women athletes as symbols of progress. But the black sport community, invested in seeing only male athletes as agents in the struggle for citizenship, did not. Illustratively, the *Defender* allowed that Elihu Latimer, not Patton, was still the "hero of the family."[76] Nonetheless, a subsequent celebration for Patton in Nashville shows that despite the black sport community's conservative, gendered conception of black women athletes, publicly honoring a black woman athlete still proved powerful, as demonstrated by "Alice Coachman Day" in Albany, Georgia. While the affair for Coachman exposed the anxiety that active and successful black womanhood caused for white America, the civic celebration for Patton had implications for ideas about race, gender, sport, and opportunity for white and black America.

When Patton arrived back in Nashville in mid-March 1951, the students and faculty of TSU enthusiastically welcomed her. TSU President W. S. Davis then led a motorcade to the city courthouse where he presented Patton to Nashville mayor Thomas Cummings, who praised the "excellent educational system of Nashville which had turned out such an outstanding citizen."[77] "Outstanding citizen" was a designation that not only conferred Americanness on Patton but also recognized black American young women as worthy of citizenship. Cummings recognized her as in possession of desirable cultural capital, which he sought to access for his city; Patton allowed Nashville to perform American meritocracy and democracy. Yet, recalling the *Albany Herald* editor James H. Gray, Cummings credited his segregated city, specifically the city's segregated educational system, for making Patton an "outstanding citizen." Cummings conveniently claimed Patton as a universal symbol of Nashville, in contradiction to her lived reality. Before he shared his statement, the marching bands of TSU, Pearl High School, and Washington Junior High School, the three black schools that Patton attended, led a parade.[78] The parading trio of marching bands exposed the optimistic inaccuracy of Cummings's words. The black educational and athletic culture of Nashville most contributed to Patton's success. These schools were products of a segregated society, yet they also were evidence of the possibilities created by black Nashvillians. Patton symbolized these possibilities.

And "Jean Patton Day" actualized the potential of these possibilities to erode the realities of segregation, or at least expose the absurdities of segregated ideologies. The celebration allowed black Nashville to experience public privileges from which they often were prohibited, freely occupying public space. Black Nashvillians lined the streets of downtown, from Sulphur Dell Park, the home

FIGURE 4. Tennessee State University welcomes Jean Patton back to Nashville following the 1951 Pan-American Games, where she won a trio of medals.
Courtesy of Tennessee State University Special Collections and Archives, Brown-Daniel Library

park for the Nashville Vols, a white minor league baseball team, and the Nashville Black Cubs, a Negro Southern League squad, to the city courthouse to the state capitol.[79] Since the parade wound through the civic center of Nashville, white Nashvillians, regardless of their opinions or preferences, also witnessed this acclamation for a black woman athlete. By dedicating public space to the celebration of Patton, the affair legitimated black women's athleticism for black and white Nashville. "Jean Patton Day" concluded with a ceremony back at Sulphur Dell Park, with Cummings and other civic leaders presenting Patton with gifts. The Birmingham Black Barons and Chicago American Giants then took to the field, as Nashville Sport Enterprise Promotions had arranged for the exhibition game between the Negro American League squads.[80] Thus, in Nashville, just as in Buenos Aires and Santiago, Patton raised questions about the relationship between race, gender, sport, and belonging for white and black American sport cultures. This inevitable questioning indicates the influence of black women's athleticism on larger understandings of American sport and society. Yet, influence did not guarantee a lack of insecurity. The status of women's track and field ahead of the 1952 Olympic Games in Helsinki was, once again, uncertain.

BLACK WOMEN TRACK STARS, THE ANTITHESIS OF THE AMERICAN WAY

As with the 1951 Pan-American Games, the 1952 Olympic Games represented a political project for the United States. But rather than establishing hemispheric authority, the US Olympic team was imagined as confirming the nation's superpower superiority. With the Soviet Union joining the Olympic Movement, the Games became a proxy battle in the Cold War. On the tracks and fields of Helsinki, American athletes would embody the democracy that aimed to defeat the communism manifested by Soviet athletes. The sporting Cold War thus had significance beyond geopolitical propaganda; it brought to the fore matters of identity politics.[81]

While the threat of communism did activate real anxieties in the early 1950s United States, widespread and ever-widening communist paranoia also spoke to insecurities about issues of race, gender, sexuality, and class within a changing US society. The sporting Cold War, like the Cold War more broadly, was a fight about content and extent of American national identity, not only as it was advertised abroad but also how it was understood and experienced at home.

As such, matters of race, gender, and sexuality were central to the American Way that the United States aimed to advertise through the Olympic Games. Black women track athletes did not easily fit with the desired image. Although the image of young black women wearing a USA uniform could counteract the accusations of racism and sexism that the Soviet Union increasingly lobbed at the United States in the information wars of the Cold War, these young women also served as reminders of the racial and gender inequities that the nation would rather ignore. As demonstrated by the cases of Coachman and Patton, the praiseworthy performances of black American track women posed complicated questions. So, prior to the 1952 Olympic Games, the USOC, once again, sought to limit women's track representation. In late 1951, the USOC announced that it would cap the number of potential Olympic women's track competitors at ten, meaning a maximum of ten track women could serve in the sporting Cold War.[82] The USOC also would require aspiring women's track Olympians again to meet strict qualifying standards. In combination, these artificially imposed policies indicate an effort to guard against the ways in which the presence and performance of black women athletes could challenge preferred perceptions of Americanness, which remained organized around whiteness and maleness.

However, the dawn of the sporting Cold War briefly appeared to offer an alternative opportunity for American track women. In anticipation of the 1952 Olympic Games, the white women who led the USOC and AAU women's track and field committees accelerated their advocacy for the sport, cleverly tapping into the ideals and fears of Cold War American society in order to argue for the appropriateness and Americanness of women track athletes. Or, more accurately, for the appropriateness and Americanness of implicitly white women track athletes. In frequent editorials for *Amateur Athlete*, the official magazine of the AAU, these women portrayed homebound young women as the antithesis of American values, instead arguing that active young women better bolstered American character. In a late 1951 editorial, Roxy Andersen, a former Canadian Olympic hurdler who recently had become the women's track and field commissioner for the Pacific AAU, pointedly pondered:

Certainly the American girl athlete is better fed, better housed, bettered clothed, and better coached than her British and European counterparts, but in the intervening years members of the fair sex across the seas have pushed our

American standard bearers well into the background when the Olympic and international medals were handed around. Surely our interest in sport has not lessened here, and from the population standpoint the United States has more to choose from and develop than Britain and Europe. What, then, is contributing to the alarming increase in poor performances by seemingly privileged American girl athlete[s]?[83]

Immediately ahead of the Olympics, she more exasperatedly asserted:

If we're going to wrap our girls in cotton wool, let's pad the pavements, flatten the hills, pull cars off our roads and eliminate the bargain counter! In fact, maybe we better just put our girls in softly padded cells, double check the air they breathe and remove them only briefly for breeding purposes! It would make just as much sense as depriving them of the healthy exercise they crave and the fun and release they long for which can be found only in women's competitive sport.[84]

Andersen implied that the bounties of capitalism and consumerism created the perfect conditions for producing elite American women track stars who then could project the superiority of American society in international competition. By not taking advantage of these circumstances, the institutions of American sport were not maximizing the benefits of consumer capitalism. They also were failing to live up to the nation's values of freedom and individualism, which seemingly required allowing young women to participate in athletics. In Andersen's estimation, developing "co-coon wrapper females who must be protected from the 'horrors' of women's competitive sport" should be an anathema for American society; they instead belonged in the sporting Cold War.

Of course, the suburbanized imagery Andersen conjured was dependent on whiteness. The whiteness of women's sport was assumed as necessary to making it "American." Yet, white Americanness was organized around certain and specific gender expectations that, despite the best efforts of Andersen and the AAU's other white women leaders, continued to make competitive sport inappropriate. Promotional materials produced by the USIA reveal the preferred conception of an American woman. For instance, a propaganda leaflet titled *Women in the United States* proclaimed, "Homemaking is still the goal of most American girls."[85] The home, not the track, remained the place where white American women should and would fight the Cold War. The ideal American woman was, or was preparing to be, a happy homemaker. Black women, in contrast, remained invisible in the gendered imagery of Cold War America. They also were absent from efforts to insert black Americans into the propagandistic image of America. As recognized by historian Laura Belmonte, USIA officials, reflecting the ideological bent of the majority of the nation's state, civic, and sporting leaders, "defined 'America' in terms that omitted many Americans."[86] For instance, Belmonte found that "US propaganda material rarely showed blacks in domestic situations." When "forced to address the gaps between democratic ideals and democratic realities," US officials did not turn to black women.[87]

The propaganda projects of the State Department instead relied on prominent black men, namely musical artists and athletes, to demonstrate the opportunities ostensibly available to black Americans.[88] The non-ideological associations of music and sport were believed to allow these men to be understood as universal and uncontroversial examples of American racial democracy. In fact, it was the confluence of certain raced and gendered assumptions that permitted black male athletes, in particular, to serve as symbols of American society. As detailed by sport studies scholar Damion Thomas, "US government officials consciously attempted to systematically promote African American athletes as examples of American willingness to incorporate people of color into the American social system."[89] Thomas identifies how the intersection of ideologies of blackness and masculinity resulted in black male athletes, such as the Harlem Globetrotters, simultaneously advertising racial integration and reasserting racial difference.[90] The Globetrotters emerged as favored goodwill ambassadors because the minstrel-like character of their brand of basketball worked, in the words of Thomas, "to give legitimacy to existing racial inequalities in American society by stressing 'progress' during the early cold war era, despite the social, political and legal barriers that hindered African-American advancement."[91]

The State Department deployed black male athletes to demonstrate that blackness was a part of Americanness, albeit doing so in a way that emphasized, rather than erased, racial differences. Blackness and femaleness, however, remained invisible in the imagery of Americanness. As discussed by historian Penny Von Eschen, the politicized and sexualized connotations of jazz made black women artists, such as composer and pianist Mary Lou Williams and choreographer and dancer Katherine Dunham, ineligible for goodwill ambassadorships in the eyes of State Department officials.[92] Because they raised questions about race, gender, sex, and nation that could not be easily constructed and construed, black women jazz artists were discomfiting representatives of American racial opportunity; they thus were unconsidered for early propaganda projects. Their absence underscores the politicalness of these supposedly apolitical national advertisements.

These projects and their preferences thus point to the power of black American women athletes, especially in the inaugural Olympic battle of the sporting Cold War. The meritocracy of international sport had allowed young black women to contest their invisibility, as shown by Alice Coachman in London and Jean Patton in Buenos Aires. In turn, sport's meritocracy had to be managed, inspiring the USOC again to impose strict women's track and field selection policies. As recognized by the *Afro-American*'s Sam Lacy, "Since the gals from Tuskegee, Tennessee State University, etc., have begun so completely to dominate the feminine track picture, there had been a marked decline in American Olympic interest in the direction," he wrote, pointing out that the "most recent announcement is that only ten gals will be taken abroad, nothing like the three-athlete-per-event which used to be the custom."[93] Nevertheless, these racially motivated restrictions would not prevent young black women from, literally, exercising their influence on the image of the American Way advertised at the 1952 Olympic Games. Through their performances, they counteracted the narrowly raced and gendered version of American identity that dominant culture aimed to consolidate through the sporting Cold War.

AGE, ASSURANCE, AND AMERICAN WOMEN'S ATHLETICISM

On July 4, 1952, approximately one hundred aspiring Olympians would take to the track and field in Harrisburg, Pennsylvania, to strive for one of the ten Olympic team slots. The July Fourth date presented coincidental yet potent symbolism. On the nation's birthday, young black women would attempt to earn the right to represent the nation that rarely claimed them. Or, from an alternative perspective, on the day also known as Independence Day, black women athletes would assert their independence from the social constructs of the sporting Cold War, using their athletic ability to establish themselves as deserving defenders of democracy.

With Jean Patton out due to injury, Mae Faggs and Catherine Hardy established themselves as the premier US talents. Since the 1948 Olympic Games, when a sixteen-year-old Faggs struggled to perform at her peak, the native of Bayside, New York, had demonstrated significant improvement as she continued to train with the PAL. Among other achievements, Faggs thrice captured the 220-yard crown at the National AAU Indoor Championships, while also leading the PAL to four straight team titles.[94] However, at the 1952 National AAU Outdoor Championship, Catherine Hardy showed greater speed than Faggs. The lone women's track competitor from Georgia's Fort Valley State College, Hardy triumphed in the 50-meter, 100-meter, and 200-meter sprint races. Her trio of victories earned her high point honors, besting the total accumulated by Faggs.[95] At the Olympic Trials, Faggs exacted a measure of revenge against her budding rival, taking the 100-meter title to earn her return trip to the Olympic Games. Hardy, however, bettered Faggs in the 200 meters, covering the distance in a swift 24.3 seconds.[96]

Three other young black track women also would claim an Olympic team berth. Barbara Jones, a fifteen-year-old sophomore at Chicago's St. Elizabeth High School who competed for the Chicago CYO, qualified as a member of the 400-meter relay squad, while Mary McNabb, a Tuskegee Tigerette from Atlanta, Georgia, was named the relay alternate. In the long jump, Mabel Landry, also a member of Chicago CYO, established a new American record as she punched her ticket to Helsinki. Four young white women—Janet Moreau, Dolores Dwyer, Marjorie Larney, and Janet Dicks—also made the Olympic team, resulting in squad with five black and four white women.[97] The interracial composition of the squad had the potential to scramble the ideological assumptions that organized American society. Racialized bodies in raced and gendered spaces was definitional to the social and cultural landscape of the Cold War United States. White women belonged in the home, visibly communicating safety, security, and stability. Black women existed outside the home, primarily performing invisible work on the margins of society. In Helsinki, the women's track and field team, regardless of the predilections of the USOC, had the potential to make visible an alternative organization of American society.

This potency remained invisible and unintelligible to the authorities of American sport culture. Instead, women athletes instinctually were understood in ways that did not threaten white heteropatriarchal power. In a report on the Olympic Trials, the New York Times led, "Youth dominated a nine-woman track and field [team] chosen tonight to represent the United States at the Olympic Games in Helsinki later this month."[98] The Times introduced the lens through which the women's track team would be understood. The idea of youth assuaged any uncertainties about an interracial cohort of young women athletes. Turning to age to make sense of something potentially unsettling also was a strategy characteristic of Cold War–era culture. Remonstrations against juvenile delinquency, the effects of momism, and fears of teen pregnancy all were anxieties about cultural change foisted onto young people.[99] Constructing youth-centric crises encouraged submission to social norms, thereby reinforcing social stability. Age served as a source of assurance in women's track. This framing expanded on the contentions about youth sport advertised by AAU leaders, including its white women officials. For instance, Catherine Meyer presented sport as a prophylactic against juvenile delinquency in a 1949 *Amateur Athlete* editorial.[100] More broadly, the AAU promoted sport as inculcating youth with cooperation, discipline, and determination.[101] Youthfulness thus provided a "safe" frame of understanding for the nation's women's track Olympians.

Making age the primary identity category through which women track athletes were understood also allowed for the elision of racial difference. While the emphasis on their shared youthfulness could be seen as progressive and integrative, it also had a regressive, color-blind function. For instance, the *Afro-American* published a photo of seven members of the Olympic team, four black and three white.[102] The photo, with black and white young women draping their arms around each other, communicated interracial sisterhood. By printing an image of girlish naivety, the *Afro-American* symbolically claimed the privileges of white feminine girlhood for young black women athletes. Yet, this image also validated the color-blind imaginings of Catherine Meyer, Roxy Andersen, and their fellow white women leaders, presenting racial difference as not determinative within the sport. Youth masked the reasons why opposition to women's athleticism remained intense. It not only ignored the sport's racialization, but also the material effects of this racialization, epitomized by the fact that the USOC only selected nine young track women for the Games.

Attention to the age of American track women also reconciled their role in the sporting Cold War. Their youthfulness, even girlishness, distanced them from the demands of the ideologically tinged athletic battle. The Cold War was a masculine rivalry, fought in the almost exclusively male arenas of politics, military, science, and sport. Ahead of Helsinki, American track and field was made to adhere to the gender distinctions characteristic of American culture, with heroic track men and happy track girls. Portraying women track stars as young girls also distinguished them from their Soviet counterparts, eliminating any rivalry between ostensibly more appropriate, girlish American athletes and the blatantly inappropriate, supposedly Amazonian Soviet ones. It is worth noting that the emphasis on the youth of the American track women did not misrepresent them, as, at twenty-two years old, Catherine Hardy was the elder stateswoman. But it did undercut their agency as athletes. These young women were trained and talented athletes, not giggling girls who just happened to run fast or jump high. The fact that the nine qualifiers exceeded the USOC's intentionally strict qualifying standards indicates as much; youth did not preclude ability and expertise. Even if they lacked international experience, they were legitimate athletes. And when they competed and succeeded, the more inconvenient aspects of their identity would become less reconcilable, making evident they ways in which young women athletes, specifically young black women athletes, challenged the raced and gendered conceptions of Cold War America.

IMAGINING IDEAL WOMEN'S ATHLETICISM

However, through the majority of the women's track and field competition in Helsinki, the image of youthful naivety that characterized American track women appeared accurate. Despite the promising performances turned in at the Olympic Trials, the international stage seemingly overwhelmed them. "American girls showed insufficient experience in the sprints," announced *Track & Field News*.[103] *Amateur Athlete* confirmed this analysis, suggesting, "The U.S. girls found the international competition far above their capabilities in most events as they wound up far behind in the team struggle."[104] Entering the final day of competition, the American track women only had secured a single point, earned by the veteran Mae Faggs for her sixth-place finish in the 100 meters.[105]

Outside of the Americans, the Helsinki program produced an array of impressive women's track and field performances. "Women athletes from Down Under are stopping the show in track," declared the *New York Times*.[106] Australia's Marjorie Jackson romped to gold in the 100-meter dash, setting a new Olympic and world record of 11.5 seconds. The track world had anticipated a showdown between Jackson and Fanny Blankers-Koen, who entered the Games intending to defend her crown. But illness ruined her Olympic fortnight. She had to withdraw from the 100-meter final before then suffering her first defeat on the Olympic stage in the 80-meter hurdles final. Her strength sapped due to sickness, she crashed into the first two barriers, failing to finish.[107] The Australian track women thus provided all the thrills in the running events. Jackson also captured the 200-meter gold in world record time. Shirley Strickland de la Hunty then grabbed a record-setting gold in the 80-meter hurdles.[108]

The mainstream American track press took an interest in the Australian duo, with the *New York Times's* Allison Danzig celebrating the twenty-year-old "fair-haired" Jackson as "the nearest thing to Fanny Blankers-Koen in these games."[109] *Track & Field News* likewise praised "Pretty Shirley Strickland de la Hunty."[110] Along with the Australians, women athletes from South Africa, New Zealand, and Germany turned in the strongest performances in the running and jumping events. Developments in Helsinki, like those in London, demonstrated that white women possessed athletic ability, refuting the fearmongering that continued to surround competitive sport for white American women. As summated by *Track & Field News*, "Anglo-Saxon girls again dominated in the sprint and hurdle races."[111] But in the strength-based field events, Soviet women took center stage. On the first day of track and field competition, Nina Romaschkova earned the Soviet Union their first-ever Olympic medal, slinging the discus further than teammates Elizaveta Bagrjanceva and Nina Dumbadze, the reigning world record holder.[112] Standing on the rostrum as the Soviet anthem played, the three women athletes presented a vision of Eastern European women's athleticism at odds with the rumored idea of illegitimate Amazonian women. The *New York Times* published a photo of three rather feminine young women receiving honorary gardenias from a Finnish young woman, a scene that complicated assumptions about athleticism, femininity, and nationality.[113]

The tall, blonde, and slim Aleksandra Chudina, who claimed a trio of medals, winning a silver in the broad jump and javelin before taking bronze in the high jump, also countered the conventional image of supposedly masculinized Soviet womanhood. Chudina instead appeared to embody idealized American athletic femininity, evidenced by the mainstream American sporting press's interest in her.[114] The javelin gold medalist attracted even more favor in the United States. The victorious Czechoslovakian Dana Zátopková was the wife of the great Emil Zápotek, who accomplished the Games' most stellar feat by winning the 5,000 meters, 10,000 meters, and marathon. Only a few hours after her husband captured his 5,000-meter gold, Zátopková heaved the javelin further than a trio of Soviet challengers. Her ability to beat the Soviets, all while advertising an appealing and appropriate image of women's athleticism, positioned her as an admiration-worthy woman athlete, both in the United

States and wider Western sporting world.[115] The response to Zátopková and others demonstrated that mainstream American sport culture could express enthusiasm about women's athleticism. Although coverage of women's track was limited, it was far from caustic.

But the open-minded attitude expressed about the triumphs of white Western and Eastern European track women did not extended to the interracial cohort of young American women. In coverage, they were almost invisible, deemed irrelevant except as apparent scapegoats. When the Soviet Union led in the overall, albeit unofficial, Olympic standings at the Games' midpoint, the *New York Times* did not hesitate to blame American women athletes, reporting on July 25 that "the Soviet women have put the USSR far in front in the team standings."[116] "An analysis tonight showed that the Communist women have scored a total of 139 points in track and field and gymnastic competition compared to one point for the United States' women," the *Times* explicated.[117] The USOC primarily was to blame, with its long-intransigent stance against women's track designed almost to guarantee a lack of success. The *Times*, notably, never protested USOC polices. Nonetheless, mainstream American sport culture readily relied on assumptions about young women athletes to explain democracy's inability to defeat communism in the sporting Cold War. However, this convenient narrative of unthreatening and overmatched American women's athleticism soon would be untenable, as the fortunes of American track women suddenly, and stunningly, would change.

THE ASPIRATIONS, ACHIEVEMENTS, AND ANXIETIES OF AMERICAN TRACK WOMEN

When the 400-meter relay team of Mae Faggs, Barbara Jones, Catherine Hardy, and Janet Moreau, a white sprinter from Boston's Red Diamond Athletic Club, stepped on the track on the final day of the women's track and field program, no expectation for excellence greeted them. But the sentiments of the sporting world did not matter to Mae Faggs. The undisputed leader of the youthful American women did not believe their shortcomings on the Olympic stage thus far guaranteed further lack of success. She sought to lift the sagging spirit of her relay-mates, insisting, "We're going to win the 400-meter!" Refusing to return home from her second Olympic adventure empty handed, she additionally implored, "I just have to go back home with a medal!"[118]

Her teammates responded. The fiery Faggs, running the first leg, did her best to position her teammates for success. Barbara Jones and Janet Moreau then followed suit, allowing Catherine Hardy to turn Australia's misfortune into America's fortune. When the women from Down Under bobbled the final pass of the baton, Hardy took advantage of her opening. Her action is illustrative of her experience as a young black woman track athlete, as well as symbolic of black American track women more broadly. A native of Carollton, Georgia, the lithe Hardy had been the lone competitor for Fort Valley State College. While the black college had claimed Hardy as their own Alice Coachman, holding a "snappy and zestful" celebration for her after she won a record-setting National AAU Indoor sprint title in 1951, she had access to little support throughout her athletic career.[119] Following her graduation from Fort Valley in the spring of 1952 with a degree in physical education, Hardy struggled to secure a job, forcing her to wrestle with an unsettled future as she prepared for Olympic competition.[120]

Nevertheless, Hardy would make the Olympic team, and then make her mark in Helsinki. Her ability to claim victory on the track mirrors her ability to claim her place in the sport, all in spite of unfavorable circumstances. Young black women who competed in elite sport similarly had to seek to make the best of less than certain situations, ever-navigating inequities of race, gender, and class. In short, young black women's consistent participation in international sport should be appreciated as just as surprising as the 400-meter relay gold secured by Hardy. They overcame exclusion, inequality, and ignorance not only to challenge elite women athletes from Western and Eastern Europe, but also to contest the imagined image of the American Way. As they danced and dallied down the track, celebrating their success, the foursome of Faggs, Jones, Moreau, and Hardy offered an alternative image of Americanness, one inclusive of the autonomy and ability of all young women.

The American sport community, however, worked to undercut any celebration of their success with various rationalizations. Writing in the *New York Times*, Allison Danzig applauded the fact that "our women's 4x100 relay team had scored an amazing victory in the world record time of 45.9 seconds." He then emphasized, "The triumph was all the more sensational because our women athletes during the entire games had tallied only one point."[121] At first glance, his analysis appears to appreciate sufficiently the surprising success of the American quartet. Yet, the specter of their shortcomings hovered over the commentary. Similarly, *Amateur Athlete* noted, "The speedy representatives of the U.S. salvaged American pride in the 400 meter relay with a sensational record-breaking win."[122] The use of the word "salvage" suggests that the American women were in dire straits, desperately needing to justify their right to compete for the United States. Nonetheless, luck, rather than ability, was understood as the reason for their win. The official report from the Helsinki Games focused on the Australian mistake more than the American success. "What might the world record for the women's 4 X 100 metres relay be but for this misfortune?," the report pondered.[123] "The USA won in 45.9. By all accounts the Australian team should have been capable of 45.4 or even better," the then report estimated.[124]

The tenuous place of women's track and field in American sport culture made this skepticism more than innocent analysis. It represented a resistance to seeing young track women, particularly young black track women, as legitimate contributors to, and thus members of, the nation. Faggs, Jones, Moreau, and Hardy were imagined as nothing more than a giggling gaggle of young American girls who consistently had been outclassed by European competitors until they happened to stumble into a gold medal. Accepting them as autonomous athletes would not have cohered with the cultural precepts of Cold War America. Ideas about women organized American society, with the delicate, submissive, and feminine white woman mirrored by the duplicitous and conniving or hardworking and homely black woman. Women's athleticism, especially the interracial relay quartet, disrupted this mythological paradigm. Thus establishment voices in American sport culture presented their 400-meter relay gold as mere luck; it was a singular moment of success that indicated nothing about the athleticism, abilities, and autonomy of American women, black or white.

It is thus important to emphasize that the American quartet did not simply benefit from the Australian mishap; the world-record time they turned in testifies to the fact that they took full advantage of a fortunate circumstance. It is not unimaginable that, had Australia's Winsome Cripps and Marjorie Jackson better executed their exchange, Hardy still could have captured gold. Only a little over a year prior Jean Patton, not in Helsinki due to injury, had beaten Jackson at the Los Angeles Coliseum Relays, stunning the track world. Hardy possessed speed that exceeded that of Patton, having set a new American 50-meter record in June. Although they performed inconsistently on the Olympic stage, American track women possessed international-level talent.

FIGURE 5. After winning the gold medal in the 400-meter relay at the 1952 Olympic Games, the American foursome of (beginning far right) Barbara Jones, Catherine Hardy, Janet Moreau, and Mae Faggs circle the track in celebration, accompanied by members of the relay teams from Germany and Britain.

BLACK WOMEN ATHLETES AND EARLY COLD WAR BLACK AMERICA

Nonetheless, only a slightly altered interpretation of the relay achievement emerged from black American sport culture. Before competition began, voices in the black sporting press offered a more favorable attitude about American women's athleticism. The *New York Amsterdam News* suggested, "The big worry is whether or not Mae Faggs, Mabel Landry, and our other distaffers can cope with the Russian excellentos in skirts."[125] In contrast to mainstream, white-defined sport culture, the *Amsterdam News* inserted black track women into the sporting Cold War, positioning them as potential contributors to the sporting nation. But as the Games unfolded, any optimism soon dampened, with voices in the black press offering rather stringent criticisms of the shortcomings of young black women athletes. After the first days of the women's track program, the *Afro-American* unsympathetically reported that "failing in their respective events were most of the American women: Catherine Hardy in the 200 meters, Mae Faggs in the 100 (she finished sixth), and Barbara Jones in the broad jump."[126]

In the context of Cold War American culture, black sport culture's adoption of the attitudes of white sport culture is understandable. As argued by historian Mary Dudziak, the Cold War structured black Americans' quest for civil rights.[127] For white-controlled American politics and culture, communism served as a malleable discourse, used to enforce social conformity and achieve social stability.[128] Thus fear of accusations of communist sympathies worked to constrict black American politics and culture. The demands of the Truman Doctrine discouraged the anti-imperialism and internationalism that had characterized the movement for civil rights, compelling the NAACP, as well as other mainstream organizations, to quiet criticisms of American foreign policy.[129] The perceived disloyalty of Paul Robeson exemplified this shift. While the Renaissance man previously had been understood as the best of black America, his words against American racial inequalities at the 1949 Paris World Peace Conference inspired an investigation by the House Un-American Activities Committee (HUAC). Through the HUAC hearing, the multitalented Robeson experienced how the Cold War enabled American state and society to impose limits on black Americans' effort for equality.[130]

Such Cold War constraints extended into understandings of sport. In the early postwar period, black track men had been avatars of a black-defined masculinity. Competing in the longer integrated sport of track and field, they had the cultural space and security to be seen as race men who expanded the boundaries of American sport and, in extension, American identity, establishing black American manhood through their athletic achievements. The escalating conditions of the Cold War, however, narrowed the racialized gender identities available to black American men, athletes or not. Performing a less assertive and more accommodating brand of black manhood served as a surer and safer strategy, guarding against accusations of communism and accentuating a commitment to the nation's values.[131] As he reintegrated Major League Baseball, Jackie Robinson modeled this cautious positioning, calibrating his every action, on and off the field.[132]

International and Olympic sport also allowed for the clear communication of patriotic priorities, as evinced by black sport culture's increased investment in black male athletes as icons of traditional American masculinity. For instance, the *Afro-American's* Sam Lacy celebrated Harrison Dillard, who would finally capture his long-sought hurdling gold medal in Helsinki, and Mal

Whitfield, who successfully defended his 800-meter gold medal, in ways that accentuated their normativity. Lacy praised Dillard for his humble, gentlemanly, and "kingly qualit[ies]."[133] Of Whitfield, Lacy rhapsodized, "He's truly an all-American, having been born in Texas, raised in California, and educated in Ohio," while also celebrating that "the world half-mile champion has 27 missions over Korea behind him, missions in which he served as a B-26 gunner."[134] Rather than celebrating them as exemplars of black athletic manhood, Lacy and his colleagues in the black sporting press made black athletes into more conservative, conventional American heroes.

This more conservative perspective also prevailed with black sport culture's interpretation of the women's 400-meter relay win. Voices in the black sport press celebrated the quartet for their surprising success, yet, like their white counterparts, not without emphasizing their previous inadequacy. The *Philadelphia Tribune* announced, "In the final day of competition, the surprise champions of the Olympics were the women's 400 meter relay foursome of the United States," before noting that it "was the only gold medal won by the American women in this meet as most of them were eliminated before the finals in most of the events."[135] The *Chicago Defender's* Fay Young somewhat sarcastically suggested, "The United States women's Olympic track team was against some big women and our 'poor little girls' did their best."[136] Although he took satisfaction in the unexpected achievement of the majority-black American quartet, he still elected to advance an infantilizing image of women track stars, rather disrespectfully dismissing their athletic agency. Similarly, the *Tribune's* Al Moses shared, "That special pet of this column, tiny Mae Faggs, Catherine Hardy, Barbara Jones, and their Nordic teammate, Janet Moreau created an Olympic and world mark in winning the 400-meter relay in 45.9."[137]

By using such language to discuss American women track athletes, these elder statesmen of black sport culture downplayed, or even denied, their athletic capacity. They were not athletes who represented the capacity of black womanhood, as Alice Coachman and Jean Patton had been, but young black girls who, along with their white teammate, happened to have run fast. These attitudes were a manifestation of, in the words of sociologist Maxine Craig, one of "the specifically gendered ways [that] racial domination expressed itself."[138] For Cold War–era black America, the effort to conform to racialized norms of uncontroversial Americanness also implicated norms of gender in ways that, more often than not, reinforced the submissive, secondary place of black women in the social and cultural spaces of black America, including spaces of sport. Instinctually obeying these ideological dictates, black sports-writers resorted to rather paternalistic analyses to attempt to make sense of the 400-meter foursome, navigating gender norms by simultaneously crediting and discrediting their unexpected gold medal effort.

BLACK WOMEN ATHLETES AND EARLY COLD WAR AMERICAN CULTURE

In total, the 1952 American Olympic experience appeared to reinforce the traditional racial and gender boundaries of American identity. As a conservative institution organized around exhibitions of masculine authority, sport primarily served as a stabilizing force, advertising and inculcating the conformity desired by the dominant institutions in the United States, both public and private. At the pre-Olympic farewell held in New York City, the white pole vaulter Bob Richards, who would win gold in Helsinki, expressed this idea to his fellow athletes, stating, "Rest assured that on the field of competition we will give our all not only as athletes but also as representatives of the highest ideals of the American way of life. In a time of international tension these games provide a medium of friendship. We intend to win, but if we lose, we will lose gracefully. I pledge that we will abide by the rules of good sportsmanship."[139]

This vision largely succeeded. The United States "won" the sporting Cold War, securing more points than their Soviet counterparts to triumph in the unofficial Olympic competition between national teams (although the Soviets declared the contest a tie).[140] In particular, Richards and his fellow American track men, responsible for the plurality of the US points, appeared to present a desirably democratic vision of American society, with the expected champions such as Richards, Dillard, and Whitfield joined by more surprising victors in Lindy Remigino, the Italian-American who won the 100 meters, and Milt Campbell, the young black American decathlete who took the silver in the Games' most grueling event.[141] A shared investment in normative manhood characterized male Olympic champions and expressed American authority.

Yet, the fulfillment of the vision described by Richards also fractured, and not due to a lack of grace or good sportsmanship. While the sporting Cold War encouraged the consolidation of the American Way, it also exposed its exclusions. The race and gender of identities of athletes who claimed victories made impossible the preferred, coherent vision of the Cold War United States, as most embodied by the triumphant track women. Thus, despite its conventional, traditional connotations, sport provided a public space in which the destabilizing potential of American women could be displayed. They exposed, however briefly, an alternative vision of America, one that the institutions that sought to establish the so-called Cold War cultural consensus would rather ignore. Mae Faggs, Barbara Jones, Janet Moreau, and, most especially, Catherine Hardy demonstrated the determination, confidence, and capacity possessed by young women, black and white. In short, a majority black, gold medal–winning women's 400-meter relay challenged the constrictions and contradictions of racial difference and gendered possibility that organized American society.

While seemingly momentary, their impact would have reverberations. The institutions of Cold War–era sport, society, and state would, albeit slowly, accommodate, incorporate, and, as would be evident with Wilma Rudolph, eventually acclaim black women's athleticism. Other dimensions of Cold War culture were scripted, thereby consigning black women's bodies to their limited role in American society in an effort to control meanings of racial and gender difference. But sport was unscripted; it provided a space in which young black women could publicly claim their Americanness. And, just as significantly, sport success encouraged American culture to begin to claim black women. The sporting Cold War would become an enabling structure for black women athletes, creating avenues of possibility among still existing constraints. The image of Mae Faggs, Barbara Jones, and Catherine Hardy joyously jumping with Janet Moreau in the summer of 1952 was not deemed emblematic of the American Way, but the image of Wilma Rudolph winning a trio of gold medals in the summer of 1960 would be. This shift indicates that the experiences of black women track stars illuminate the negotiations and renegotiations of race, gender, and national identity that defined the United States during the 1950s, not only as the Cold War escalated but also as the direct-action movement for civil rights emerged. Moving forward, the demands of these movements, in combination with the performances of black women track athletes, pushed and pressed the boundaries of American belonging.

3

PASSING THE BATON TOWARD BELONGING

MAE FAGGS AND THE MAKING OF THE AMERICANNESS
OF BLACK AMERICAN TRACK WOMEN, 1954–1956

Four years after leading the American women to an unexpected gold medal in the 400-meter relay, Mae Faggs again found herself on the Olympic track. Instead of Barbara Jones, Janet Moreau, and Catherine Hardy, her teammates now were a trio of young Tigerbelles: twenty-one-year-old Margaret Matthews of Atlanta, Georgia; fifteen-year-old Wilma Rudolph of Clarksville, Tennessee; and nineteen-year-old Isabelle Daniels of Jakin, Georgia. As she completed the first leg of the relay final, Faggs passed the baton to Matthews. Matthews and Rudolph both ran sufficiently speedy legs before Rudolph and Daniels executed their exchange, readying Daniels to finish the race. In a tightly contested final sprint, Daniels sought to establish separation from her Australian, British, and the Soviet competitors. She proved unable to best Australia's Betty Cuthbert or Britain's Heather Armitage, leaving the American foursome with the bronze. The time of 44.9 seconds recorded by the quartet of Tigerbelles improved upon the 45.9 seconds of their 1952 Olympic predecessors.[1]

Faggs, however, was frustrated. She blamed herself for the inability of the Americans to claim a brighter medal, believing she should have emphasized to Daniels the necessity of leaning toward the tape, a tactical adjustment that may have allowed her teammate to take the silver or even the gold. On the whole, a sense of dissatisfaction dominated Faggs's third Olympic experience.[2] Deemed the "Mother of the Tigerbelles" by TSU coach Ed Temple, Faggs took her leadership, or mothering, responsibility seriously.[3] Before and during the Olympic fortnight, she devoted her energy to preparing her teammates to perform at their peak, doing so at the expense of her own condition. Faggs had hoped finally to claim an elusive individual medal. Yet, when at the starting line for her 200-meter semi-final race, Faggs found herself overtrained, resulting in her failing to advance to the final. She later recollected, "I was just so interested in my teammates, and helping them, and I was running so hard because I wanted us to get a medal. This shouldn't bother me but it still does."[4] Nonetheless, Temple later declared the 1956 Olympic team "the foundation" of modern American women's track and field, recognizing that the nine young black women who competed for the nation in Melbourne made possible the more celebrated successes to come.[5] Albeit in different tones, Faggs's dissatisfaction and Temple's satisfaction both capture the raised expectations and expanded opportunities for black American track women in the mid-1950s.

The collision of the Cold War and civil rights movement explains these changed circumstances.[6] Through an emphasis on nonviolent direct-action protest, the civil rights movement effectively illuminated the absolute insufficiency of American democracy. The Soviet Union, in turn, trumpeted this evidence of American hypocrisy. In response, black American track women were enlisted in the sporting Cold War. As the civil rights movement showed, respectable women, such as Rosa Parks, and ambitious girls, like the many who aimed to integrate public schools, powerfully could communicate that black Americans deserved full citizenship. Somewhat similarly, black women athletes, who also were respectable and ambitious, could demonstrate that the United States was making progress toward racial equality. At the 1955 Pan-American Games in Mexico City and 1956 Olympic Games in Melbourne, black American track women were inserted into the image of Americanness. Black American sport culture also altered its appraisal of black women track stars, now understanding them as race women who contributed to the quest for equality. In Mexico City in 1955, Barbara Jones and Mildred McDaniel achieved victories that led to their acclaim as both American and black American athletic heroines. A year later in Melbourne, McDaniel and a sextet of TSU Tigerbelles again inspired the enthusiasms of American and black American sport cultures.

But even as black women track stars began to earn unprecedented recognition as representatives of American sport, black America, and America at large, such praise and promotion ultimately did not alter ideal American identity.

The intersection of their racial and gender identities simultaneously enabled and constrained their representational influence. The young black women who represented the United States in the 1955 Pan-American Games and 1956 Olympic Games emerged as athletic icons because they expertly abided by normative, white-defined gender expectations, as strategized by Ed Temple.[7] The performance of gender normative whiteness, rather than assertions of black femaleness, permitted the perceived Americanness of black American track women. Thus, by following the "Temple Way," young black women helped to inscribe a certain, circumscribed American identity. The highly gendered understanding of them confirmed, rather than challenged, the social order that organized mid-1950s American society.

However, beneath this conservative and conventional imagery, black women athletes exercised influence, as most exemplified by the unapologetic and outspoken Mae Faggs. She was the "Mother of the Tigerbelles" not simply because she served as the model of the Temple Way, but because she shaped the Temple Way to meet the needs and desires of young black women, introducing a sense of "entitlement" into the culture of black women's track and field.[8] It was this entitlement that made, and would continue to make, American sport culture recognize, accommodate, and begin to appreciate the athletic ability and American identity of young black track women. Faggs's influence is most evident in the attitudes expressed by her talented younger teammates, Wilma Rudolph and Willye White, at the 1956 Olympic Games. However, Faggs's frustrations also indicate the continued uncertainty and insecurity facing black American track women. Her 1956 Olympic experience encapsulated the new possibilities and enduring precarities that were produced by the collision of the Cold War and civil rights movement.

THE TEMPLE WAY AND THE AMERICAN WAY

In the fall of 1952, not long after returning from Helsinki, Mae Faggs headed south, matriculating at TSU and joining new head coach Ed Temple's Tigerbelle track and field program. At TSU, Temple adopted and perfected the Tuskegee model, combining a commitment to education, athletics, and appearance to create opportunities for young black women.[9] Although only twenty-six years old when he assumed head coaching duties, Temple, who also served as a sociology instructor at TSU, acutely understood how ideologies of race, gender, and sexuality would be ascribed to his athletes, potentially delegitimizing them, as well as black America more broadly. In response, he established the Temple Way, an intentionally-strict suite of policies and practices that served to preemptively protect his athletes from racist, sexist, and homophobic stereotypes. The mantra "ladies first, students second, and athletes third" governed all Tigerbelles.[10]

To ensure this standard was met, Temple issued many heavy-handed mandates. Because dominant ideas about female promiscuity were racialized as black, Temple prioritized guarding against any such perceptions. He thus prevented Tigerbelles from riding in cars with any romantic suitors or attending extracurricular dances. Yet, more than wanting to discourage any overly sexualized understandings of his athletes, he sought to encourage appropriately feminized understandings of them. Temple demanded that Tigerbelles expertly perform traditional, heterosexual, white-defined femininity. "I want foxes, not oxes" became a famous (or infamous) Temple maxim.[11] For instance, Tigerbelles were required to style their hair and apply makeup immediately after meets, an effort to imitate ideal white womanhood. Temple would later clarify, "What I wanted was that no matter where we went, people, perfect strangers would wonder what my young ladies did . . . I wanted folks to be surprised to discover they were members of an athletic team."[12]

In her autobiography, Tigerbelle Wyomia Tyus, who would win back-to-back gold medals in the 100 meters at the 1964 and 1968 Olympic Games, expressed frustration with, but also understanding of, these performative requirements, writing, "Whatever 'ladylike' meant. We knew that it meant you had to carry yourself a certain way." She continues, "If you look at pictures of when the Tigerbelles traveled as a team, you can see that we were always decked out in our finest. That was a big part of the program. Tigerbelles had to dress up to get on a plane. That was it. We had to conform to the social idea of what it meant to be a lady—or at least Mr. Temple's idea of what it meant."[13] Like athletic director Cleve Abbott and the authorities at Tuskegee, Temple understood that young black women were "symbolic material" who could "rearticulate the meaning of black in American society."[14] The Tigerbelles, like the Tigerettes, exemplified the assimilative ideology of black American citizenship.

The purpose of the strict rules, regulations, and restrictions that composed the Temple Way extended beyond the symbolic. As Temple realized, "Every single one of these girls had never really been away from home. I was responsible for them. I felt responsible for them. I had promised their parents I would look after them and that's just what I did."[15] Temple's policies and practices made sport a safe and suitable space through which young black women could improve their life station. Athletic achievement allowed young black women to access opportunities otherwise unavailable, especially educational opportunities. As Temple recognized and reiterated, "Athletics opens up doors for you, but education keeps them open."[16] He rightly promoted the power of education and athletics to together "uplift" poor, rural, and presumably unrefined young black women. The recollections of Tyus confirm Temple's effectiveness, as she notes, "Some people claim Mr. Temple controlled us, but I don't think so. I think he tried to create a safe place where we could learn our own minds."[17]

Not insignificantly, Temple's policies did not prevent TSU from becoming a women's track juggernaut. He carefully attended to the athletic development of each Tigerbelle. As he would tell the *Philadelphia Tribune*, "I am a perfectionist and I believe in lighting [sic] starts and correct body movements."[18] Tyus remembers expertly organized practices, focusing on fitness, technique, and other specialties. Temple also would film these practices, later providing pointed criticisms of any flaws in an athlete's form.[19] This programmatic philosophy resulted in TSU dominating women's National AAU championships and populating the rosters of Olympic teams from the mid-1950s through the 1960s. The Tigerbelles appeared to exemplify the belief that femininity and athleticism were compatible. Still, the Temple Way seemed to put black women athletes in a curious position. Temple's gendered strictures required young women to subsume their own priorities to perform a certain image of a supposedly appropriate and American womanhood, which was defined as, and thus perpetuated the privileged status of, normative, middle-class white womanhood. In order to experience uplifting athletic and educational possibilities, young black women had to sacrifice their self-determination. Tyus, however, understood it more nuancedly. Of Temple's attitude and impact, she asserts:

> He knew that Black women wanted something other than just a sedentary-type life, that track gave us an opportunity to do extraordinary things, and that there was more for us to do than be a teacher or a nurse—although if that was what you wanted to do, he would encourage you to do it. I never thought a Black woman with some schooling could have an occupation other than those two until I went to Tennessee State and got to talk to Tigerbelles who had gone places and done things—things I had just heard about or maybe read in a book. Mr. Temple got us to see beyond what society expected of us at the time, and if had done nothing else, that still would have been enough.[20]

Nevertheless, the public performance of the Temple Way mostly masked this progressivism. Instead, it appeared to align with, and thus helped entrench, the ideology of the AAU and USOC. As discussed, the actions and attitudes of the white women leaders of the USOC and AAU reveal their instinctive prioritization of white women athletes. From her perch at the AAU, Roxy Andersen continued to pen editorials that imagined women track stars as exemplars of an implicitly white all-American womanhood. In a July 1954 *Amateur Athlete* op-ed, she introduced sport as an incubator of cooperation, community, ingenuity, and voluntarism, the values that defined citizenship for (white) women in the 1950s.[21] Of former women track athletes, Andersen asserted, "The same urge that drove them to the top in their respective fields of sport has also helped them to become leaders in their communities today. The well-learned lesson of good sportsmanship is now being applied to everyday living," thereby injecting sport with social purpose.[22] Similarly, former Olympian and new AAU women's track and field committee chairwoman Frances Kaszubski insisted that "all girls who participate in the sport of track and field and especially those who enter AAU track meets are classified as modern Cinderellas" who were "worthy of knowing, cultivating, promoting, or meriting recognition or attention."[23] By abiding by the Temple Way, Tigerbelles encouraged the administrators of women's track to begin to celebrate them as sporting Cinderellas. Of course, Alice Coachman, Jean Patton, and other black American track women from the late 1940s and early 1950s also had been subject to the intersectional pressures of race and gender, which they navigated by comporting themselves with calm and class. However, historical circumstances endowed the Tigerbelles who practiced the Temple Way with propagandistic power, which in turn allowed black American track women to begin to emerge as examples of the American Way.

The intensification of the Cold War and the acceleration of the civil rights movement motivated a reappraisal and revaluation of the Americanness and feminineness of young black track women. As emphasized by historian Mary Dudziak, the Cold War and civil rights movement inextricably were intertwined. "The Cold War created a constraining environment for domestic politics. It also gave rise to new opportunities for those who could exploit Cold War anxieties, while yet remaining within the bounds of acceptable 'Americanism,'" she argues.[24] The conditions of the Cold War helped enhance the effectiveness of the emerging nonviolent direct-action civil rights movement of the 1950s. Civil rights activists, especially those involved with the campaigns organized by

Dr. Martin Luther King Jr. and the Southern Christian Leadership Conference, demonstrated "acceptable" Americanness by exhibiting the behaviors and values understood as indicative of white middle-classness, from gendered dress to protestant Christian values to a desire to participate in the consumer capitalist economy.[25] Yet, southern white reactionaries responded to their efforts with violent resistance, severely exposing the incompleteness of American racial equality. In the context of the Cold War, the Kremlin easily could distribute images that highlighted the hypocrisy of American democracy. In response, the United States government would redouble its reliance on cultural propaganda, including that provided by the sporting Cold War. Enter black American track women.

As bearers of the double burden of race and gender, black women track stars could signal that American society was overcoming its racial inequities. With their impeccable behavior and highly gendered presentation, these young women athletes, like civil rights activists, advertised their Americanness. Whether practiced by civil rights activists, black women athletes, or the gay rights activists of the early homophile movement, this performative strategy was not unproblematic, as it inscribed the values of normative, middle-class whiteness as coterminous with all-Americanness.[26] Nonetheless, by following the Temple Way, young black track women would be ready to represent the American Way when the conditions of the sporting Cold War called them do so. And the institutions of American sport soon would call, beginning with the 1955 Pan-American Games. The AAU and USOC, and even the Department of State, would accommodate rather than ignore the achievements of black women track stars, including them in the identity of American sport. The place of these young women in mainstream American sport culture thus modeled the management of racial difference in an America wrestling uncertainly with the demands of democracy.

THE PLACE OF BLACK AMERICAN TRACK WOMEN IN PAN-AMERICAN PROPAGANDA

At the 1955 Pan-American Games in Mexico City, American sport aimed to more prominently promote an image of racial equity. In combination with the decision in *Brown v. Board of Education*, which, in overturning the doctrine of "separate but equal," seemed to show the world that the nation was on the path to racial equality, the achievements of black athletes were imagined as further refuting accusations of American racial inequality.[27] However, just as the more liberal sectors of US sport and society, mostly motivated by Cold War–related concerns, were beginning to recognize the accomplishments of black Americans as signs of the nation's democratic character, the sport of track and field also directed intense attention to white male runners, from emerging sprint star Bobby Morrow to four-minute-mile prospect Wes Santee.[28] This attention exposed the deep and still-dominant desire for white male athletes to show themselves the nation's superior athletes and, in doing so, solidify the authority of white American manhood more broadly.[29] The emotional investment in the abilities of Morrow, Santee, and other white male runners mirrored a wider cultural interest in white male athletes. While white stars such as Mickey Mantle offered a sense of stability in an increasingly integrated Major League Baseball, the search for masculine white male heroes was reflected most in the increasing popularity of collegiate and professional football.[30]

This emphasis on white male athletes represented a reaction to a larger sense of crisis surrounding white American manhood, from anxieties about softness to hysteria about homosexuality.[31] Such apprehension and uncertainty partly derived from fears of the perceived power of black masculinity. Among other incidents, the brutal murder of fourteen-year-old Emmett Till in the summer of 1955 laid bare white American fear of black masculinity. In order not to activate white anxieties of race and gender, excellent black male athletes, as implicit icons of black masculinity, had to follow the model established by Jackie Robinson. However, Robinson, as well as fellow baseball star Larry Doby and boxing champion Floyd Patterson, endured the difficulties of navigating black expectations and white fears.[32] As further indication of this fraught social environment, officials of American sport took care to celebrate "good Negros," meaning the black male athletes who most displayed the traits of the white American middle class, at the 1955 Pan-American Games. Favored black sporting stars were the light-skinned Korean War veteran and middle-distance runner Mal Whitfield and the highly educated and well-mannered decathlete Rafer Johnson, both of whom later would serve as goodwill ambassadors for the State Department.[33]

In contrast to earlier international competitions, black American track women also would be incorporated into the image of American sport, a reflection and extension of how respectable black women and girls had gained representational purchase in an American society navigating the intersection of the Cold War and civil rights movement. As schools, however slowly, began to integrate, young black women became activists, visibly leading the national effort for educational equality.[34] The Montgomery Bus Boycott likewise demonstrated that the bodies and behaviors of black women could communicate the rights deserved by all of black America.[35] Because of white American alarm about black manhood, seemingly reserved and respectable women, epitomized by the perception of Rosa Parks, represented "safer" symbols through which to demand racial equality. The sense of safety read into well-mannered black women encouraged mainstream American sport culture to begin to abandon their entrenched resistance to recognizing black women track athletes as American athletes. Unlike their male counterparts, black women athletes did not appear to threaten to rearrange the racialized gender order, which was important for an American society wracked by a web of racial and gender tensions.

Nonetheless, giving attention to black American women athletes still raised certain social discomforts. Although largely silenced, the specter of mannishness still hovered over women athletes, especially black women athletes who competed in the supposedly masculine sport of track and field.[36] But because they represented the nation, there was no incentive for American sport culture to cast overt aspersions on their womanhood.[37] That black sport culture, exemplified by the ideology of Ed Temple, demanded that black women athletes perfectly perform traditional womanhood also guarded against any negative notions. Furthermore, because the institutions of American sport considered the Pan-American Games less prestigious, a mere precursor to more prominent and important Olympic competition, it provided a space where US sport more comfortably could begin to praise the contributions of black women athletes. Their youthfulness also allowed their athleticism to be understood as temporary and, thus, unthreatening. So, feminine in presentation and young in age, black women athletes could be accommodated as rather uncontroversial avatars of Americanness in ways that preserved traditional racial and gender hierarchies, similar to "good Negroes." They served as safe signifiers of the nation's commitment to equality.

The organization and interpretation of the Pan-American Games women's track and field qualifying meet, which also served as the 1955 National AAU Indoor Championships, evinced the AAU's, USOC's, and mainstream American sport culture's altered perspective of black women athletes. The AAU selected Joe Robichaux, the black coach of the interracial Chicago Comets (formerly the Chicago CYO) to direct the Pan-American qualifying meet, which was held at the University of Chicago Fieldhouse in early February 1955.[38] That National AAU president Louis G. Wilkie attended demonstrates the degree of official investment in the effort not only to enhance the sport's domestic credibility but also to situate young women athletes to find success in Mexico City. The meet received raving reviews. AAU chairwoman Frances Kaszubski enthused, "It seemed like a dream, compared to other meets, in that everyone in the Field House was wearing his Sunday SMILE and MANNERS!"[39] She continued:

> Real spectators, who paid admission to see the girls compete in Track & Field! There was Dave Albritton, one of the greatest male track stars, doing the announcing! The lady officials added considerable charm and color to the event with their attractive uniforms (red blazers and white skirts) while performing with an air that bespoke of confidence and experience. And, in the distant, upper row, a most impressive group of scholarly-like newspaper reporters were clicking the keys of their typewriters, with ear-phones attached, as they covered the results of the various events and individual performances.[40]

After finishing one-two-three in the 60-meter dash, a trio of Tigerbelles—Isabelle Daniels, Mae Faggs, and Margaret Davis—entered the stands, collecting contributions needed to fund the women's track team's trip to Mexico City. That women's track and field still did not receive sufficient financial support from the USOC underscores their still partial, incomplete place in the American sporting nation. Nevertheless, considering that only four years prior the USOC had attempted to prohibit women track athletes, particularly black women track athletes, from representing the United States in Buenos Aires, three young black women collecting funds from primarily white fans for the American women's athletic effort signaled significant progress.[41] Overall, the meet offered an idealized image of a democratic, inclusive, and cooperative American athletic culture, aligning almost perfectly with the optimistic and propagandistic imaginings of US sport and state. Led by Daniels and Faggs, a team of sixteen young track women, nine black and seven white, would make the trip to Mexico City, where events would permit women's track and field to begin to be promoted as a safe and sensible representation of American opportunity and equality.

When reporting on the 1955 Pan-American Games, the US sporting press would not exalt the accomplishments of young black American track women with overt enthusiasm. However, the understated, straight-forward recognition they would receive represented a significant shift. Recall the USOC

FIGURE 6. The Tigerbelles who finished first, second, and third in the 60-meter sprint at the 1955 Pan-American Games trials, Isabelle Daniels, Mae Faggs, and Margaret Davis (right to left), accept congratulations from AAU President Louis G. Wilkie.
Courtesy of Tennessee State University Special Collections and Archives, Brown-Daniel Library

attempted to prevent young track women from participating in the inaugural edition of the Pan-American Games, perceiving them as a threat to the version of American identity that the United States aimed to advertise in 1951. Now, four years later, the ideological recalculations that resulted from the intersection of the Cold War and civil rights movement allowed them to be seen as less contested and more appreciated contributors to the United States' Pan-American effort. On March 17, a *New York Times* headline declared, "Three U.S. Aces Win in Mexico City," with the accompanying article announcing that "Rod Richard, Barbara Jones, and Bob Backus won championships for the United States in the Pan-American Games today."[42] Reporting on her win in the 100-meters, the *Times* did not classify Jones as a "girl" athlete, which would have communicated that her achievement was less legitimate than or separate from those of American men athletes. Rather, the nation's leading newspaper introduced the seventeen-year-old Chicago Comet sprinter as equal to her male counterparts. She was an athletic "ace," a designation that signaled her status as a talented, unquestionably American athlete. In her qualifying heat, Jones had registered an 11.6-second effort, a time that approached the 11.4-second world record held by Australia's Marjorie Jackson.[43] Aided by the high altitude of Mexico City, Jones bettered her time in the final, covering the 100-meter distance in 11.5-seconds to best teammate Mae Faggs by one-tenth of a second. The exertion such speed required, in combination with the high altitude, resulted in her collapsing almost as soon as she crossed the finish line. According to her hometown *Chicago Defender*, Jones "collapsed shortly after crossing the finish line. She was revived by oxygen and given glucose tablets, but fainted a second time and had to be carried on [to the] team's locker room."[44]

Somewhat surprisingly, Jones's collapse did not inspire excessive consternation from the sporting press. The collapse of multiple women at the end of the 800-meter race at the 1928 Olympic Games in Amsterdam represented a seminal moment in the history of women's sport, repeatedly recycled by opponents of women's athleticism to limit, or even eliminate, competitive opportunities.[45] But Jones's collapse would not be used to delegitimize her athletic ability, or the athletic abilities of all women athletes. That numerous male athletes, including black American middle-distance man Lou Jones, who set a new 400-meter world record in Mexico City, and 400-meter hurdles gold medalist Josh Culbreath, also suffered from altitude's ills likely helped inoculate Barbara Jones from any hysteria about her health.[46] Nonetheless, it still was significant that Jones was treated as an athlete, with her ability to strive, struggle, succeed, and recover respected. The following day, she simply stated to reporters, "I am proud to have come here to win for my country. I feel fine now."[47] In her confident and concise statement, Jones asserted her status as an American athlete.

Three days following her 100-meter triumph, Jones anchored a come-from-behind win for the American women in the 400-meter relay. After Isabelle Daniels, Mabel Landry, and Mae Faggs had completed their legs, the United States trailed Argentina by approximately three yards. Jones, showing no fear about again pushing her ability in the high altitude, grabbed the baton from Faggs, quickly closing the gap to give the United States the victory in a new meet record time of 47 seconds.[48] Along with Jones, Mildred McDaniel positioned herself as an American athletic icon with her Pan-American performance.

The day after Jones received prominent praise in the *New York Times* for her century sprint win the paper gave headline billing to McDaniel for her gold medal victory in the high jump. "U.S. Team Wins 3 More Track Titles to Increase Pan-American Games Lead; Miss M'Daniel High Jump Victor," announced the *Times*. After registering the new Pan-American record of 5 feet, 6¼ inches, a mark that exceeded the existing one by almost 9 inches, McDaniel did not rest on her laurels, instead thrilling the thousands of Mexican fans by attempting to best the world mark, then held by the Soviet Union's Aleksandra Chudina.[49]

The individual golds earned by McDaniel and Jones were two of the ten medals secured by black American women track athletes in Mexico City.[50] However, more significant than the victories these athletes scored was the symbolism the victories communicated. Mexican sportswriter Hugo Aguilar described the US team as the exemplar of the spirit of diversity, equality, and understanding that characterized the Pan-American fortnight. "The people forget their frontiers, men forget the color of races, politics, economic differences, the struggle for commerce and trade, and the different manner of thinking which divides the world. There is only an appreciation and admiration of the strength and skill of the athletes. All are free. All are equal. All are brothers," wrote Aguilar.[51] Aguilar's understanding of the American Pan-American performance aligned with US propagandistic priorities. American athletes associated the nation with the values it proclaimed, a victory in the context of the sporting Cold War. Black American sport culture also took particular pride in the Pan-American event, celebrating black athletes and their achievements as exemplars of American democracy. In his analysis of the Games, ANP Pan-American correspondent Earl Morris quoted the Gettysburg Address, writing, "The world will little note nor long remember what (was said) here, but it can, never forget what they did here."[52] He also equally included black women athletes in this optimistic vision of American sport, asserting, "Then there were my countrywomen who are rated as the world's fastest women. Among them were Isabel [sic] F. Daniels, Mabel Landry, Mae Faggs, and Barbara Jones."[53]

These analyses reflect that black women track stars had become integrated into the imagery of American athleticism and, in extension, American identity. This shift proved noteworthy not only for mainstream American sport culture but also black American sport culture. Support for black women athletes had always been circumscribed. Black American women athletes were seen as distinctly different from their male counterparts, viewed mainly through the lens of their gender identity. Black male athletes were race men; black women athletes were not race women. Yet, the Pan-American Games marked a point of change. The liberalized attitude toward women's sport adopted by the mainstream sporting press encouraged the world of black sport similarly to reconsider the possibilities of its women athletes.

REIMAGINING BLACK AMERICAN TRACK WOMEN AS RACE WOMEN

Black American sport long had recognized and emphasized men's sport as a space of black activism, with the triumphs of black male athletic stars understood as puncturing white supremacy and displaying black capacity. By the mid-1950s, the black sport community began to grasp the activist-like potential of black women track athletes, motivated by the women and girls who increasingly were on the frontlines of the movement for civil rights. Black American sport culture began to appreciate these young women as athletic activists, realizing that their athletic achievements could enhance the causes of black America. Thus, before the Pan-American Games began, the black press shared their excitement for the prospects of young black American track women.[54] Celebrating the nine "sepia distaff runners," the *New York Amsterdam News* predicted that their success would surpass that achieved at the 1951 Games.[55] In the aftermath, the speedy Barbara Jones earned the most attention for her efforts in the altitude of Mexico City. Both the *Philadelphia Tribune* and *Chicago Defender* certified the high school senior from Chicago's St. Elizabeth's School as a black American athletic star.[56] The *Tribune* noted, "The Pan-American Games at Mexico City brought some unknown Negro stars to the spotlight. A girl, 17-year-old Barbara Jones of Chicago's St. Elizabeth High School, set a new Pan-Am games record when she raced the 100 meters final in 11.5 seconds."[57] "Barbara Jones Sparks Tan Pan-Am. Stars," declared the *Defender*, describing her as "sensational" for her near world record effort in the 100-meters.[58] The paper also suggested that "Miss Jones' record-setting spree tended to overshadow" other performances.[59]

Along with athletic excellence, Jones also possessed a feminine flair that much satisfied black sport culture. Although not (yet) a Tigerbelle, Jones appeared to obey the Temple Way. The *Chicago Defender* eagerly described her as "an attractive, charming, and effervescent female" who "presents a pleasing personality and laughs readily even when the joke's on her."[60] But, in contrast to years prior, recognition of Jones's femininity did not replace recognition of her athletic ability. While the black sport community primarily had presented

Alice Coachman as a reserved and respectable young black woman who just so happened to jump high, they celebrated Jones as an excellent young woman athlete who also was engaging, energetic, and fittingly feminine. As the *Defender* headline declared, "Barbara Jones, Nation's Fastest Female, Proves Feminine, Too." Thus, when the paper posited "that March [1955] was the greatest month of achievements in the history of Negro athletes," the accomplishments of Jones and other black track women at the Pan-American Games were included.[61] Later that year, the *Philadelphia Tribune* similarly declared, "The Golden Age of the Negro in Sports might well have already started."[62] The promise of such a possibility partly derived from the performances of black women track stars, especially Jones, at the Pan-American Games. Mildred McDaniel's world-class high jumping ability also received positive appraisal. In short, the black press had begun to recognize that Jones, McDaniel, and other young black track women could help prove to the athletic publics of the United States and the world the capacity of black Americans.

Such emerging enthusiasm continued to be expressed as the 1956 Olympic Games approached. The *Philadelphia Tribune* predicted, "The United States Women's Olympic team will make the best showing at Melbourne since Uncle Sam's girls captured four gold medals at Los Angeles in 1932."[63] At the *Atlanta Daily World*, sports editor Marion E. Jackson suggested that "Uncle Sam's nieces are going to give the global games a fit."[64] Voices in the black sport press also boosted black women track stars as the only young women who possessed the determination and desire necessary for athletic achievement. The *Afro-American's* Sam Lacy stated, "No white girl has given the U.S. a gold medal in the Olympic Games since Helen Stephens scored in Berlin."[65] "As a matter of fact, without colored girls in general, Uncle Sam would occupy an extremely embarrassing position in the world of women's track," he further propounded.[66] Others in the black press even began to imagine that young black women athletes might best their Soviet counterparts. While noting that "those European gals are a sturdy lot," the *Defender* predicted "that the US will win the sprints this year," insisting, "we have two of the best in the world in Mae Faggs and Isabell [*sic*] Daniels of Tennessee State university [*sic*]. The paper further proclaimed that "the McDaniels [*sic*] girl from Tuskegee looks like a certainty in the high jump," before expressing the hope that "perhaps a few more will improve by the time the Olympics opens in Melbourne, Australia."[67]

These expectations were justified, much due to the TSU Tigerbelles. At the 1956 National AAU Championships in Philadelphia, Mae Faggs took a trio of titles to lead the Tigerbelles to their second consecutive national champion-ship. The meet also introduced a pair of intriguing new stars. Competing for the Tigerbelle junior squad, two teenage talents—Clarksville, Tennessee, sprinter Wilma Rudolph and Money, Mississippi, long jumper Willye White—offered an enticing preview of their international potential, each setting a new record in their specialties.[68] At the 1956 US Women's Olympic Track and Field Trials, held in Washington, DC, a week after the national title meet, Faggs, Rudolph, and White then would score the victories needed to make the 1956 Olympic team. Tigerbelles Isabelle Daniels, Margaret Matthews, and Lucinda Williams also would earn Olympic berths, resulting in a record six Tigerbelles securing spots on the 1956 Olympic squad. Even Fay Young, the curmudgeonly *Chicago Defender* sports columnist, favorably appraised the Tigerbelles for this accom-plishment, writing, "At no time in the history of the Olympics has any one team qualified that many girls on a team representing this country. Thus the triumphs of the Tennessee State girls is really a first in the annals of American track and field competition."[69] The *Afro-American* echoed Young, exclaiming, "In the greatest single demonstration in modern women's track meets, the Tennessee track girls won seven of nine places to dominate all running events in which they participated."[70]

Ed Temple referred to his six Tigerbelle Olympians as "my dream team," insisting they were the "greatest of them all."[71] "This is more than I expected. I came here with six and was going to put six on the boat," he additionally enthused.[72] He could unapologetically tout the ambition and ability of his athletes because of their image; their amenable femininity made acceptable the appreciation of their athleticism. Furthermore, by presenting himself as the prideful patriarch, the personable Temple allowed the leading voices in black sport culture to accept the aspirations of his athletes and acclaim their accumulating achievements. It was his overt paternalism that established the structure of permission that allowed black American sport culture, which retained conservative gender notions, to embrace young black track women as elite athletes and racial activists. A photo published in the *Defender* soon after the US Women's Olympic Track and Field Trials communicated this un-derstanding. While the caption praised the quality of the interracial team of sixteen, the photo showed the nine young black women outfitted in dresses more feminine than the skirts and shirts worn by their seven white team-mates.[73] Thus, ahead of the Olympic Games, the black sport community did not hesitate to praise the nine young black women, especially the sextet of Tigerbelles, as athletes who were appropriate, ambitious, and American.[74]

THE ENTITLEMENT OF BLACK AMERICAN TRACK WOMEN

However, black American track women did have agency in their representational reevaluation. They were not simply symbols, subject to the ideological priorities that the confluence of the Cold War and civil rights movement produced. It was their achievements and attitudes that forced both mainstream and black American cultures to accommodate them. Even if these sport cultures made the meanings of black American track women match their political prerogatives, young black women also made the sport of track meet their needs. And much of this overlooked influence was due to the unapologetic Mae Faggs. From the moment she arrived in Nashville in 1952 to enroll at TSU and compete for the Tigerbelles, the native of Bayside, New York, did not hesitate to exercise control over her athletic career. Foremost, Faggs did not so easily accept Temple's often paternalistic overtures. "At times I did question Coach Temple, and I'd challenge him," she later asserted.[75] Faggs proudly expressed her sense of independence. When it came to her athletic career, she saw herself as an equal to Temple, as well as the other much older male athletic officials at TSU and in the black sport community.

For example, when the TSU athletic department decided not to send Faggs to the 1953 National AAU Indoor Championship in Boston, where she could have won the 220-yard national title for the fifth-straight year, she did not hesitate to share her disappointment, inspiring Temple to agitate for funding from the athletic department. Motivated by Faggs, Temple would become an incessant advocate for equal support for his athletes, increasingly, and proudly, annoying the TSU administration, which believed in devoting the majority of resources to men's football and basketball. "The basic and most important thing to me is to have equal opportunities for the women," Temple asserted in his 1980 autobiography.[76] In 1953, his efforts on behalf of Faggs were unsuccessful. Soon thereafter, the TSU athletic department also refused to allocate the resources needed to allow the Tigerbelles to compete in the 1953 National AAU Outdoor Championship in San Antonio. This decision further frustrated Faggs, leading her to consider leaving the school to find a program more willing to provide the sporting support she believed she deserved.[77]

Faggs shared her feelings of frustration with the *Chicago Defender*'s Fay Young, who took umbrage with her unappreciative attitude. In May 1953, Young devoted his weekly column, "Fay Says," to a dressing down of Faggs. "There is something that a youngster doesn't always get in college that he or she certainly will need later on in life. That 'something' we have in mind is attitude—and you can spell it with capital letters," led Young.[78] Recalling his conversation with Faggs at a mid-winter basketball tournament held at TSU, Young wrote, "Miss Faggs seemed to be upset about two things. They were (1) that she wasn't sent to Boston to defend her title in the indoor meet because Tennessee State's athletic director did not see the need of spending that much money as no provisions had been made for such trips and (2) $10 per month had been cut from her scholarship allowance."[79] Young then described the ways in which he explained the TSU athletic department's reasons to Faggs, which, much to his dismay, she did not readily accept.

To further illustrate Faggs's perceived attitude problem, Young also recounted the occurrences at the 1953 Tuskegee Relays. TSU disputed Tuskegee's 114 to 112 victory, insisting that a Tuskegee athlete, Annie Gordon, competed in more than the four events permitted by AAU rules. Tuskegee, however, declared that their relays were not subject to AAU standards, defending their team title as legitimate. After the meet, Young and the head referee were discussing the issue when Faggs entered the conversation to offer her opinion. Young reported his disgust with her action, "But Miss Faggs proceeded to butt into the confab which (1) showed she had little manners and (2) proved that she has the wrong attitude. She blurted out, 'If you are running the meet according to AAU rules then this girl should have all the places taken away from her.'"[80] According to Young, he again explained the situation to Faggs who, impatient with his paternalistic preaching, then commented, "I realize that this is a Negro college, etc etc."[81]

Young, somewhat understandably, took offense at her retort. Her words tapped into tensions of gender, generation, and region that had been intensified by the civil rights movement, as the effort by black Americans to earn full inclusion in mainstream American society could (and often would) have the unintended consequence of destabilizing and delegitimizing black institutions. Young's attack on Faggs reflected these intersecting sensitivities and uncertainties. "What we would like to know is didn't Miss Faggs who came from Staten Island, New York state, know that when she came to Tennessee State that it was a Negro college and where has she been all these years that she hadn't know that Tuskegee also is a Negro institution?," he sarcastically supposed.[82] But more importantly, his words indicate how appalled he was that a young black woman would bluntly express her opinion to her black male superiors. He did not respect her right to share her ideas, regardless of their rightness or wrongness. So he tore her down. "We know she wouldn't have stalked into a conference of a New York white coach to challenge any AAU official. We are wondering why, with all the prestige a woman should have after being a member of two United States Olympic teams, she had come to 'a Negro college' for an education," he wrote.[83] He then concluded, "Those of us who have seen 40 years in helping Negro youngsters in northern as well as southern schools aren't so seedy that we have to take any suggestions from any youngster who feels his or her importance because she is a damnyankee [sic]. NewYorkers [sic] don't worry us one bit, neither does any upstart who hails therefrom."[84]

Young's rather vicious reaction indexes the influence of Faggs, as well as black women's athleticism more broadly. His words reveal the lingering discomfort that the relatively conservative male figures of authority who controlled the black sports world held about black women's athleticism. Women's sport disrupted the middle-class black community's long-established gender order, not only because women were allowed to enter the mostly male space of sport but also because sport endowed them with a sense of assurance deemed off limits to young women. Faggs clearly showed this confidence and independence. Seeing Faggs's attitude as a threat to both his authority and his ideas, Young reasserted his power, and the traditional, gendered, and generational power structure of black American culture, by not taking her seriously. Young black women track stars' status as race women, while increasingly recognized, remained tenuous.

Nevertheless, Faggs fought the hierarchy that governed the black sport community. She did not reflexively genuflect to the institutions of black sport, instead insisting that they respect and respond to the desires and demands of young black women athletes. By stating, "I realize that this a Negro school," Faggs boldly called out the organizational shortcomings of black collegiate sport, holding TSU, Tuskegee, and other black colleges to the higher standards she believed were needed to prepare women athletes to achieve national and international success. Faggs forthrightly expressed her entitlement, living the theory of sociologist Aimee Meredith Cox. In her study of twenty-first-century black girls at a Detroit homeless shelter, Cox reconceives entitlement as "an empowered statement that disputes the idea that only certain people are worthy of the rights of citizenship and the ability to direct the course of their lives."[85]

Respecting Faggs's ambition and attitude, Ed Temple loosened his paternalistic strictures in order to take advantage of her experience and expertise. He willingly learned from her, incorporating the priorities of young black women into his program. Although Temple still would enforce respectability politics, requiring his athletes to obey an array of rules and restrictions, he also was a relentless advocate for their equal right to sport. Wyomia Tyus's reflections of Temple hint at the influence of Faggs, as she notes of the coach, "There was something about him that made it possible for us women to accept him, to let him be a part of our lives. Even with some of his antiquated ideas—and you know we disagreed with some of them—we still allowed him to be who he was and accepted what his program was about. Because we all had to give a little so that we could work together to get what we wanted."[86] As Tyus's words indicate, teammates, as well as future Tigerbelles, also would take their cues from Faggs. She created space for black women athletes to self-determine their athletic, academic, and extracurricular collegiate experiences by negotiating, and sometimes even ignoring, Temple's strictures. For instance, because many Tigerbelles played basketball in high school, they excitedly joined intramural teams, albeit making sure to evade Temple when doing so since, due to concerns about injury and stamina, he prohibited his athletes from participating in intramurals.[87] They also strategically stretched the limits of his rule against riding in cars with potential male suitors, with future Tigerbelle Willye White, in particular, defying Temple's dating dictates.[88] Tyus's conception of what it meant to be a Tigerbelle shows Faggs's lasting imprint. In her autobiography, she writes, "For me, the Tigerbelles were the essence of being a woman who was going places and getting things done. It wasn't just about being able to run—you had to have goals in life."[89]

The significance of Faggs's spirit of self-determination also is evident in the increasing success of the Tigerbelle track squad, highlighted by their first National AAU Championship in 1955. The small squad of six Tigerbelles—Faggs, Isabelle Daniels, Lucinda Williams, Martha Hudson, Patricia Monsanto, and Ella Mae Turner—traveled to Ponca City, Oklahoma, and trounced a talented cohort of 135 aspiring track stars from the United States and beyond.[90] "In the home of the Pioneer Woman, Tennessee State university AC made a clean sweep of the 1955 girls and women's AAU track and field championship," declared the *Chicago Defender*.[91] Faggs turned in one of the most impressive performances of her career at the Ponca City championship meet, winning the 100- and 200-yard dashes, in addition to anchoring a record-setting 440-yard victory, as she captained TSU to their first (of many) national titles. According to *Sports Illustrated*, "As expected, the star of the show was 23-year-old Mae

FIGURE 7. Mae Faggs, the "Mother of the Tigerbelles" and top competitor at the 1955 National AAU Championship, refines her form at a 1954 practice.
Courtesy of Tennessee State University Special Collections and Archives, Brown-Daniel Library

Faggs, a senior at Tennessee State University and veteran of two Olympic Games. The best woman sprinter since Stella Walsh, Mae Faggs ticked off a new American record of 10.7 seconds in the 100-yard dash, won the 220-yard dash and anchored the fastest 440-yard relay (49.1) ever run in this country by women."[92] Faggs later said of her performance, "Any girl in the United States that ran past me in the 100 meters or ran by me in the 200 meters knew that they were the best in the United States, because I was the best at the time."[93]

However, the TSU athletic administration failed to fully value the school's first National AAU Championship. According to Ed Temple, "In 1955, we won our first outdoor national championship. It was a great thrill for me, but it was a disappointment too." Echoing the frustrations of Faggs, he further asserted that "the people at Tennessee State didn't appreciate it. They were still thinking of us as [a] black team who won the black championship. They didn't know the significance of being a national champion. Really, we just advanced too fast for the school at the time. There is no doubt about it. We were ahead of them."[94] Nonetheless, in the dominant narrative of black American women's track and field, it is the institutions of TSU and Tuskegee, helmed by black male coaches and administrators, that have been most credited for the national, as well as international, athletic achievements of young black women. These institutions are imagined as enabling such successes. In large part, the black sporting press, populated by mostly conservative male sportswriters, produced and perpetuated this perspective. For instance, following the Tigerbelles' 1955 national championship, Fay Young, ignoring the documented apathy, congratulated the TSU administration, not Temple nor his athletes, for the Tigerbelles' inaugural title, writing, "But without the school and its far seeing president who could have cold watered the idea of women's track and field athletic activities who gladly went along with the idea, there wouldn't have been any Tigerbelles."[95]

Yet, as exemplified by Mae Faggs, young black women athletes shaped the culture of women's track in a way that allowed them to find success. Faggs did not simply take advantage of the opportunities generously opened to her— she directly demanded such opportunities. Her influence would be evident in the attitudes expressed by her teenage teammates Wilma Rudolph and Willye White at the 1956 Olympic Games. The agency of Faggs and other young black women track athletes forced black American sport culture, as well as mainstream American sport culture, to accommodate and appreciate them as athletes. In short, the "Faggs Way," in combination with the Temple Way, required that black American track women become part of the American Way during the sporting Cold War. The symbolism of black American track women, however, would obscure this instrumental influence. Rather than figures of black female autonomy, they were made into models of normative young women, racialized imitations of idealized white American womanhood.

THE AMERICAN IMAGERY OF BLACK AMERICAN TRACK WOMEN

It was this imagery that allowed AAU chairwoman Frances Kaszubski, ahead of the 1956 Olympic Games, to excitedly exclaim about "the American track and field (feminine) stars," suggesting that the sextet of Tigerbelle Olympians

were "the number one topic of conversation among athletes of other countries."[96] The actions of Voice of America indicate she was not exaggerating, at
least not all that much. As reported by the AAU, the propagandistic program
"requested and obtained a ten-minute tape recording for broadcast to Europe
on the results of the 1956 National Championships and Olympic tryouts."[97]
Not insignificantly, the USIA decided to advertise America through the athletic
exploits of young, primarily black, women. The broadcast, in combination
with Mae Faggs's participation on a State Department–sponsored goodwill
tour in the spring of 1956, reflects to degree to which black women athletes
had become accepted identifiers of American identity.

In March 1956, Faggs became only the second black woman athlete to be
included in a State Department tour when she, along with the white javelin
thrower Karen Anderson and six male track stars, three white and three black,
traveled to West Africa.[98] Only two years prior, the AAU had resisted sending Faggs to British Guiana for a similar such tour. In the spring of 1954,
the British Guiana Amateur Athletic Union invited Faggs to compete in its
annual All-Women International Games. Due to concerns about financing,
the AAU rejected the invitation on Faggs's behalf, with evidence suggesting
the organization did not even inform Faggs of this opportunity.[99] While the
lack of financial resources served as a convenient excuse for the AAU failing
to seriously consider sending Faggs, the prospect of a black woman athlete
individually representing the AAU, and thus the United States, in an international competition likely inspired trepidation. Such an opportunity would
have served as an implicit recognition of the autonomy and independence of
young black women, a destabilizing proposition for US sport and society.

In the intervening two years, as the movement for civil rights increasingly
complicated Cold War aims, US sport and state had begun to see black women
athletes differently. As bearers of the double burden of race and gender, they
helped doubly to counteract continued Soviet criticisms of the American "democracy," seemingly showing that the nation provided opportunity for all,
regardless of race or gender. And because black women track stars followed
the Temple Way, with their careful, conventional comportment, they safely
could serve a recognized representational role, whether at the Pan-American
Games or in West Africa. So Faggs now had propagandistic purpose, as her
success and symbolism permitted the United States to advertise its claimed
commitment to equality without overtly threatening traditional racial and
gender arrangements. To further alleviate any lingering anxieties, she would
travel to West Africa as part of racially balanced and sex-integrated track team,

meaning a young black woman would not singularly stand as an officially sanctioned symbol of American sport and state.

On March 23, Faggs, Anderson, Josephine Robichaux, who was the wife of the Chicago Comets head coach Joe Robichaux and the women's chaperone, and the six black and white track men departed New York, arriving first in Monrovia, Liberia. After the athletes conducted local clinics and competed in an official meet, the institutions of Liberian sport and state hosted a "bon voyage" party for the American contingent, where the secretary of state of Liberia read a message from the Liberian president that thanked the United States and its athletes for their friendliness and generosity. The group then headed to Accra, Gold Coast, leading a series of clinics before competing in the Gold Coast All-Comers Meet. The *Daily Graphic*, the local newspaper, reported that the American athletes "gave a wonderful display by creating six new Gold Coast All-Comers Records."[100] In Lagos, Nigeria, the third and final stop, the American athletes led skill and strategy demonstrations for young athletes. They also attended a reception with Nigerian and European athletes. Reportedly, the American athletes infused the affair with liveliness, engaging all attendees in the singing of popular American songs. The chairman of the Lagos Sports Council expressed appreciation for the spiritedness shared by the American athletes, commenting to a US official, "We [meaning Nigerian athletes] work together fine, but we've never before been able to have fun together. We've found out now that we can enjoy each other. Credit goes to your American kids for that."[101] Such positive sentiments and scenes much pleased the institutions of US sport and state, expanding on and aligning with the ideological aims of athletic diplomacy. Faggs's inclusion in this successful initiative thus conferred legitimacy on her and, in extension, other black women athletes. Faggs's experience, along with the USIA film of the 1956 National AAU Championship, certified black women athletes as state-sanctioned, admiration-worthy American citizens, allowing them to advertise the sensibility and possibility of the American Way during and after the 1956 Olympic Games.

THE AMERICAN ATHLETICISM OF BLACK AMERICAN TRACK WOMEN

"They knew we were there!" announced Pacific AAU chairwoman Roxy Andersen in *Amateur Athlete* soon after the 1956 Olympic Games. Her "we" included black women athletes, as she applauded the accomplishments of the bronze medal–winning 400-meter relay team of Mae Faggs, Margaret Matthews, Wilma Rudolph, and Isabelle Daniels, long jump silver medalist Willye White, Earlene Brown for her fourth-place finish in the discus and sixth place in the shot put, and, especially, Mildred McDaniel for her gold medal victory in the high jump.[102] In the high jump competition, McDaniel not only claimed the gold medal but also the world record. Before the Games, *Sports Illustrated* predicted that McDaniel would become the first woman athlete to break the 6 foot barrier.[103] While her leap did not exceed that lofty mark, she raised the world record from 5 feet, 8¾ inches to 5 feet, 9¼ inches.

The *New York Times* also offered much enthusiasm for the efforts of McDaniel, reporting, "Mildred McDaniel, a 23-year-old Tuskegee Institute student from Atlanta, fulfilled the prediction that she would have the best chance of any of our women track and field athletes to win gold."[104] By identifying McDaniel with Tuskegee, the paper coded her as black but not with the intent to delegitimize her. McDaniel, instead, was the most talented of *"our* women track and field athletes" (emphasis added).[105] Subtly but significantly, the paper positioned her as an American athlete, an identity not encumbered by her blackness or femaleness. The *Times* celebrated that she "far exceeded expectations," describing the "great burst of applause" that erupted "as the Atlanta girl sailed over the bar."[106] The paper also emphasized "the rapt attention of more than 100,000 persons as the United States' long-limbed and graceful high jumper, Mildred McDaniel, set a world record of 5 feet, 9¼ inches in winning the women's high jump."[107]

Of course, this attention to McDaniel paled in comparison to that given to the likes of Bobby Morrow, the speedy white farm boy from west Texas who, after winning three track medals in Melbourne, would grace the cover of multiple national magazines.[108] Nonetheless, recognizing McDaniel as an American Olympic icon represented the first time the mainstream American sport community had chosen to see a young black woman athlete as such. Recall how Alice Coachman's historic gold medal was all but ignored, earning only a single sentence in the nation's paper of record. Mainstream American sport culture instead indulged in the excellence of Fanny Blankers-Koen, devoting almost all coverage of women's track and field at the London Games to the "Flying Dutch Housewife." The Melbourne Games produced a new white women's track star in Australia's Betty Cuthbert. While she did not replicate Blankers-Koen's four-gold-medal feat, she won three medals as she and her Australian teammates swept the women's sprints. Cuthbert, even more than Blankers-Koen, offered an idealized image of women's athleticism. A pert and perky blonde-haired and blue-eyed eighteen-year-old, Cuthbert, unsurprisingly, emerged as the darling of the host nation. Yet, showing the significant ideological shift that had occurred since 1948, the US sport press only perfunctorily reported on Cuthbert's accomplishments, adding none of the extra flourish expected by past precedence.[109] The Cold War and civil rights context that surrounded the 1956 Games explains this editorial choice. Because of her racial and gender identities, McDaniel powerfully communicated the purported possibilities of American democracy. In the friendly confines of Melbourne, the high-achieving McDaniel offered an idealistic image of US citizenship. Critically, it also was her understood ability to adhere to white-defined gender norms that allowed McDaniel to serve this symbolic role. The performance of gender norms acted as a salve for her racial difference. Racialized gender expectations permitted her to be seen as an avatar of American identity.

Unsurprisingly, McDaniel's hometown of Atlanta expressed even more enthusiasm for her Olympic accomplishment. As they had done with Alice Coachman, Atlanta's black community excitedly organized honors for McDaniel, along with Margaret Matthews, the TSU Tigerbelle and bronze-winning relay member who also was an Atlanta native. However, the tone of the recognition for the two differed from that given Coachman. Coachman was interpreted as an icon of black womanhood, with her broader significance as an American athlete, black American athlete, or black American not emphasized. In contrast, the affair for McDaniel situated her as symbol of American athleticism, black American athleticism, and black American citizenship. An editorial in the *Atlanta Daily World* introduced her as "a symbol of courage" who displayed "fierce pride and titanic determination."[110] The editorial explicated, "Miss McDaniel shows the spirit of her people. She grew up in the Southland. She has watched the grim patterns of race relations which chained their progress but not their competitive spirit. She refused to bow to the mandates of second-class citizenship and bridled competition."[111] "Georgians are proud of Miss McDaniel and her achievement in sports and as an ambassador of goodwill," the editorial concluded.[112]

Atlanta's black public further made evident their sense of pride in McDaniel by turning out in droves for the civic celebration held in her honor in mid-December 1956. While resembling those held to honor Coachman and Jean Patton, the public parade for McDaniel and Matthews was of a different scale. According to the *Daily World*, a crowd of more than five hundred fans, along with "photographers, reporters, radio announcers and civic leaders," "virtually mobbed" McDaniel as she stepped off of the Crescent Limited train car at Atlanta's Terminal Station.[113] A collection of police cars then escorted a motorcade featuring McDaniel and Matthews through the city's five neighborhoods to Hurt Park. It was, in the words of *Daily World* sports editor Marion E. Jackson, an "exuberant procession" for "the two Atlanta prides."[114] At the gathering at Hurt Park, Mayor William B. Hartsfield offered his appreciation for McDaniel and Matthews, recognizing the two young women as civic and racial icons. The mayor told the assembled Atlantans, "I am happy and proud of your achievements. It has always been the role of Atlanta to produce champions."[115] He continued, "We are happy and proud of the honor that you have brought to your race, the city and country. I am proud that you have upheld the good name of Atlanta."[116] Hartsfield thus used the two black women track stars to enhance Atlanta's image as "the city too busy to hate." The words of the white mayor also indicated an understanding of the role of black track women in advancing racial equality.

A similar scene occurred in Nashville, with the city's broader black community honoring the six Tigerbelles with an extended affair. The *Afro-American*'s Mabel Crooks emphasized the team's historic character, writing, "The girls scored three outstanding 'firsts' in the history of the Olympics: (1) This was the first time that any school or club had six members to qualify for Olympic competition in any sport. (2) This was the first time that all four members of the women's relay team came from the same school. (3) This was the first time that three teams broke the world's record in the same event."[117] But more than their history-making achievements motivated such celebration. They received such recognition because, in victory and defeat, their class and comportment allowed them to be understood as proving the Americanness of black Americans. Not dissimilar from the young black women who donned their Sunday best to sit at lunch counters or ride interstate buses, young black track women advanced awareness of the rights deserved by all black Americans.

Yet, like Christian civil rights activists who participated in the nonviolent direct-action protests, the image of and honors for the Tigerbelles, as well as Mildred McDaniel, communicated a certain version of black American belonging. Their performance of traditional gender roles expressed the potential of racial equality, thereby fulfilling the democratic demands of the Cold War and the civil rights movement. The inherent racialization of gender, however, would protect against a meaningful rearrangement of America's inequitable racial realities. Nonetheless, the experiences of black American track women Down Under also introduced alternative possibilities. International athletics also served as a space of entitlement for young black women athletes, including the teenaged Wilma Rudolph and Willye White.

THE AUTONOMOUS ATHLETICISM OF BLACK AMERICAN TRACK WOMEN

As the 1956 Games approached, sixteen-year-old Wilma Rudolph retained the insecurities that derived from a childhood of struggle. The twentieth of twenty-two children born to a handyman and domestic worker in Clarksville, Tennessee, Rudolph not only encountered the poverty produced by the segregated South but also suffered from polio and related illnesses until age twelve. Her self-understanding began to change when, in the summer of 1956, she joined the summer training program established by Ed Temple for Tigerbelles and future Tigerbelles. When refereeing a girls' high school basketball game, Temple witnessed the speed of the then-raw Rudolph. Almost immediately, he all but insisted that Rudolph train with the Tigerbelles. That summer, he would prepare her, as well as his other charges, for the National AAU Championship in Harrisburg, Pennsylvania, the Olympic Trials in Washington, DC, and, most importantly, the Olympic Games in Melbourne, Australia.

But for all her talent, Rudolph first frustrated Temple. She lacked a killer instinct, showing a tendency to please rather than push her teammates in training. Her hesitancy, however, makes sense. Long excluded from neighborhood sprint races as a young girl because of her illnesses, pleasing others likely seemed the safest strategy to make sure she remained included; it signaled her appreciation of the simple opportunity to participate. Recalling a 1956 practice race with Isabelle Daniels in her 1977 autobiography, Rudolph wrote:

> I matched her stride for stride, and I realized, for the first time, that I could pull away from her any time I really wanted to. But I didn't. Just knowing that I could was enough for me. So I held back and let her win. There was no advantage for me in beating her, because it would have caused hard feelings; I thought if you're a high school kid you don't go around showing up established stars by beating them.[118]

Mae Faggs, whose own athletic ability had encouraged her to develop a stubborn and strong self-esteem, recognized Rudolph's ingrained, gendered hesitancy and uncertainty. So she began cultivating the confidence of her protégé. After asking Rudolph if she desired to make the 1956 Olympic team, Faggs firmly told her, "All right, all you have to do to make this team is stick with me. Put everything else out of your mind and concentrate on doing nothing else but sticking with me. You stick with me in the race, you make the team."[119] The Olympic veteran soon began telling the teenage talent, "Wilma, you really have the ability to perform as an individual."[120] During the 200-meter race at the Olympic Trials, Faggs implored Rudolph to reject her inhibitions and unleash her speed. Faggs recalled yelling "Come on!" to Rudolph as they together entered the final turn. Rudolph replied, "I'm coming Mae!" But, much to Faggs's frustration, Rudolph did not come all the way. According to Faggs, "I just barely got her. It shocked her that she had pulled up so quick next to me." She added, "Later I told her, 'Why did you hesitate? You don't ever do that!' I fussed at her for doing it. 'You saw your chance, you should have blown past me!'"[121] Faggs addressed Rudolph as an athlete, encouraging her to see that she could, and should, want to win. She was entitled to athletic excellence.

Eventually, Rudolph began to understand, recognizing and realizing her individual potential. "Then it started sinking in—performing as an individual. An individual. Up to that point, all I was concerned about was fitting in with all the rest of the girls."[122] In other words, she realized individual athletic achievement and ambition were her right. As a poor young black woman not only raised in a southern society organized by racism but also in a black southern society that honored patriarchal privilege, Rudolph had inculcated the understanding that her race, gender, and class had fated her for a limited life. The exclusions she had experienced because of her physical disabilities had further discouraged Rudolph from developing personal ambition. Individualism, in short, seemed off-limits. Faggs, however, made Rudolph aware that she had the capacity to create her own fate. And her athleticism, particularly her potential for Olympic achievement, offered an avenue.

In addition to introducing Rudolph to new perceptions of her person and possibilities, her Olympic adventure exposed her to unfamiliar, intriguing material advantages. The women's Olympic Village in Melbourne was an idyllic space. According to a press release from the Organizing Committee, "Homes in this section are finished and painted in striking shades of yellow, blue, red, dark purple, gray and pink. They make a colorful picture, set off by lawns and gardens." The athletes' bedrooms featured beds with "cottage weave bedspreads" and window curtains with "modern patterns and colors."[123] In total, the village resembled a modern suburban community, highlighted by a full shopping center that included a beauty shop, concert hall, post office, bank, souvenir shop, milk bar, and travel bureau.[124]

For the black American track women, the Olympic Village provided an opportunity to experience the material privileges of middle-class whiteness denied to them in the United States.[125] Their equal and unfettered access to these consumer comforts translated into further physical and emotional comfort. Rudolph and her teammates experienced the Melbourne Olympics as an integrated, inclusive community that equally respected the wants and needs of all athletes. "I was overwhelmed by the different kinds of people," Rudolph remembered. Her Tigerbelle teammate Margaret Matthews likewise emphasized that "everybody was so nice to all of us."[126] Soon after her return from Melbourne, Willye White told the *Afro-American*, "It was a tremendous thrill. It was really wonderful just being there."[127] Later recalling her experience, White insisted, "The Olympic village was unity. The only place in the world where there was peace. It was home."[128]

Like Rudolph, White experienced the opportunities that came with her elite-level athletic ability as a stark departure from life she knew in her hometown of Money, Mississippi, the place where fourteen-year-old Emmett Till had been murdered just over a year before White would journey to Melbourne. According to her recollections, she had internalized the sense of physical and psychological deviance that white racial violence desired to communicate to black Mississippians. In 1991, she commented in the *Chicago Tribune*, "I felt that I was very unattractive. I was the little pale-skinned black girl with gray-green eyes and funky red hair." She further recalled, "As a child, I always wore high-top shoes and overalls. The parents in my neighborhood forbade their children to play with me because I was a tomboy."[129] White's childhood, similar to that of Rudolph, was defined by her embodied difference, inculcating her with a lack of self-esteem that, slowly but steadily, her participation in competitive sport would counteract. "Running gave me the confidence I needed. I realized I had athletic ability, something no one could take away from me," she asserted.[130] She certainly displayed such confidence and comfort in Melbourne. The reputation that young black American track women, particularly White, established for dancing confirm the invigorated attitude the Olympics allowed them to access and express. At evening gatherings in the Olympic Village lounge, White reportedly led the informal dancing lessons that the young black American track women offered athletes from other nations, including the Soviet Union. The *Philadelphia Tribune* described White as "the little Miss who tried to teach the Russians the 'rock and roll.'"[131] According to Isabelle Daniels, "We had dances almost every night," allowing her and her teammates also to learn new dances from Italian and Canadian athletes.[132]

The array of adoring international fans also boosted the esteem of the young black track stars. "I was asked for my first autograph at the Village, and no matter what anybody says, it does make you feel important and nice, when somebody asks you for your autograph," Rudolph recollected. The requests made Rudolph realize that she and her teammates were understood not only as athletes but also as authoritative representatives of America. That Rudolph and her teammates excitedly spent more than an hour a day willingly signing autographs indicates the impact of this notoriety. Rudolph later wrote, "After a while, all of us girls on the US team would spend an hour every day outside the gate of the Village, signing autographs for whoever wanted them. We did that because we wanted to, not because anybody told us to." "So many people wanted the autographs of Americans that we usually wound up staying more than just an hour, and once or twice we signed for almost two hours," she further shared.[133] The personal, intimate interest expressed by the Olympic fans altered Rudolph's self-understanding. Yes, the rhetoric and imagery of mainstream American sport culture increasingly recognized black women track stars as symbols of the nation and its possibilities. Yet, Rudolph and her teammates did not often experience such possibilities in the United States. The policies and practices of their home country consistently denied their Americanness. In contrast, their experiences in Australia provided them with the sense that they were full Americans.

The young black women who would represent the United States witnessed, experienced, and even indulged in a way of life Down Under different from the one prescribed by the US sociopolitical order. As Willye White powerfully would put it years later:

> Being in Australia was quite an experience. I discovered there were two worlds. There was Mississippi and the other world. (In) the world outside of Mississippi, blacks and whites socialized together, they danced and ate together, even dated each other. Had I not had the opportunity to experience that, I could have spent the rest of my life thinking that the world consisted of lynching, racism, murder, and cross-burning.[134]

Rudolph later shared similar sentiments, asking herself, "Is this all one big dream?"[135] She remembered, "I started to realize a little about what Mae Faggs had told me about the knowledge you get from traveling, and how she valued that more than her Olympic medals."[136] This exposure to diverse persons and places made Rudolph and White aware of alternative cultural and social possibilities that increased further their confidence in themselves. Their reactions to their athletic performances demonstrate as much.

Rudolph advanced to the semi-finals of the 200 meters, where, in her estimation, "This is where I blew it."[137] "I really don't know what happened, except that I did not run as fast as I should have, I finished third and was eliminated from the 200," she explicated. In her autobiography, Rudolph explained her personal devastation, writing, "I asked myself over and over, 'How will I ever be able to face them again back home? I'm a failure.' I didn't go out of my room, I just sat there and felt miserable."[138] Of course, it should not necessarily be significant that Rudolph felt such frustration; it is expected that Olympians who do not medal experience doubt and disappointment. Yet, only months prior, Rudolph simply was happy to be running, resisting exerting the effort needed to defeat her teammates in training sessions. Now, Rudolph exactingly reexamined her race. She demanded better of herself, a notable attitudinal shift. "A couple of days later, I forced myself to go to the Olympic Stadium, and watch Betty Cuthbert run," Rudolph later shared, explaining, "I sat there in the stands watching her, and I said to myself, 'You've got four years to get there yourself, but you've got to work hard for those four years and pay the price.'"[139] Because of her broader pre-Olympic and Olympic experiences, Rudolph had cultivated the confidence needed to engage in such self-criticism and establish such expectations. She did not question her ambition; she unapologetically asserted it. As Rudolph later stated, "I was disappointed, yes, but on the other hand, I wasn't disappointed," for, as she suggested, "how could I be disappointed in the whole experience itself? The travel, the glamour, the excitement that goes with being a part of an Olympic team."[140]

Willye White exhibited a similar attitude. First, the Olympic environment allowed her the time and space needed to refine her long jumping technique. She later shared, "In Melbourne, every morning I would go out to the track and watch the foreign athletes train, and later that day I would come back and emulate whatever I saw them doing earlier. I did not have a coach, so I visualized. If the world record was 20 or 22 feet, I would practice until I could beat that."[141] This process of self-instruction made her expect perfection, which she almost achieved when she secured what was one of the most surprising American achievements. Leaping 19 feet, 11¾ inches, White won the silver medal. But her success did not encourage satisfaction. Her reflections reveal apparently contradictory emotions about her performance, both frustration and inspiration. "It was almost an embarrassment, coming in second. Worth one line in the paper. Second best in the world is treated like a shame," White asserted years later.[142] "I was bitter for months," she admitted, "even years."[143] However, she converted her disappointment into determination. She recalled, "After the summer of '56, I returned to Mississippi and knew that I must succeed in athletics; not only would it free me, but it would offer the opportunity to travel all over the world as well."[144] And she would, participating in international athletic competitions for two decades.

Rudolph similarly channeled her dissatisfaction back into the sport. Before she would tally three gold medals at the 1960 Olympic Games in Rome, she helped the US track women claim a medal in the 400-meter relay in Melbourne. However, according to Rudolph, the indomitable Mae Faggs was most responsible for the relay bronze. Like Rudolph, Faggs was displeased with her inability to advance to the final in the individual sprints. From the perspective of Rudolph, Faggs admirably overcame her disappointment to direct her focus, as well as that of her teammates, on the relay race. Rudolph insisted, "She was the motivator for us." "She was very good at having a calm and cool exterior when she was nervous. She really psyched us up that day; she went around telling us, 'Let's go get 'em, let's give it all we've got, let's make it into the top three and win ourselves a medal.' Soon, we all started picking up on that, and we were actually hyper, telling ourselves that we really were about ready to go out there and upset somebody," Rudolph remembered.[145] Spurred by the spirit of Faggs, the quartet of four American Tigerbelles nearly grabbed the gold. Rudolph swiftly completed her third leg and cleanly passed the baton to anchor Isabelle Daniels, who fell just short of Britain's Heather Armitage and Australia's Betty Cuthbert in a photo finish.[146]

Yet, as noted, Faggs experienced the relay bronze rather differently. Disappointment defined her time Down Under. While frustrated that she did not achieve her long-sought individual medal, her failure to guide her teammates to the relay gold caused her more consternation. She believed herself obligated to be the unimpeachable "Mother of the Tigerbelles." Her attitude about her responsibility resembles the social role expected of women, especially black women. Service trumped self. So for all the ways in which Faggs understood that athletics could, and should, raise her teammates' awareness of the rights, opportunities, and recognitions that they deserved as American athletes and

American citizens, retrogressive and restrictive attitudes still mediated her mindset. Faggs lived this tension; she constantly negotiated social conventions in order to assert her self-confidence.

Of course, one may question Faggs's recollections, as well as those of Rudolph and White. Yet, their narratives, even if inexact or exaggerated, reveal how they chose to make sense of their experiences. They show the ways their sport success changed their understandings of the rights, opportunities, and recognitions that they deserved not simply as athletes but as athletes who represented America. Rudolph and White both positioned their time in Melbourne as transformative, altering their expectations for themselves and, in turn, the trajectory of their lives. In other words, their self-reported stories demonstrate that sport offered them a new understanding of their identity. Faggs's story, however, introduces the limitations of alternative, autonomous self-understandings. The enduring obligation to and investment in performing traditional gender roles, due both to dominant American gender ideologies and the expectations imposed on race women, foreclosed a real reconfiguration of American belonging. Moving forward, through the 1958 US–Soviet Union dual track and field meet and the rise of Wilma Rudolph, black American track women further would help establish a rather exclusive "foundation" of American identity.

4
WINNING AS AMERICAN WOMEN
THE HETERONORMATIVITY OF BLACK WOMEN
ATHLETIC HEROINES, 1958–1960

The August 1958 cover of *Amateur Athlete* featured Isabelle Daniels, Lucinda Williams, Barbara Jones, and Margaret Matthews. For the first time, the foremost amateur sport organization in the United States chose to advertise itself through black women athletes. The Tigerbelle quartet ostensibly earned their cover shot for winning the 440-yard relay at the 1958 National AAU Outdoor Championship in Morristown, New Jersey. During the relay final, the foursome was in top form. They flawlessly executed their three baton exchanges—from Daniels to Williams to Jones to Matthews—allowing them to establish a new AAU record of 46.9 seconds. Unsurprisingly, the four also racked up individual honors. Daniels, Williams, Jones, and Matthews represented each other's stiffest competition as they led the Tigerbelles to a fourth straight team title, winning by a margin of more than sixty points.[1] However, the Tigerbelles graced the cover of *Amateur Athlete* not because of their ability but because of their image. Outfitted in their crisp and clean TSU uniforms, the quartet smiled as they embraced each other, communicating camaraderie and charm. An engagement ring, visible on the ring finger of Matthews, further indicated their appropriate femininity. In short, the young black women track stars successfully performed white-defined gender norms. They thus were understood as eligible exemplars of Americanness.

In the late 1950s, this image had particular propagandistic power. Identifying black American track women as symbols of the best of the American Way offered a resolution to the demands that the Cold War and civil rights movement imposed on American sport and society. Young black track women were imagined as embodied evidence against the (accurate) accusations of American inequality increasingly publicized by the Soviet Union. Because the combination of blackness and femaleness long had represented the antithesis of ideal Americanness, black women athletes appeared to powerfully communicate the opportunities proclaimed as available to all in a democratic nation. When outfitted in the uniform of the United States, especially when competing in the sporting proxy wars of the Cold War, these young women served as proof of the increasing inclusivity of American identity. But because the understanding of their Americanness was premised on their ability to perform, perfectly, white-defined femininity, recognition of their Americanness always worked subtly to reassert the traditional racial, gender, and sexual orders of the United States. They presented an optimistic image of equality, albeit one that actually worked to reinforce the hierarchies that differentially determined Americanness.

The perceived and, more critically, promoted normativity of black American track women demonstrates how US culture effectively managed the boundaries of American identity. The symbolism of the likes of Daniels, Williams, Jones, Matthews, and, soon thereafter, Wilma Rudolph permitted US sport and society to perform, but not practice, democracy. While this process had begun in Mexico City and Melbourne, it would be consolidated in Moscow, before then culminating with Rudolph in Rome. Black American track women no longer were a threat to the normative boundaries of American belonging; they were constitutive to a conservative vision of America. The experiences of black American track women thus reveal the exclusionary character of normative Americanness. Although the surprising success achieved by the Tigerbelles in the inaugural US–Soviet Union dual in Moscow would pave the way for Wilma Rudolph to be proclaimed as an admirable, all-American heroine, Rudolph herself was unable to participate in the Moscow meet due to an imperfect, inconvenient aspect of her life, an unplanned pregnancy. Additionally, the strategic visibility and invisibility of Earlene Brown in the imagery of American sport exposes the ingrained inequities that still structured American identity.

Thus, the experiences and interpretations of young black American track women surrounding the 1958 US–Soviet Union dual and 1960 Olympic Games illuminate the centrality of heteronormativity to idealized American identity, highlighting how it operated (and operates) capriciously to preserve and protect the nation's entrenched inequalities. The ideology does not simply express the importance of heterosexuality to US society; rather, it is an implicitly racialized ideology that privileges and prioritizes traditional, heterosexual white-defined gender roles. Yet the ostensible ability of all Americans to perform normative gender roles made (and makes) fulfilling the expectations of heteronormativity and, in turn, American citizenship appear equally possible to all. The young black women athletes who represented the United States in international track and field events in the late 1950s and early 1960s effectively advertised this possibility. Their role in these ideologically tinged athletic battles thus reflects the broader effort of dominant American culture to reconfigure the image, but not the actualities, of American belonging in the late 1950s.

THE PROPAGANDISTIC POWER OF A COLD WAR SPORTING SHOWDOWN

In July 1958, the United States and Soviet Union would face off in the first head-to-head dual track meet between the two nations, an initiative organized on the American end by the State Department in cooperation with the AAU. While a seemingly straightforward opportunity for the United States to use athletic achievement to assert the supposed superiority of democracy, the increasingly visible and violent reactions of white Americans to black Americans' claims to civil rights made the meet a more pressing, and potentially problematic, propaganda opportunity. Since the 1956 Olympics, the movement for civil rights had inspired intensified reactions from white Americans. In particular, white Americans resisted the desegregation of schools required by the ruling in *Brown v. Board of Education*, culminating with the violent resentment provoked by the integration of Central High School in Little Rock, Arkansas. The images emerging from Little Rock appeared to refute any and all of the idealistic claims made by the United States. In this complex, changing sociopolitical context, black women athletes, marked by racial and gender difference, would seem to raise further discomfort about the content and character of American identity.

Yet, black women track stars, especially when they wore the uniform of the United States, served a propagandistic purpose, permitting US sport culture to navigate the contradictions and tensions of American democracy.

As documented by sports studies scholar Damion Thomas, the intersecting events of the Cold War and civil rights movement encouraged the State Department increasingly to task black athletes with counteracting images of the nation's enduring inequities. The government sent "good Negroes," namely Mal Whitfield and Rafer Johnson, on goodwill tours around the globe, relying on them to reassure people of color of America's rightness. Thomas writes, "In the post-*Brown* environment, the State Department wanted Whitfield to take a tour precisely because of his stature as a 'man of color.'"[2] Building on the strategies introduced at the 1955 Pan-American and 1956 Olympic Games, US sport culture likewise positioned black women track stars as symbols of unfettered and uncontroversial American possibility. This approach relied on, and thus reinforced, the centrality of the ideology of heteronormativity to American identity.

AAU organizers named the performatively patriarchal Ed Temple head coach of the US women's team for the 1958 dual.[3] His reputation, as the author of the Temple Way, worked to reinforce the appropriate gendering of the American women track athletes. The eighteen young women who would compete in Moscow were assumed to acquiesce to the authority of a fatherly figure, thereby not threatening the traditional American gender order. The believed contrast between sufficiently submissive American women and their supposedly too-independent Soviet counterparts also underscored this understanding. As recognized by historian Laura Belmonte, American Cold War cultural propaganda long had critiqued the Soviet Union for permitting, even encouraging, women to "work as stevedores, street cleaners, and forge operators."[4] The perceived masculinization of Soviet women was enhanced for athletes, who were described, by both the white and black presses, as "husky" and "Amazons."[5] In his 1980 autobiography, Temple himself endorsed these ideas, quipping, "This was during the time of the famous Press sisters. They had more muscles and whiskers than I had. They were something to deal with until they started these hormone tests, and the Press sisters just disappeared from the competition scene."[6] Temple's reflections are indicative of the belief that the conventionally heterosexual comportment of American women, including black American women athletes, made them and, in extension, their country superior, regardless of what happened on the track or field. Heteronormativity was a sign of American superiority.

Yet, somewhat surprisingly, the American team included six white women, a circumstance that seemingly would trouble Temple's paternal position and the United States' ideological calculations. However, the ideological gymnastics permitted by the flexibility of heteronormativity made Temple's position possible. That Temple received this role thus provides insight into the complicated, intersecting dynamics of race, gender, and sexuality that structured American sport and American society in the late 1950s. First, that the AAU chose Temple as coach reflects the degree to which the US women's track and field team was understood and, more critically, accepted as a "black" team. Having increasingly established their dominance of the sport, black American track women had defined American women's athleticism as black American women's athleticism. Importantly, as they did so, they contested long-standing negative stereotypes, subtly, steadily, and successfully presenting an image of black women's athleticism that was understood as acceptably American. Yet their racial difference was not irrelevant. Rather, their racial identity ensured their femininity would remain seen as secondary to that of white women, regardless of how perfectly they appeared to perform femininity. Participating in competitive athletics thus did not jeopardize black women athletes' gendering.

White women, in contrast, still were seen as forsaking their femininity by entering competitive sport. Despite the efforts of the white women leaders of the AAU, participation in track and field still was understood to stain the femininity of white American women. The uncertainty surrounding the US women's basketball teams that, beginning in the mid-1950s and continuing through the 1960s, engaged in international competitions, including against the Soviet Union, likewise demonstrates how ideas about femininity complicated the place of white women athletes in the imagery of American sport. According to historian Kevin Witherspoon, "The physical of nature of these contests [between the United States and Soviet Union] became problematic, particularly for American officials, who struggled to achieve a balance between success on the court and upholding traditional American expectations for femininity"; in turn, "American officials elected to minimize the significance of the women's games and eventually to discontinue them altogether."[7] So even as white women continued to compete in track and field at the national and international levels, they were rendered all but invisible in the imagery of American sport. Because of the combination of their racial, gender, and sexual identities, they lacked propagandistic purpose, offering no representationally relevant response to the concerns raised by the Cold War–civil rights context.

In sum, the perceived heteronormativity and predominant blackness of American women's track and field meant that the squad assembled for the inaugural US–Soviet Union dual aligned with the American social order. Institutions of US state and sport accepted black women athletes as appropriate representations of womanhood, especially in comparison to their Soviet counterparts. But they still were black, which placed them well outside of idealized white American womanhood. Although part of America, black American track women still were not fully American. Nevertheless, in Moscow and across Europe, the bodies of the eleven black American track women would continue to do political work, amenably managing the extent and content of American democracy.

THE 1958 US–SOVIET UNION DUAL AND THE IMAGE OF AMERICAN DEMOCRACY

Their abilities, however, were not deemed as necessary to the ideological athletic battle. Little expectation greeted American track women in anticipation of the dual. Despite their ever-improving effort, it was unquestioned that the ostensibly invincible Soviet women would crush their American counterparts. In turn, the AAU mandated sex-segregated scoring for the meet, guaranteeing that the assumed dominance of the Soviet women would not allow the Soviet Union easily to claim an overall victory. Of course, it remained unsaid that the United States' long underinvestment in women's track and field made these scoring machinations necessary. The Soviets, unsurprisingly, protested this arrangement, but the United States would get its way.[8] Unfazed by scoring methodologies or ideological priorities was the indomitable Ed Temple, who had high expectations for his squad. "The United States women's coach, Ed Temple of Tennessee State University, warned that his girls should not be underrated," noted the *New York Times*.[9] The coach told the *Philadelphia Tribune's* Claude Harrison, "We have a 50–50 chance against the Russians with our hopes mainly resting on the dashes, relay and broad jump. The Russians will have a big edge in most of the weight events."[10] Temple's belief in his athletes would prove far from misguided.

After a ceremony featuring much pomp and circumstance opened the much-anticipated meet, a young black woman from Chicago provided the first spark.[11] Barbara Jones, now a TSU Tigerbelle, out-sped Vera Krepkina in the 100 meters, with Isabelle Daniels finishing a close third. Jones and Daniels then joined Margaret Matthews and Lucinda Williams, captain of the US women, to execute an almost perfect performance in the 400-meter relay, finishing clear of their Soviet competitors by almost a full second. The foursome that had appeared on the cover of *Amateur Athlete* registered a new American record, the only record-breaking performance of the competition's first day. In the field events, Earlene Brown, a black beauty shop employee from California, also claimed a surprising second place in the discus throw, denying the Soviet women their assumed sweep.[12] These opening-day achievements of black American women athletes thus ensured that they could not be ignored. Contravening the separate scoring structure, their efforts inserted the women's competition into the center of the sporting Cold War. Ignoring the AAU's scoring preferences, the *New York Times* estimated, "Hopes for an American team victory will ride largely with the girls tomorrow." The paper then suggested a win in the 200-meter sprint and 80-meter hurdles would, in combination with the points expected to be earned by the US men, give the Americans the overall victory that the AAU had considered impossible.[13]

On the second day of competition, Lucinda Williams won the 200 meters before Earlene Brown put the shot further than Galina Zybina and Tamara Press. Yet, the total four firsts won by the US women did not prove enough; they fell short of the Soviet women by a score of 63 to 44. Nonetheless, only excitement surrounded their performance. Ed Temple remembered thinking, "We shocked the U.S. men and we shocked us. We didn't know we was good. But we really showed out."[14] The AAU likewise asserted, "Our girls surprised all hands by winning four of the ten events and holding the Russians to 63 points to our 44."[15] This enthusiasm extended to the black sporting press. The *Chicago Defender's* Robert Musel trilled, "But Uncle Sam's girls humiliated the husky competitors by winning two of the first five events in the women's competition."[16] He happily explicated:

> The Russians obviously figured their women would pick up enough points to enable them to win the meet. But the underdog Yank gals may have thrown a monkey wrench into that plan when Barbara Jones of Chicago won the 100-meter dash in 11.6 seconds and then ran a brilliant anchor leg to give the United States a victory in the women's 400-meter relay with a 44.8 second clocking.[17]

Somewhat contradictorily, the American women's admirable defeat enhanced their reputation as exemplars of their nation as much as, perhaps more than, a win. Such a respectable showing strategically satisfied the

FIGURE 8. Martha Hudson, Lucinda Williams, Isabelle Daniels, and Margaret Matthews (left to right), all members of the American team that competed in the 1958 USA-USSR dual track and field meet in Moscow, show off the medals won under the direction of coach Ed Temple.
Courtesy of Tennessee State University Special Collections and Archives, Brown-Daniel Library

ideological aims of the Cold War–civil rights moment. First, losing to the Soviet women preserved believed differences between American and Soviet women. As noted by sports studies scholar Lindsay Parks Pieper, sporting officials and journalists in the United States did not hesitate to "disparage" Soviet women athletes, readily questioning their biological womanhood.[18] In turn, the inability of black American women athletes to equal women athletes who supposedly had renounced their femininity through their aggressive commitment to athletics suggested that, despite participation in competitive sport, they retained feminine character. That black women scored all the victories for the United States also signaled American racial equality. Yet, at the same time, the achievements of black American women again served as a reminder of their supposedly inferior femininity, as the six white American women athletes who competed in Moscow did not come close to claiming a victory. The striving efforts by black American track women thus protected the nation's racialized gender hierarchy in a way that appeared inclusive. The remainder of the track and field tour codified this imagery. Victories and defeats in front of hundreds of thousands of Western Europeans established and entrenched black American track women as salvific symbols of US democracy, promisingly performing equality in a way that nonetheless preserved inequalities.[19] One member of the US women's team would seem ineligible to serve such a symbolic role. But the body of Earlene Brown still had ideological purpose.

THE INELIGIBLE AMERICANNESS OF EARLENE BROWN

At the 1956 US Women's Olympic Track and Field Trials, Earlene Brown introduced herself to the world of American sport. A twenty-one-year-old shot putter and discus thrower from Compton, California, Brown attracted attention for her ability but also for her identity. Bespectacled and big-boned, Brown, who worked in a local hair salon to support herself and her young son, offered an image of a black woman athlete at odds with the highly tailored TSU model.[20] She thus challenged the athletic ideology of black American sport culture. Even if black women track stars had begun to be recognized as legitimate athletes whose accomplishments could accrue respect for the race, this liberalized perspective relied on the expectation that all black women athletes abide by the "politics of respectability." Brown's physical being, in combination with her lived experience, placed her outside of black American respectability. In short, the Temple Way was the only way. So, although Brown was embraced by the Los Angeles black community, black American sport culture more broadly regarded her with trepidation, remaining rather silent about her performance and prospects.

After the 1956 Olympic Games, Brown was absent from the array of celebrations held in the black communities of Atlanta and Nashville. Geography partly explain her absence, as Brown was a native of California. But the articles of acclaim penned by the black press barely mentioned the "matron" of women's track, even though she nearly medaled in the discus and finished a more than respectable sixth in the shot put. For instance, the *Chicago Defender*'s Fay Young blithely noted, "Oddly enough, Mrs. Earline [sic] Brown . . . placed in the shot put."[21] The silence surrounding her speaks volumes. As a heavy-set single mother who worked in a beauty salon, she exceeded the imagined gendered, sexed, classed, and corporeal parameters of heteronormativity and respectability. In turn, she was understood as unable to embody black Americans' hopes for full citizenship.

In contrast, Brown served a significant symbolic function for mainstream American sport culture. "Mrs. Brown Betters Two Track Records," announced the *New York Times* on the first page of the sports section following the conclusion of the 1956 US Women's Olympic Track and Field Trials.[22] The *Times* detailed the impressiveness of Brown's performance:

> Mrs. Earlene Brown, who has been a practicing athlete only three and one-half months, set two American records today in winning a place on the United States women's Olympic track and field team. Mrs. Brown, 21, far from a polished track performer, used sheer power to throw the discus 145 feet 4 1/2 inches and the shot 46 feet 9 1/2 inches. She used the 226 pounds on her 5-foot 7-inch frame to send the weights to record-shattering distances.[23]

Although recognizing Brown's ability, the *Times* made sure to emphasize her physicality. She was presented as the stereotypical laboring black female body, albeit inserted into the space of sport, thus making her a curiosity. Ahead of the 1958 US–Soviet Union dual, the *New York Times* again underscored her exceptional strength, noting her swift improvement in a way that served to exoticize her: "She achieved 50 feet for the first time in her life a week ago and has improved on that steadily in daily work-outs."[24] The *Times* also published a photo of Brown receiving instruction from Parry O'Brien, the two-time Olympic shot put gold medalist from Southern California who embodied traditional white American masculinity.[25] While the image showed the inclusivity of the American squad, it also was somewhat provocative, as O'Brien guided Brown's arms as he stood behind her. Yet, in a 1950s white America that feared miscegenation, this image did not activate such anxieties.[26] Rather, O'Brien and Brown could be photographed interacting in such a way because of her supposedly excessive blackness. She would be understood as unfeminine, even unsexed. It was assumed that she could, and should, throw like a man.

Of course, this image of black women's athleticism contrasted with that of the Tigerbelle quartet that appeared on the cover of *Amateur Athlete*. This difference had ideological utility. In their analysis of the meanings of Wilma Rudolph, sport studies scholars Rita Liberti and Maureen M. Smith recognize that the juxtaposition of Rudolph with Brown after the 1960 Rome Olympics was constitutive to popular perceptions of Rudolph's femininity.[27] "As a study in contrasts," they write, "Rudolph is made more appealing to white audiences *because* of Brown's ongoing presence in the media."[28] Brown, however, served this function for the broader population of black women track athletes beginning in 1956. Often described as jolly and jovial, she evoked the Mammy stereotype, a seemingly primitive figure from the black American past. Her rapid rate of improvement also underscored the belief in the inherent, even abnormal athleticism of black women. Because of her supposedly unfeminine physicality, Brown made more evident the appropriate femininity of other black women track stars.

In contrast, the slim and shapely sprinters and jumpers who competed for TSU and Tuskegee embodied the progress of black America. The likes of Mae Faggs, Isabelle Daniels, and Mildred McDaniel, as well as Rudolph, signaled the social progress supposedly made possible by the democratic institutions of US sport and state. Their image reinforced that Americanness was something to be earned; more specifically, it was something to be earned through an adherence to normative values and behavior. At the same time, Brown's over-embodied blackness also served as a reminder of the ostensibly inherent differences between black and white American women. Although black women track stars may represent the nation, Brown made evident that the womanhood and, thus, the Americanness of black American women remained insufficient. By serving as the specter of the too independent and too autonomous black woman, she signaled how heteronormativity appeared to tame black women, making them appropriately, but never fully, American.

The juxtaposition of Brown with fellow discus thrower Olga Fikotová Connolly further illustrates the limited American identity that the majority of black American track women advertised. At the 1956 Olympic Games, the twenty-four-year-old Czechoslovakian not only bested the favored Soviet women to steal the gold medal in the discus, but she also stole the heart of American hammer thrower Harold Connolly. Their courtship presented a seemingly perfect Cold War fairy tale, with the attractive and impressionable Eastern European young woman charmed not only by a strong American man but also by his free and democratic country.[29] The *New York Times* devoted much coverage to the Connollys, including detailing the geopolitical difficulties they navigated ahead of their wedding in Prague in the spring of 1957.[30] That US Secretary of State John Foster Dulles sent his wishes to the couple upon their wedding highlights the interest in the Connolly affair, as well as the propagandistic pleasure US officials took in it.[31] As a white, attractive woman athlete whose story advanced the US Cold War cultural agenda, Connolly stood as the unfulfilled yet ideal (white) American woman athlete.

Having relocated to the United States, Connolly began to compete in national AAU-sponsored events, including the 1957 National AAU Championship in Shaker Heights, Ohio. As the organization announced, "The meet will be enlivened by a discus throwing duel between Mrs. Harold Fikotova [sic] Connolly, Olympic champion in the event and Mrs. Earline [sic] Brown, fourth in the Olympic competition."[32] Identifying Connolly through her husband's name, in contrast to Brown's unnamed husband (from whom she was separated), underscored her superior, implicitly white, femininity. Her matrimony made safe her athletic ability, allowing her to earn praise for besting Brown in their showdown. *Amateur Athlete*, however, did not draw attention to the strength her win required, instead describing the "chummy and friendly" rivalry that developed between the black woman athlete often described as "popular" but "portly" and the pretty, happy Czechoslovakian.[33]

But this pair of opposites was not just a curiosity. When competing against each other in national and international meets the two women served as embodied boundaries, influencing how the majority of black women track stars could be seen as symbols of American citizenship in a way that was uncontroversial, as well as rather conservative. Brown accentuated the slimness and suaveness of the majority of black American track women, showing that they possessed traits that proved their appropriate femininity and, in turn, earned them their Americanness. Yet, she also served as a reminder of the seemingly inherent unfemininity of blackness. Connolly, in contrast, advertised the ideal womanhood that, due to racial difference, black women athletes, no matter their ability to abide by gendered conventions, never would meet.[34] The bodies of women athletes thus performed the possibility of Americanness for black Americans, all while still communicating the racialized limits of full American belonging. This dynamic was in effect at the three-way meet between the United States, Czechoslovakia, and Hungary in Budapest in the summer 1958.

A few days after their admirable effort in Moscow, black American women dominated the track and field in Budapest, winning seven of the eleven events.[35] In the discus, Brown claimed the victory over Connolly, heaving the discus approximately 6 inches further than the Czechoslovakian. Otherwise, Margaret Matthews turned in the most impressive performance. At the previous meet in Poland, Willye White won long jump by leaping a new American record of 20 feet and just over 2½ inches.[36] Her mark appeared to erase Matthews from the record book, until Matthews exacted quick revenge in Budapest. She reclaimed the record by leaping 20 feet and 3¼ inches.[37] In total, the gracefulness of Matthews contrasted with the girth of Brown, accentuating her appropriate femininity that, nonetheless, did not match the quintessential femininity of Connolly.

Thus, throughout the summer of 1958, the bodies of women athletes, especially black women athletes, did political work. Because of Earlene Brown, the sprinters and jumpers who always obeyed the Temple Way more effectively advertised that Americanness was something to be earned through heteronormative comportment. Brown thus enhanced the propagandistic propagation of a conservative understanding of American citizenship. For the normativity of her teammates that she accentuated still was racialized, meaning that the full Americanness that attractive black women athletes appeared to promise for black Americans always would remain out of reach. And it would be Wilma Rudolph who most would live this cruel reality. Following her Roman romp at the 1960 Olympic Games, Rudolph would ascend to American iconicity, a celebrated demonstration of the democracy's supposed superiority. Yet her absence from the 1958 summer tour, including the seminal Moscow meet, introduces the ways in which the insidious inequities of heteronormativity undermined the optimistic equality that she advertised. Rudolph lived the increasingly imagined but ever-unfulfilled belonging of black women athletes. In contradistinction to her image, she intimately experienced the impossibility of unfettered Americanness for those marked by race, gender, and other minority identities.

THE IDEOLOGICAL IMPORTANCE OF WILMA RUDOLPH'S ABSENCE

In the summer of 1958, when black American women track stars "showed out" in Moscow, Rudolph was in her hometown of Clarksville, Tennessee. Even though the then-eighteen-year-old had yet to establish herself as an undisputed spiriting superstar, Ed Temple still could have used her services. Yet, she was not eligible to compete to for a spot on the squad due to pregnancy. She was unfit, both physically and representationally.

By the late 1950s, unwed black mothers had been inscribed as pathological, examples of the supposedly inherent cultural deficiencies of poor black Americans. This understanding not only was a product of racialist white ideologies but also was endorsed by the black middle class, which sought to enhance their own fitness for full American citizenship by distinguishing themselves from purportedly immoral poor black Americans.[38] As put by sociologist Maxine

Craig, "The practice of making distinctions among black people, who whites treated as indistinguishable, was another manifestation of black racial pride."[39] This shared social belief about illegitimacy involved a tangle of gender, race, sexual, and class expectations that would ensnare Rudolph, influencing not only her eligibility for the summer track and field tour but also shaping her subsequent story. Her unwed pregnancy and single motherhood would be excised from her all-American image, an inconvenient, irrelevant, and ignorable instance. It is rather ironic that Rudolph, the athlete who supposedly symbolized the possibilities of the American Way, most experienced its limitations. The lived realities of her pregnancy and motherhood thus further illuminate the problematic aspects of black American track women's acceptance as exemplars of ideal Americanness. The American identity they advertised was exclusionary and disciplinary, as the treatment of Rudolph's pregnancy and motherhood demonstrates. Her experience highlights how the ideology of heteronormativity, while allowing black women athletes to be included in a diverse, democratic image of Americanness, ultimately reinforced restrictions on full belonging.

Scholarship on Rudolph primarily has reproduced this inconvenient understanding of her pregnancy and motherhood. In analyses of her emergence as an American icon, the episode often has been elided or quickly explained away, an assumedly unfortunate event that, fortunately, did not disrupt her athletic career.[40] However, such interpretations implicitly reify the idea that her heteronormative identity is intrinsic to her historical relevance. The dominant understanding of Rudolph, from her 1960s moment through historical memory, thus reflects the unquestioned prominence, power, and policing function of the ideology of heteronormativity. Pausing on Rudolph's pregnancy and motherhood instead provides a critical perspective of the centrality of heteronormativity to American identity. Furthermore, Rudolph devoted much detail and description to her pregnancy in her 1977 autobiography, suggesting it was an experience critical to her self-understanding. The trials and tribulations she experienced as a young, unwed black mother required her to reckon intimately with the intersecting, yet often contradictory, expectations of race, gender, sex, and class that categorize and circumscribe citizenship.

According to Rudolph, she immediately, and instinctively, felt shame upon learning of her condition. "I was mortified. Pregnant?" she recalled, continuing, "Pregnant. I refused to tell a soul."[41] Aware of the classed expectations of a black middle-class institution such as TSU, Rudolph especially feared sharing her condition with Ed Temple. She wrote:

> One day Coach Temple showed up at my house. He sat down with me and my mother and father, and said he had come over from Nashville because he had just heard some startling news. He said he heard I was pregnant. We all nodded. Then I went and hid. I couldn't face him. When I finally came out of hiding, he said, 'Wilma, I still want you to come to Tennessee State after the baby is born.' I was overjoyed when he said that, because I already knew that Coach Temple had a standing rule than [sic] he never took a girl into his track program who had a baby. So he was breaking one of his own rules for me, and that made me feel absolutely great.[42]

Her narration illuminates the racial, gender, and class tensions that structured the black community, as well as introducing how she lived these tensions. While possibly exaggerating her embarrassed reaction, the recollection nonetheless reveals her intense sense of class-based shame. Expectations of gender combined with those of class to make her question her place at TSU. Yet, by bending his rules, Temple provided an opportunity for redemption. That he made such an exception often has been understood as a sign of her exceptionality, as if the coach discarded his policy because he foresaw her world-class promise. And it was remarkable that Rudolph not only continued, but accelerated, her athletic career following her early pregnancy, a clear, yet quiet, defiance of gender norms. As she wrote in her autobiography, "I really didn't want to become a housewife at such an early age, I knew I could still be a runner, and I wanted to be able to go to the Olympics in 1960."[43] Nonetheless, her ability to disregard expectations was premised on perfectly obeying the paternalistic policies of Temple. He established rules for Rudolph, permitting her possible redemption. He insisted upon treating her like all other Tigerbelles, meaning he prevented her from caring for her daughter during the track and field season. In short, if she wanted to be a Tigerbelle, she had to put full-time motherhood on hold. Her unwed motherhood was all but was erased in service of her Olympic potential.

Rudolph's circumstance thus required that she navigate constantly a web of gendered, raced, and classed norms, publicly abiding by dominant expectations even as she privately defied them. But this dynamic was far from easy. Even though she did not want to be a housewife, she wanted to be a mother. Yet her desire to be an athlete and a student, roles that came with certain classed associations, precluded her fulfilling her mothering role. During her freshman year, Rudolph's older sister Yvonne, who lived in St. Louis, took care of her daughter, Yolanda. This distance, in addition to Rudolph's academic and athletic obligations, prevented her from ever seeing her daughter. At the close of her first semester, Rudolph, knowing she only had a three-day holiday break due to Tigerbelle training sessions, asked Temple for extra days off so she could travel to St. Louis and see Yolonda. Temple refused. As Rudolph described it:

> So I went to Coach Temple, and I asked him for a couple more days off, and told him I want to see my baby in St. Louis. 'She's five months old now and I haven't seen her since back in September.' Coach Temple said absolutely not; he said he was going to treat me just like everybody else, three days off and that's it, no special favors. I accepted that, since I knew I was lucky to be there in the first place, having had a baby and all.[44]

Her initial thoughts suggest that she had internalized the presumably necessary gratitude for Temple's generosity. However, when Yvonne proposed adopting Yolanda, Rudolph did not hesitate to disobey her coach's demands. She quickly contacted Yolanda's father, her former boyfriend Robert Eldridge, hatching a plan to head to St. Louis and, in her words, "steal our baby back." Their effort, somewhat surprisingly, succeeded. After the emotional episode, Rudolph's father and mother agreed to keep Yolanda in Clarksville, thus easing Rudolph's mind about her status as Yolanda's mother. Nonetheless, she still struggled to balance her multiple roles, writing in her autobiography:

> I was a freshman and that was a hard adjustment for me, I was running track, and that took up a lot of my time. I had to keep a two-point average in the classroom to keep my scholarship and stay in school, and that meant I had to study." She continued, "I was also a mother, and I wondered a lot how my baby was doing back home. Robert was dropping hints that I should drop out of school, quit track, and become a full-time wife and mother. It was tempting at times, I admit it. There were millions of times I just wanted to quit school and take the easy way.[45]

Somewhat understandably, ceding to a conventional lifestyle, rather than one characterized by a complicated combination of expectations and obligations, appealed to Rudolph. She wanted a "normal" American life. Of course, before the end of the next year, Rudolph, although living far from a "normal" American life, would stand as an icon of ideal Americanness. Despite her real-life struggle to fulfill raced, gendered, and classed proscriptions, she would emerge as a model of American identity, one ostensibly unencumbered by any tensions or contradictions. The invisibility of her pregnancy and daughter were essential to this imagery. And the choices of the very middle-classed black sport culture were critical to making it possible.

Although Temple and TSU accepted Rudolph in spite of her status as an unwed mother, black American sport culture did not abandon their classed ideas about illegitimacy. In the black press, Rudolph's identity as a young, unwed, but nonetheless doting, devoted, and determined mother was erased. This perspective is understandable. In seeking to earn citizenship, absolutely embodying the moral values proclaimed by white America represented a viable, explainable strategy. The black middle class consistently strove to exceed the social expectations that white Americans believed they could not meet; providing any ammunition for white prejudice was not an option. So Rudolph's motherhood was kept secret, allowing her to appear to emerge easily, uncontroversially, and unprecedentedly as an American icon. But the gap between Rudolph's imagery and reality exposes the insidiousness of this stance. Aspirational black Americans, intentionally or not, participated in the formation and consolidation of a citizenship that, ultimately, always would limit the full belonging of black Americans. Gendered normativity was understood, and thus inscribed, as the salve for racial difference. Yet gender norms themselves already were racialized, making impossible the irrelevancy of racial difference to an American citizenship organized around gender conventionality.

Notably, the mainstream, white-controlled American press also would not expose Rudolph's status as an unwed mother. Rather, she would be presented as a great and graceful young woman who perfectly and pleasantly proved the opportunities American democracy provided for all. That her status as a mother remained silenced suggests the degree to which Rudolph emerged at the ideal moment, when the confluence of the Cold War, civil rights movement, and contingent circumstances of sport encouraged her to be seen as the foremost symbol of American citizenship. The seemingly easy elision of Rudolph's unwed motherhood, highlighted by her unexplained absence throughout the 1958 summer track and field tour, emphasizes the ways in which mainstream and black American sports cultures simultaneously navigated expectations of race, gender, class, and nation in a way that enshrined a certain vision of Americanness, one that would be symbolized by Rudolph. But first, she had to position herself for such recognition.

WILMA RUDOLPH, READY FOR ROME

In the popular imagination, Wilma Rudolph seemingly rose from nowhere, suddenly running with speed, grace, and élan. Not only were the inconvenient aspects of her life erased but so was her history of athletic improvement. For all the importance of her image and understandings of it, it is necessary to appreciate how Rudolph's ability made her prominence possible. Although aspects of her past and present would be emphasized or obviated so that she could symbolize the supposed best of American society, it ultimately was her athletic agency that set the stage for her ovation.

Following the birth of daughter, Rudolph returned to the track in January 1959, debuting as an official TSU Tigerbelle at the National AAU Indoor Championship in Washington, DC. The Tigerbelles triumphed for their fifth-straight indoor title, with Rudolph contributing a win in the 50-yard dash before running the lead leg of TSU's 440-yard relay victory.[46] In her autobiography, Rudolph claimed, "My speed was tremendous after I had the baby; I was much faster than before."[47] Her performance at the National AAU Outdoor Championship in Cleveland in June of 1959 suggests she was not exaggerating. She out-sped veteran teammate Lucinda Williams to take the 100-meter title.[48] This performance encouraged Ed Temple to tout her talent ahead of the second US–Soviet Union dual track meet, held at Philadelphia's Franklin Field in mid-July. "I have a sprinter that has all the potential for greatness. She has a fast start, long stride and a great desire to win," Temple told the *Philadelphia Tribune*, insisting, "For this meet she'll be at her best."[49]

Unfortunately, muscle spasms prevented Rudolph from fulfilling Temple's predictions.[50] Overall, the US women failed to reprise their surprising performance from the previous summer. Barbara Jones repeated in the 100 meters, and Williams did the same in the 200 meters, but otherwise the Soviet women won with ease. At September's 1959 Pan-American Games, held in Chicago, Rudolph returned to the track, running well but not yet matching Temple's lofty proclamations. Instead, Lucinda Williams served as the star of the American women's side, winning the 100-meter and 200-meter sprints. Rudolph finished second in the 100 before teaming with Williams, as well as Isabelle Daniels and Barbara Jones, to triumph in the 400-meter relay.[51] About nine months later, at the 1960 National AAU Indoor Championship, Rudolph finally began to fulfill the sprinting potential promoted by Temple, leading the Tigerbelles to their sixth-straight indoor title. As described by *Amateur*

Athlete, "The 19-year-old sophomore from Clarksville, Tennessee won the 50-yard dash and then returned to set marks in the 100 and 220 yard dashes. Miss Rudolph thus became the second woman to win three events in National AAU women's competition."[52] The *New York Times* also made note of Rudolph's trio of triumphs, declaring her an "Olympic candidate."[53] In early July, Rudolph asserted her outdoor excellence. Running at a pre-AAU Championship meet in Cleveland, Ohio, she broke both the 100-yard and 220-yard outdoor marks. According to the *Afro-American*, "Rudolph became the first woman athlete to hold the indoor and outdoor records for both the 100 and 220 races in more than a quarter-century."[54] The following weekend, she again romped. At the 1960 National AAU Outdoor Championship in Corpus Christi, Texas, she set the record for a curved 200 meters, tied the record for the 100 meters, and ran anchor for the Tigerbelles' record-setting 400-meter relay. Unsurprisingly, Rudolph propelled the Tigerbelles to their sixth-straight AAU team title.[55]

Seeing Rudolph and her teammates in action encouraged AAU women's track and field committee chairwoman Frances Kaszubski to declare the Corpus Christi championship "the most successful national meet for our women in history," insisting it proved that the Olympic prospects for American women "look better than ever."[56] This passel of promising American track women then decamped for Abilene, Texas, for the 1960 US Women's Olympic Track and Field Trials, which were held the following weekend. Here, Rudolph won the 100-meter and 200-meter sprints, establishing herself as the most talented, and most touted, of the thirteen young American women who would head to Rome. Nine other young black women earned an Olympic berth—Earlene Brown, Barbara Jones, Lucinda Williams, Willye White, Shirley Crowder, Martha Hudson, Ernestine Pollards, and Neomia Rogers.[57] Yet, black sport culture increasingly had enthusiasm only for Rudolph.

"You haven't seen it in the dailies, but a 17-year-old sophomore at Tennessee State College is the swiftest female in the world. She is Miss Wilma Rudolph," declared the *Afro-American*.[58] The paper then proclaimed, "The men did very well, we all thought [alluding to the performances of black athletes at the US Men's Olympic Track and Field Trials], but now that we have looked at the girls' performance, we realize our young men must be content with second place."[59] Rudolph's world-class quality performances certainly justified this excitement, but as was already becoming clear, it was her beauty as much as her speed that encouraged the interest of the black American sport community. Seemingly, her appearance overshadowed the athletic ability of her teammates.

For instance, the *Philadelphia Tribune* asserted, "The United States Women's Olympic track and field team is expected to make its best showing since 1932. And the main reason for this bright outlook is Tennessee State's flying lass, Wilma Rudolph."[60]

Within black American sport culture, the individualized iconization of Rudolph began before Rome, suggesting black sport culture realized the potential of her image to express black ability and equality, albeit a certain vision of black ability and equality. Captivated by her seemingly perfect combination of attractiveness and athleticism, the black sporting press, understandably, exalted her as a perfect representation of black American womanhood and, in turn, American womanhood. The individualized image of Rudolph, akin to the public presentation of other attractive black women, "was one act of intervention in a long struggle over the representation of the race in which the image of the black woman was a focal point." "The black woman was in turn represented as the irreproachable symbol of successful assimilation," asserts Maxine Craig.[61] Black America's perspective of Rudolph exemplified the degree to which gender conventionality was understood as essential to black American citizenship. Their interpretations of Rudolph also established the dominant but limited understanding of her and, in turn, the idealized, yet circumscribed, American identity she would embody. However, Rudolph's experiences and performances in Rome again evince the alternative Americanness that, while often overlooked, she lived and represented.

RUDOLPH RISES IN ROME

"If my girl (Rudolph) can sprint among the first three in the Olympic final I'll be happy," Ed Temple, who served as coach of the sprinters and jumpers for the 1960 US Women's Olympic Track and Field team, confidently insisted ahead of the Games.[62] Such expectations did not cause Rudolph to quake. In the Olympic Village, she reportedly felt confident. Similar to the situation in Melbourne, Rudolph and her teammates experienced the Olympics as an empowering environment. Although mainstream America sport culture imagined the 1960 Games as an opportunity to certify the superiority of a democratic society, black American track women found them to be a space that better fulfilled the promises of democracy than the United States. As Rudolph stated, "My first impression of Rome was that it was a storybook city come true; seeing the Coliseum, the catacombs, the Vatican, was like seeing the pictures come to life."[63] Her autobiographical recollections resemble those she shared about Melbourne, reflecting the resonance of, as well as the importance she placed on, simple, satisfying pleasures. "The atmosphere in the village was more fun, too. We could eat anytime we wanted to eat, there was a recreation hall which everybody hung around in, and every night there was dance," Rudolph remembered.[64] Black American track women again led these festivities. According to Rudolph, "Since all the athletes from other countries wanted to learn the latest American dance steps, we were all in popular demand. We gave them the latest steps we learned from 'American Bandstand' on television back home."[65]

This supportive, celebratory atmosphere contributed to Rudolph's readiness for competition. "Myself, I felt loose and free," she asserted. Temple also aimed to reinforce her self-belief. As Rudolph recounted in her autobiography:

One day, Coach Temple sat me down, and we had a very serious talk. He said that he thought my chances were very good for winning three gold medals, and then he told me about this dream he had been having. He said that for two and three nights in a row, he had dreams that I actually did it, won three gold medals and became the first American woman in Olympic history to have done that. I felt good about that, because I knew I was running well.[66]

Regardless of the veracity of Temple's tale, he effectively raised Rudolph's self-esteem. She reported, "My practice runs were great, and the weather in Rome was perfect for me—the temperatures in the 100s, and it felt just like it felt down in Tennessee, where I had been running in hot weather for years. My body was used to the heat, and the hot weather actually helped put me in a good frame of mind."[67] Her attitude offers a perspective of her ambition, a characteristic that, while necessary to her athletic success, would be erased in the image of Americanness that she soon would embody. However, the unlucky whims of sport almost foiled her. When training on a field behind the Olympic Stadium the day before her first race, Rudolph stepped in a hole and turned her ankle. It immediately bruised and ballooned, appearing to jeopardize her readiness to run the next day. Fortunately, after a night of icing and elevation, the worst of the swelling had subsided. According to Rudolph, "When I got up, I put my weight on it and, thank God, it held. I said to myself, 'Thank God, it's only a sprain, I can handle that because I don't have to run any curves today, just the straightaway in the 100.'"[68] This ankle episode again demonstrates the confidence she had cultivated. Rudolph asserted, "I knew I could run, and since I was going to be running the 100, I knew the ankle wouldn't hamper me that badly."[69] The shy and passive sprinter from rural Tennessee believed in her ability to run her best, despite injury. She was living the alternatives that sport had made imaginable.

She maintained her sense of self-confidence as she entered the Olympic Stadium for the 100-meter qualifying heat. Rudolph recalled, "When I got into the tunnel, a strange calm came over me. I was nervous in a sense, yes; but I also got a chance to take a look at the runners I would be going up against, and I felt, deep inside, that I could beat any of them."[70] The enthusiastic Italian fans further increased her self-assurance. As she entered the starting blocks, many of the eighty thousand Olympic observers chanted, "Vilma . . . Vilma."[71] This excitement made both the mainstream and black American press aware of the wider popularity of Rudolph, introducing her propagandistic power as a representative of America and black America. Her performance also augmented her seemingly self-evident appeal. She easily won both her first, second, and third qualifying heats, quickly establishing herself as the gold medal favorite. Her effort in the fourth qualifying heat confirmed her status. She sped down the track in 11 seconds flat, a new world record. But the IOC disallowed it, determining she had the assistance of a breeze over two miles per hour. Denied official recognition of this achievement, Rudolph entered the final with extra motivation. Describing her pre-race experience, Rudolph wrote in her autobiography, "I was not afraid or intimidated in that tunnel. I never talked, but I always looked the others straight in the eye."[72] Rudolph took this focus onto the track, unfazed by the many thousands of fans again cheering, "Villma. . . . Vilma."

Although a notoriously slow starter, she cleared the blocks cleanly when the starting gun sounded, an early indication that she soon would fulfill expectations. As she later recalled, "When I reached the fifty meters, I saw that I had them all, and I was just beginning to turn it on. By seventy meters, I knew the race was mine, nobody was going to catch me."[73] And no one did. She easily bested Britain's Dorothy Hyman and Germany's Jutta Heine by more than 5 yards. She also claimed the world record denied to her the day prior, again covering the distance in 11 seconds flat. Although overjoyed by her victory, and overcome by the number of telegrams from well-wishers that soon flooded her room in the Olympic Village, Rudolph immediately directed her attention to the 200-meter competition. After breezing through the qualifying rounds, she believed no one could beat her, despite the dismal weather that arrived on the day of the final. Rudolph recalled thinking, "The 200 was mine.

FIGURE 9. Wilma Rudolph powers past Germany's Jutta Heine on her way to a gold medal in the 200 meters at the 1960 Rome Olympics.

I loved it more than anything else. A little rain was nothing to me. I was saying to myself as a way of psyching up, 'There's nobody alive who can beat you in the 200. Go get it.'"[74] Untroubled by her ankle or her challengers, Rudolph grabbed the 200-meter gold. Yet, somewhat surprisingly, she was not entirely satisfied. She later shared, "The time was 24 seconds flat, and that was like walking. I was disappointed, because I had been doing a consistent :22.9 in the 200, and 24 flat was embarrassing."[75] Rudolph's attitude again exemplifies the often unrecognized ambition that she discovered and developed because of her athletic abilities and opportunities. She thus set her sights on the 400-meter relay, telling herself, "That's two gold medals down and one to go."[76]

Nonetheless, the US women did not enter the 400-meter relay final favored. Outside of Rudolph, American women had struggled to find success. In the 100 meters, neither Martha Hudson nor Barbara Jones made the final, while in the 200 meters, Lucinda Williams and Ernestine Pollards likewise failed to advance to the final. The understated expectations also reflect the presumed exceptionality of Rudolph; she was the singular US women's athletic star, far superior to her teammates. The Soviet Union, Germany, and Britain thus seemed better prepared to win the team event. According to Rudolph, "The teams everybody was talking about were Russia, West Germany, and Britain. Well, we wiped them all out, and we set a world's record in the process."[77] As the *Chicago Defender* put it, "The Tennessee Tigerbelles—Pee Wee, Skeeter, Beejay, and Lucinda—did proud by Uncle Sam."[78] The foursome of Martha Hudson (Pee Wee), Barbara Jones (Bee Jay), Lucinda Williams, and Rudolph (Skeeter) not only won gold but also broke both the Olympic and world records with their time of 44.4 seconds.[79] The nicknames indicate the solidarity of the American relay squad, a closeness cultivated through their extensive, exacting training. This experience assured Ed Temple. "I told the girls to go out for a record and that's just what they did. With no mistakes," Temple later shared.[80] The team of Tigerbelles navigated the potential precarity of the relay, carefully and conscientiously passing the baton before swiftly covering their segment of the track. Rudolph rather nonchalantly claimed, "It was an easy race for us; everybody ran their best, and we won it going away."[81] The accomplishment also endowed her with a tangible claim on her Americanness, something that, in her words, "nobody could ever take away from me, ever."[82]

When she dismounted the medal rostrum upon receiving her relay gold, an American official presciently told her, "Wilma, life will never be the same for you again."[83] This statement was both true and untrue. Organizations across the United States and world soon would seek to celebrate her, calling on her to provide her presence for particular ideological purposes. Through these public appearances, she introduced a new perception of American women athletes, black American women athletes, and black American women. These developments were not insignificant. However, she primarily would be understood as defining and delimiting an exclusive American identity. Both black and white Americans would impose on her their priorities, together establishing a conservative construction of Rudolph and, by extension, Americanness. All the more, she still would experience barriers of race, gender, and class, ensnarled in the boundaries of American belonging that she appeared to exceed.

5
"OLYMPIAN QUINTESSENCE"

WILMA RUDOLPH, ATHLETIC FEMININITY,
AND AMERICAN ICONICITY, 1960–1962

In the spring of 1961, the London wax museum, Madame Tussauds, debuted a collection of statues that celebrated sports heroes. Included was one of Wilma Rudolph, making her the first, and only, American athlete to achieve this somewhat curious honor.[1] Unintentionally but appropriately, the wax statue encapsulates the dynamics of her developing iconicity; it appeared to be the real Rudolph, but, of course, was unreal. The understandings of her that emerged after her 1960 Roman triumph operated similarly. Rudolph was molded into an idealized exemplar of Americanness by both mainstream and black America. In an early 1960s America still wrestling with the confluence of the Cold War and the civil rights movement, the combination of her racial and gender identities made her symbolically potent, yet, simultaneously, her identities made her a readily accessible and always malleable figure, as biases of race and gender resulted in a discounting of, or even disrespect for, her personal, physical autonomy. Voices in the mainstream and black presses thus shaped their specific Rudolph statutes, disregarding her lived realities or personal preferences in order to use her experiences and image to press and protect their own priorities. The configurations of Rudolph exemplify the constant, complicated intersection of ideologies of race, gender, and sexuality, an amalgam that, like wax, could, and would, be mixed and molded to attempt to make a certain, universal American identity seem real.

Sports Illustrated titled the blurb announcing the reveal of the Rudolph statute "The Frozen Face of Fame."[2] The frozenness of the wax statute also symbolizes the effects Rudolph would have on American belonging. For both black and mainstream America, the celebration of Rudolph codified and consolidated a conservative model of Americanness. The centrality of white-defined gender conventionality to representations of Rudolph guarded against the progress she ostensibly embodied, instead protecting the status quo racial, gender, and sexual structures of US society. Although the acclaim for Rudolph appeared to indicate the inclusiveness of American identity, understandings of her in fact inscribed a disciplinary, exclusive model of Americanness. Rudolph's self-understandings and struggles demonstrate this restrictiveness; she sought to assert her autonomy and Americanness as she experienced the enduring limitations of race, gender, sex, and class during and after her athletic career. Her story thus illuminates the complicated progress achieved by black American women athletes who had passed the baton. In over a decade of international track and field competition, where they challenged the boundaries of American belonging through their excellence, their efforts did not render these boundaries irrelevant. Rather, these boundaries were reconstituted, with representations of black women athletes, especially Wilma Rudolph, critical to this reconstitution by making full Americanness more imaginable, yet still impossible, for those marked by race, gender, sex, or class.

WILMA RUDOLPH'S ALL-AMERICAN ICONICITY

As they watched Wilma Rudolph receive the 200-meter gold medal on the rostrum in Rome, American fans unofficially inaugurated her as national icon. According to the *New York Times*:

> When winning medals are presented at the Olympic Games, the national anthem of the victorious nation is played in abbreviated form. But this was not good enough today for thousands of United States tourists. When Wilma Rudolph of Clarksville, Tenn., received her gold medal for winning the 200-meter dash, the Yanks in the stands sang the anthem—and carried right on without benefit of accompaniment when the band left off with 'rockets' red glare.'[3]

The leading tribunes of American sport culture continued this acclamation. When introducing her to the American public, the *Times* announced, "This queen of the 1960 Olympics is a slender beauty whose eyes carry a perpetual twinkle, as if she were amused, and a little puzzled, at what is going on around her."[4] The paper also insisted that "the Tigerbelle looked more like a homecoming queen than a woman athlete."[5] *Sports Illustrated* likewise declared her "America's lovely, graceful girl sprinter," stating she "proved herself not only a magnificent athlete, but a gracious lady."[6] The magazine further proclaimed, "With her lissome grace and warm smile, Wilma was not only a winner, she was delightfully American as well."[7] The nation thus embraced a black woman athlete as an admirable exemplar of all-American femininity.

Whereas the young black women who competed in track and field in the mid- to late 1950s received a modicum of recognition, Rudolph earned repeated, full-throated endorsements for her femininity, a rather radical proposition. Yet, this radicalism ultimately had conservative implications. Rudolph resembled other black women widely recognized by white America for their beauty, such as Lena Horne, Dorothy Dandridge, and Diahann Carroll. As a "light-skinned black woman with European features," Rudolph, like her Hollywood counterparts, "reinforced the message that beauty was found in light skin, straight long hair, thin lips, and a narrow nose."[8] In their deconstruction of the images and memories of Rudolph, Rita Liberti and Maureen M. Smith analyze how her cultural positioning resembled that of Dandridge, identifying how "classed notions of respectability" were intrinsic to the "allure" of both women.[9] They conclude, "Like Dandridge, Rudolph's appearance fit fairly neatly within the established standards of white hegemonic beauty, and the press's fixation on her beauty continually reinforced these standards."[10] However, as an acclaimed athletic representative of the United States, the image of Rudolph did more than reify respectable white femininity; she also fortified the relationship between respectable white femininity and American identity. As the above quotations from mainstream journalists indicate, Rudolph's conventional beauty confirmed her Americanness. In turn, celebrating Rudolph's womanhood also served as a means to celebrate America's supposed democracy. Fast yet feminine, she was understood as implicit proof of the nation's democratic possibilities, as the equal opportunities offered by US society ostensibly allowed Rudolph to emerge as such an attractive and excellent athlete. She was a powerful, seemingly self-evident symbol of American possibility and progress.

An almost unending array of ever-exaggerated effusions thus emphasized her womanhood. She was a "delightfully graceful, pretty girl."[11] Seeing her at an awards ceremony in New York City, *New York Times* sportswriter Robert Lipsyte took care to note, "Miss Rudolph, 5 feet 11 inches tall, looked chic in a brown-and-white checked cotton suit," further sharing, "She said it was more comfortable than track clothes."[12] When later announcing that the Associated Press had selected her as "Athlete of the Year," the paper published a photo of her posed in a floral skirt, thereby advertising her athletic femininity.[13] All the more, her individual biography combined with her athletic excellence and feminine attractiveness to make her a more potent example of democracy's promises. As *Sports Illustrated* explained:

> Wilma, who has the carriage 'a queen should have,' as an English writer said, is all the more remarkable because she was crippled by a childhood illness and was in bed from the time she was 4 until she was 8. She is one of 19 children, from very poor parents. Her father is an invalid and her mother takes in laundry and does day work to support the family. Wilma was discovered by Tennessee State Coach Ed Temple. She cannot explain her extraordinary ability. 'I just run,' she says. 'I don't know why I run so fast.'[14]

The excessive public attention she earned affirmed her Americanness. As described by the *Times*, "For since her coronation as queen of the spiked-shoe set last summer, loyal subjects and overzealous sycophants have combined to keep her sprinting around her pedestal. Some merely want her autograph or opinion; others her hand in marriage."[15] States, cities, and civic organizations thus showered Rudolph with honors that underscored her admirable, feminine Americanness.[16] The *Ladies Home Journal* expressed the sentiments of many, with an editor writing, "I've seen Wilma Rudolph run like a gazelle, walk like a queen and smile like an angel, and I wonder if she doesn't do as much for equality and freedom as Lumumba, Tshombe and Kasavubu combined."[17] Rudolph, in short, was the "right" kind of black American; her conventional attractiveness, resembling white femininity, made her be understood as worthy of imitation, unlike the assertive independence leaders of Africa who had begun to gain purchase in black America.[18]

Unsurprisingly, officials of US state and sport aimed to take advantage of her appeal. In 1961, the USIA produced a film, *Wilma Rudolph: Olympic Champion*, which emphasized her ability to overcome childhood illness to achieve athletic and academic success. Distributed abroad and shown domestically, the film forthrightly presented her as a figure of American individualism who proved the possibilities available to all, regardless of race or gender, in a democratic society.[19] In April 1961, Vice President Lyndon B. Johnson invited her to the White House, where, upon meeting her, he insisted she also meet President

FIGURE 10. President John F. Kennedy and Wilma Rudolph chat in the Oval Office in the spring of 1961.
John F. Kennedy Presidential Library and Museum, White House Photographs

John F. Kennedy, resulting in a photograph of the new president and Olympic champion.[20] For a young president invested in his inspiring image, yet resistant to truly engaging with the movement for civil rights, inviting Rudolph into the Oval Office provided an opportunity for Kennedy to present himself as committed to racial equality. She allowed him to safely but not substantially signal his support for black Americans. The photograph of the two also defined American identity around the exemplification of racialized gender norms. As Kennedy and Rudolph appeared to demonstrate, earning full Americanness required perfectly embodying the traits valued by white America. Of course, Rudolph herself did not match this standard. Her status as an unwed mother, if made public, would have stained her. Yet, her secret remained silenced, suggesting the degree to which the institutions of American sport and state wanted to believe in a certain version of Rudolph. She symbolized the best of the American Way, seeming to show the nation's progress toward unfettered democracy all while also protecting an American social order that remained undemocratic.

WILMA RUDOLPH'S BLACK AMERICAN ICONICITY

Critically, black America's celebrations and conceptions of Rudolph did not challenge mainstream America's idea and image of her. As noted, the black sporting press had begun to celebrate Rudolph for her femininity in anticipation of the 1960 Olympic Games. After her triple-gold triumph, black America entirely embraced Rudolph, exalting her femininity and envisioning her as an ideal representative of black Americans' fitness for citizenship. The *Afro-American* asserted, "As graceful as a kitten, the fastest woman in the world is a very charming person. She walks with grace and holds her body erect at all times."[21] The paper's society columnist, Lula Garrett, also named Rudolph to her "'60's Top Ten," whom she "selected because of the strictly feminine subtlety with which they initiated moves that have or will have national and international influence."[22] Garrett's counterpart for the *New York Amsterdam News,* Thomasina Norford, similarly noted, "The ultra femininity of Wilma Rudolph, Olympic track star, was a delightful surprise."[23] The black press also emphasized how her femininity inspired her international popularity. The *Chicago Defender* delighted in reporting, "Her long legs, which won her three Olympic medals, couldn't keep her away from a flock of Italian cameramen, the most persistent on earth," while the *Atlanta Daily World* happily shared, "The Italians called her the Black Pearl. She was singled out as the coolest thing in the American camp at Rome."[24]

The extended attention given to Rudolph's rumored relationship with black male track star Ray Norton further illustrates the effort to affirm her femininity.[25] As the *Philadelphia Tribune* quipped, "Wilma Rudolph, winner of three gold medals for dear ole Uncle Sam that is, had denied an Olympic romance with Ray Norton, who twice finished last in the men's sprints. That is credible because Norton obviously didn't have the speed to run around with Wilma."[26] According to the *New York Amsterdam News,* "She's too busy pledging to Delta sorority" to bother with Norton.[27] *Jet* magazine also was eager to share that "Olympic track star Wilma Rudolph has had to answer 'no' to more than 75 marriage proposals."[28] When Rudolph actually would marry, wedding William

Ward, a fellow TSU student, in the fall of 1961, the black sporting and social presses offered much coverage of her wifehood.[29]

Albeit seemingly frivolous, anecdotes that underscored Rudolph's femininity had political purpose. Through Rudolph, black America sought to claim the appearances, activities, and, by extension, privileges of white femininity for young black women. Albeit a conservative point of emphasis, it could have progressive effects. As the movement for civil rights progressed, women occupied increasingly public roles, although the path to such publicity was premised on the performance of appropriate womanhood. Conventional femininity could enhance one's activism, as demonstrated by Diane Nash.[30] Approximately nine months before Rudolph captured three gold medals and countless hearts, Nash, the leader of the Nashville Student Movement, leveraged her beauty, charisma, and light skin to encourage the integration of the lunch counters of the city that she and Rudolph called home. The black press understood and identified her beauty as integral to these efforts, with *Jet* referring to her as "a former Chicago Miss America beauty contestant."[31] This emphasis was not necessarily misguided, as Nash's attractiveness assuaged the racial anxieties of white Nashvillians, including Mayor Ben West.[32]

A similar dynamic developed with Rudolph. As discussed, mainstream America enthusiastically embraced Rudolph, with interest in her serving as seeming proof that she could contribute to the erosion of racial barriers. Soon after returning to the States, she succeeded in doing as much. When her hometown of Clarksville, Tennessee hoped to honor her for her Olympic achievement, Rudolph mandated that the festivities be integrated. Her hometown accepted these conditions since Rudolph presented a rather uncontroversially appealing figure through which the intransigent southern town could claim, however temporarily, its status as a racial democracy.[33] As described by Rudolph in her autobiography:

> As it turned out, this particular parade had a social significance beyond the welcoming of Wilma Rudolph back home. Clarksville, at the time, was still a segregated city, and [the] parade actually was the first event in the history of the town. So was the banquet they gave for me that night; it was the first time in Clarksville's history that blacks and whites had gathered under the same roof at the same event.[34]

The success of the celebration certified Rudolph's importance to black America. She thusly received a seemingly never-ending array of honors from black American organizations. Most prominently, the NAACP named her a guest of honor for their annual Freedom Fund dinner. President Roy Wilkins considered her an apt guest "at a time when young people are playing such a prominent role in Negro America's march on dignity."[35] According to the *New York Amsterdam News*, "A highlight of the dinner was the introduction of Miss Wilma Rudolph," who "received a thunderous applause."[36] An accompanying photograph featured Rudolph in an evening gown, with strings of pearls draped around her neck, conversing with Wilkins and fellow-honoree Lena Horne. Similarly, in an *Ebony* magazine photo essay accounting "Negro Progress in 1960," a photo of Rudolph, sharply dressed in a suit as she sat atop a convertible and waved to an interracial audience of approximately forty thousand Clarksvillians, served as the leading image.[37] As put by Marion E. Jackson in the *Atlanta Daily World*, the achievements of Rudolph and other black Olympians represented "proof positive that our national vigor is firm

FIGURE 11. Coach Ed Temple looks on as well-wishers entreat Wilma Rudolph for her autograph.
Courtesy of Tennessee State University Special Collections and Archives, Brown-Daniel Library

and strong. We are not weaklings and this melting pot land of ours needs to use all of its resources. Were it not for our bronzed ambassadors of goodwill who wear spiked shoes, where would our country be[?]."[38]

However, black America's widespread exaltation of and infatuation with Rudolph presents a conundrum. Rudolph's perceived femininity, or, more precisely, her proximity to white femininity, would mediate most all of the praise for her. While opening some progressive possibilities, the attention to her attractiveness ultimately reinforced an adherence to racialized gender roles as a requirement for Americanness. In short, she underscored that idea that heteronormativity was essential to black American citizenship. This sociocultural circumstance resembles that surrounding black beauty queens who participated in integrated contests in the 1960s. As explained by sociologist Maxine Craig:

> Black contestants challenged the content of the contest but not its form. On the contrary, their demands for inclusion reinforced the legitimacy of beauty contests as institutions that celebrate women. Black beauty queens were always symbols of both defiance and conventionality. When they entered beauty contests, they challenged nothing about the construction of gender except the color of beauty and femininity. These women saw the Miss America title and the contest itself as a symbol and a ritual that could be claimed by black women and used to assert the dignity of the race.[39]

With Rudolph, conventionality trumped defiance. Although she potentially provided black American sport culture an opportunity to advocate more assertively for social change, such would not be the case. In the summer of 1963, Rudolph led a direct-action protest in her hometown of Clarksville. Accompanied by approximately three hundred Clarksvillians, she attempted, unsuccessfully, to integrate a local Shoney's restaurant.[40] Somewhat surprisingly, her effort did not inspire any agitation or receive much attention, suggesting her activism exceeded the role envisioned for her.[41] As the effusive coverage of her indicates, it was believed that Rudolph, like black beauty queens, could affect more change by simply smiling, changing hearts and minds with her charm. The traditionally gendered worldview of black America discouraged any consideration of alternative opportunities she possibly presented. Interpretations of her instead inscribed a restrictive conception of American identity, one that complemented, rather than challenged, mainstream American prerogatives. She was understood as athletic, individualistic, feminine, and, more importantly, American. Except by Rudolph herself.

THE INCOMPATABILITY BETWEEN ICONICITY AND AUTONOMY

Rudolph wrote in her autobiography, "Everybody was making decisions for me; I never had to think about anything else but looking pretty and smiling a lot."[42] Yet, she was not naively "looking pretty and smiling." Not only did Rudolph's lived experiences not match her symbolism, but she also did not endorse her established image. Before she returned from Rome, she told the *New York Amsterdam News*, "It's going to all but kill me to have to go back home and face being denied this, that, and the other because I'm a Black American."[43] She additionally asserted, "In America, they push me around because I'm a Negro, here in Europe, they push me to the front."[44] But the black press did not pay much attention to her more forthright criticisms of the racial realities of the United States, instead allowing her to offer an ostensibly universal image of American opportunity. Rudolph's status as a widely celebrated American heroine also did not protect her from continued violations of her independence and integrity. While her beautiful, black athletic body communicated the possibilities of American citizenship, she had not gained the foundational right of citizenship—full autonomy over her body. Although her proven talent and appealing traits opened new opportunities to her, these opportunities came with exacting expectations.

First, Rudolph's appeal encouraged traditionally men-only track meets to include (or re-include) women's exhibition races, with Rudolph featured as the star talent who presumably would speed past a slate of selected young women opponents. Pincus Sober, chairman of the AAU men's track and field committee, aptly asserted, "The Olympic Games made the name of Wilma Rudolph mean something to people. Suddenly she's a star, with glamour, voted Athlete of the Year in Europe. She'll run at the Millrose Games and at Los Angeles and maybe in a couple of other meets. She's going to create a lot of interest."[45] The black press also excitedly anticipated her appearances. As predicted by Claude Harrison in the *Philadelphia Tribune*, "Wilma, however, will be the star of the 1961 indoor season. Everyone will be out to see the young lady who was responsible for the greatest American women's track showing since 1932."[46]

Rudolph thus was expected to run and smile and run and smile on tracks across the nation. Based on reports, she did not disappoint. In January 1961, more than thirteen thousand fans packed the Los Angeles Memorial Sports Arena to witness Rudolph in action at the second annual Los Angeles Invitational.[47] As announced by *Sports Illustrated*:

Indoor track meets used to run off an occasional race for women just to fill a gap in the program and to lend a note of variety to the succession of events. But the promoters of the second annual Los Angeles Invitational meet last week scheduled a 60-yard dash for women as the feature of the evening and reached a long arm all the way across the country to Tennessee to fetch its prize entrant: the beautiful Olympic medalist, Wilma Rudolph.[48]

Reporting on the action in Los Angeles, the magazine's James Murray noted, "Wilma, who appeared to be having the time of her young life, showed up poised, friendly, innocently flirtatious," but nonetheless "had no trouble disposing of the world record in her event in both the heat and finals."[49] He then rapturously concluded, "It really was wonderful Wilma's night. Indeed, it might be her decade," for "everyone in the massive sports arena, possibly excepting the girls she defeated, was quite in love with Wilma Rudolph."[50] Rudolph then traveled to New York for the nation's top indoor track meets, the New York Athletic Club meet and the Millrose Games.[51] Her appearance at the Millrose Games, the most prestigious of meets, particularly testified to her popularity. As the *New York Times* recognized, "It's strictly a personal tribute to Miss Rudolph that there's a distaff act on the program. Women had been persona non grata to the Millrose management since 1930–31, when Stella Walsh was the world's fastest female."[52] *Sports Illustrated* likewise noted, "The usual host of male stars will be on hand for the winter program, but a happy new note will be added by a woman—Olympic heroine Wilma Rudolph. This is the first time since the early '30s, when the Polish-American Olympic star Stella Walsh ran indoors, that a female has challenged the traditional box-office strength of the men."[53]

These unprecedented racing opportunities, a product of her exceptionality, also perpetuated Rudolph's apparent extraordinariness. According to the *Times*, "The 14,5000 spectators who braved swirling snow also were treated to world record-equaling performances by Wilma Rudolph," who "equaled the women's indoor 60-yard dash record she set at Los Angeles two weeks ago in the semi-final as well as the final."[54] The *New York Amsterdam News* similarly gushed, "Queen Wilma, her graceful stride flowing as smoothly as the waters of the Cumberland River that runs near her alma mater, twice cruised to an effortless 6.9 to equal her own world record and defeat her teammate, Vivian Brown."[55] Rudolph was presented as uniquely fast, fit, and feminine, even though her fellow Tigerbelles also competed in these indoor meets. This perception thereby curtailed the potentially progressive possibilities of these expanded athletic opportunities. Rather than demonstrations of the athletic potential of young women, especially young women of color, these events served as celebrations of Rudolph's athletic femininity, thereby reinforcing the centrality of gender normativity to the ostensibly inclusive American identity that Rudolph advertised. Furthermore, the dominant, highly gendered understanding of Rudolph disregarded her individual autonomy and her physical capacity, as first became evident when she headed south to Louisville, Kentucky, in February 1961 to compete as the featured star at the inaugural Mason-Dixon Games.[56]

Although Rudolph's undefeated indoor record remained unscathed in Louisville, she did not. According to the *New York Times*, "Miss Rudolph bruised her hip when she crashed against a guard wall beyond the finish."[57] In addition to this injury, her indoor running schedule also had begun to wear on her. At the National AAU Indoor Championship in Columbus, Ohio, in March 1961, Rudolph at first seemed her always speedy self. In the 220-yard trials, Rudolph set a new world record, covering the distance in 25 seconds flat.[58] She then won the 100-yard title, also in a record time of 10.8 seconds.[59] However, in the 220-yard final, Rudolph appeared unable to access her speed, falling to teammate Vivian Brown for her first loss since before Rome.[60] More disconcertingly, she collapsed soon after the crossing the finish line.[61] Nonetheless, she still ran the anchor leg for the Tigerbelles' 440-yard relay team, but, still surprisingly, she did not deliver them to victory.[62] Upon her return to Nashville, Rudolph immediately entered the hospital, suffering from a stomach disorder.[63] As reported by the *Atlanta Daily World's* Marion E. Jackson soon thereafter, "Olympic gold medal winner Wilma Rudolph has been advised to take a rest from the banquet and track trail. The triple gold medal winner recently collapsed from exhaustion in Columbus, Ohio."[64] Jackson further described Rudolph's grueling schedule of on and off the track appearances:

> Fame is costly—America's most publicized woman star is attractive Wilma Rudolph, the triple gold medal winner of the XVII Olympiad. Miss Rudolph has been constantly on the go since her triumph in Rome, Italy last year. The Tennessee State star has been on coast-to-coast television and radio, given countless interviews, guested at more banquets than we can count, and performed week after week in the indoor track circuit. During all of these weeks, Miss Rudolph was besieged by magazine writers and reformers who wanted her to tell all. A very gracious young lady, Miss Rudolph tried to accommodate everyone, but the strain was more than even an athlete could endure.[65]

In his autobiography, Ed Temple echoed Jackson's analysis, writing, "When we returned to the States there were parades, award ceremonies, speeches, interviews," but "everyone was exhausted and wanted to go home, see their families, and rest awhile. The strain the girls had been through was just too big for the people here to understand—everyone thought they should be all bubbly and 'Miss Personality Plus.'"[66] Rudolph's exhaustion and hospitalization, however, was about more than the burdens of her fame. Her body seemingly belonged to others. A spectrum of sport and civic organizations sought to access her symbolic capital, desiring that she perfectly perform her combination of athleticism, femininity, and Americanness.

Notably, Rudolph consistently voiced her displeasure with running indoors. As she succinctly stated to *Sports Illustrated*, "I don't like it. Too many people. I don't like it."[67] Madison Square Garden particularly bothered her due to the cigarette smoke that wafted from the stands to the track. "This smoke is just too much. I can hardly breath or keep the tears from clouding my eyes. They shouldn't allow the fans to smoke in here," she told the *Philadelphia Tribune*.[68] Rudolph reiterated her dislike in her autobiography, asserting, "I felt like an Amazon in an arena, performing for the blood-thirsty crowds. Nevertheless, no matter what city I was in, or what arena I was in, people turned out to see me run. So I felt I owed them the very best performance I could possibly give on that particular night—and I delivered it."[69] Rudolph further shared the pressure she felt to always perform. Recalling the headlines that declared, "What's Wrong with Wilma?," when she lost, she explained, "Nothing was wrong. I just got beat that night, fair and square. I didn't run fast enough, and you can't win them all. But people couldn't accept that; they figured that if I won three gold medals at the Olympics, I should be able to win in a little old meet."[70] "That's the kind of pressure I was under," she emphasized.[71] Rudolph's reflections reveal the lack of ownership over her body that she experienced. It was for the pleasure of others, the role long provided by women's bodies, particularly black women's bodies.

During this time, Rudolph also entered a relationship with William Ward, a fellow TSU student. In October 1961, they wed.[72] Somewhat surprisingly, they kept their nuptials a secret for almost two months.[73] Rudolph told *Jet*, "Everyone knew everything about my life. I wanted to keep my marriage a secret so I could have this one thing for myself."[74] Her secrecy speaks volumes; it was an effort to reclaim her autonomy. Her status as mother also remained a secret, even though she did not intentionally seek to keep it as one. To reiterate, the black press was most responsible for making invisible her motherhood. For instance, soon after the revelation of her marriage, *Afro-American* sportswriter Sam Lacy asserted, "The Wards—Wilma and William—have no immediate plans to raise a family. But they have no plans not to raise one, either."[75] The perception of Rudolph as a newlywed with a family as a future prospect, rather than present reality, exemplifies her performative role. Both black and mainstream sport culture intentionally imagined Rudolph as significant of normative Americanness, regardless of evidence to the contrary.

Ultimately, Rudolph did not question her performative, public role. Although not always enthused, she dutifully acceded to these demands. In the spring of 1961, she recovered from her exhaustion and returned to the track, becoming the first woman athlete to run at the Drake Relays in Des Moines, Iowa, the top track meet in the midwestern United States.[76] Through her presence and performance, she again advertised appropriate Americanness. And she continually would be called on to model ideal American identity, especially in the summer of 1961, when she returned to the track wearing the uniform of the United States for the first time since Rome.

THE WONDER OF WILMA RUDOLPH IN THE SUMMER OF '61

In January 1961, the AAU announced, "The home-and-home series of dual track and field meets with the Soviet Union most likely will be renewed this summer with a match at Moscow July 15–16."[77] "The US squad traveling to Moscow will also meet squads representing West Germany and Great Britain and possibly other countries as the AAU intensifies its program of international competition this year," the organization further clarified.[78] Inspiring the most interest ahead and during this international jaunt was, unsurprisingly, Wilma Rudolph. After continuing to struggle with nagging injuries throughout the spring of 1961, Rudolph entered the National AAU Outdoor Championship, which served as qualifying for the aforementioned AAU international track tour, not in top form. Nonetheless, more than eight thousand packed Gilroy Stadium in Gary, Indiana, eager to watch her run. Participating only in the 100-meter competition, Rudolph won with relative ease, tying the AAU record in the process.[79] Despite her tiresome schedule, she expressed excitement about the opportunity to compete abroad, especially in Moscow. As she told the *Philadelphia Tribune*'s Claude Harrison, "I've never been to Russia and I'm looking forward to it."[80] She also asserted, "I'm sure I'll be in top shape in about a week."[81] Her comments likely pleased officials in the AAU and mainstream American sport culture for, in their estimation, only Rudolph's condition mattered when it came to the US women's squad.

Of the American women, *Sports Illustrated* suggested, "None of them can stay within an impala's side of Wilma Rudolph."[82] Such a statement recalls past assertions about women's track, when the AAU, USOC, and leading voices in the mainstream American sport community preemptively predicted the inadequacy of women athletes. While Rudolph was world class, her teammates also were worthy of respect. The 1961 women's track and field squad included not only Olympic veteran Willye White but also members of the rising generation of Tigerbelles in Vivian Brown and Edith McGuire, as well as emerging talents in Chicagoan Lacey O'Neal and Billie Pat Daniels, a white, teenaged middle-distance runner from California.[83] However, by not seriously considering the abilities of other American track women, US sport culture exaggerated Rudolph's exceptionality. This cultural positioning resembled that of black American women who found fame in the movie and music industries in the 1960s. Of such women, historian Ruth Feldstein notes that critics and commentators saw them "in isolation," even as she documents the talented cadre of black women whose performances had collective political power. Feldstein explicates, "When critics praised any one artist as unique, they elided the important similarities among black women entertainers and their strategies for performing black womanhood."[84] In the world of international sport, isolating and individualizing Rudolph made her more propagandistically potent. She spoke to the ideology of American individualism, albeit in a way that did not disrupt the status quo of American society. Rudolph was imagined as advertising the opportunities available to all, but at the same time, because she was seen as such an exception, she did not appear to presage the wider potential of women, especially black women. The celebration of Rudolph's singularity thus did not threaten the nation's prevailing racial or gender orders. She could offer an ostensibly democratic, but exclusively defined, example of national belonging.

Rudolph's on-track efforts did nothing to counteract this understanding. The women's 100-meter sprint served as the opening event of the third US-Soviet Union dual meet. Rudolph began things with a bang. In front of the more than seventy thousand spectators in Lenin Stadium, Rudolph blazed down the track in 11.3 seconds. According to the *New York Times*, "Miss Rudolph

was clearly in command of the women's 100 meters after the first thirty meters. She sped home a comfortable winner."[85] *Sports Illustrated* thus deemed
her "wondrous Wilma Rudolph."[86] Yet, the self-assured Rudolph reacted nonchalantly to her record-tying effort, telling reporters, "I was very surprised to
equal the record because I haven't been running that hard and haven't been
too well—but I'm very pleased."[87] Her performance in the 400-meter relay
likely further pleased her. It also provided more proof of her exceptionality. As
discussed in the introduction, she showed incredible speed in order to atone
for a bumbled baton exchange. *Sports Illustrated* narrated the scene:

> Wilma fumbled the hand-off slowed and looked around. By the time she began
> to chase the Russian anchor girl, Tatiana [*sic*] Shchelkanova, she was fully five
> yards behind. At first it appeared that this was too far even for Wilma. She closed
> very slowly for the first 30, 40, 50 yards. But then something happened. Wilma
> went zoom. She passed Shchelkanova as if the Russian were nailed to the track
> and won by three yards. The time was 44.4, breaking the old record of 44.5.[88]

Even the Soviets seemed swayed by her speed. According to the magazine,
Rudolph "captur[ed] the hearts of Muscovites as she had captured the hearts
of Romans."[89] These sentiments indicate that Rudolph served as the ideal
athletic ambassador in this era of the sporting Cold War. More than defeating
communism on the athletic field, officials of US sport and state desired to use
the dual to foster friendship and understanding, enticing their Soviet rivals
through democracy's appeal. Rudolph achieved this aim. As *Sports Illustrated*
further claimed, "no one was too concerned over the final score," only with
Wilma Rudolph.[90] Rudolph again was unfazed by her own excellence, simply
stating, "I guess that last leg was as fast as I ever ran."[91] Her comments reflect
her self-confidence; she expected to triumph. However, to outside observers, her quiet confidence was read as a charming sense of calm and class, an
unthreatening example of women's athletic excellence, as well as feminine
American womanhood.

After the dual in Moscow, the US squad headed to Stuttgart for a match with
West Germany, where Rudolph consolidated both her athletic and symbolic
value. The meet program did not include a 100-meter dash for women in its
official roster of events, but in order to satisfy the West German sports fans
intent upon seeing Rudolph run, officials added it as an exhibition. The informal race overshadowed the official competition. Moreover, Rudolph did not
simply run to appease adoring fans; she ran to set a new world record, blazing

down the track in 11.2 seconds. According to the *New York Times*, "Willowy Wilma" won over the crowd, as they "cheered her lustily for many minutes," after her scintillating sprint.[92] The scheduling of a special race for Rudolph, in combination with her display of record-breaking speed, appeared to affirm her unmatched, extraordinary ability. However, teammate Willye White demonstrated that Rudolph was not the only world-beating black American woman athlete. White not only established a new American long jump record, but just as impressively, she also showed elite speed in the 100 meters, running shoulder-to-shoulder with Rudolph.[93] Rudolph actually gave White credit for helping her secure the world record. She later told reporters, "Willie [*sic*] and I had been kidding one another all day about which one of us would win the race, as we do. We decided that we might as well go after a record. So Willie [*sic*] pushed me as hard as she could, or I might not have done so well."[94]

But White received little in recognition from international audiences or the mainstream American press. A combination of political priorities and cultural preferences explain her invisibility. First, White overtly lived out the entitlement inculcated in her by Mae Faggs. Recall, before finding success in sport, she was ashamed of her identity, as her light skin, green eyes, and short red hair had made her feel like an outsider in the black community of rural Mississippi. Athletics endowed White with evident self-assurance. She now exuded confidence, increasingly embracing her black female autonomy and rejecting the "politics of respectability." For instance, at the 1960 Rome Olympics, White sought to cultivate interracial solidarity among the women's track team. In particular, she mentored Billie Pat Daniels, a white teenage 800-meter runner. Years later, White would note, "I saw myself in this big, oxey white girl who never wore makeup. Wild. Vulnerable. A need to be embraced."[95] But this relationship would make Daniels's parents, as well as US Olympic officials, uncomfortable, resulting in White's expulsion from the Olympic team. White, in short, did not reflexively perform heteronormativity, willingly disregarding the submission expected of women athletes, especially black women athletes. She herself admitted, "I was headstrong. They needed to break me."[96]

But White would not bend or break; she instead was committed to self-defining her sporting experience. Soon after the 1960 Olympic Games, she would leave TSU, refusing to remain bound by Ed Temple's paternalism. "Coach Temple wanted to control every aspect of your life, training, classes, who you dated, and I was too much of a free spirit for that," White later recollected.[97] She would chart her own athletic course, relocating to Chicago to compete for the Mayor Daley Youth Foundation track team. All the more, White, in contrast to Rudolph, did not project conventional femininity. She not only embraced her self-described "funky" red hair but also experimented with different colors. She also expressed an electic sense of style, donning kerchiefs or other flashy accoutrements.[98] Rather than attempting to imitate white femininity, White made visible her brand of alternative, black womanhood.

Secondly, regardless of the degree to which White did or did not obey expectations, her success belied the preferred narrative of Rudolph's iconicity. Such emotive interest could be invested in Rudolph because she was understood as unique, an unthreatening representative of the belief that US democracy provided equal opportunity for black Americans determined enough to apply their abilities. By "overcoming" poverty and polio to become an excellent and attractive athlete, Rudolph advertised an equality that was highly individualized. This idea of Rudolph also complemented the increasingly prominent belief that America's racial problems would be rectified at the personal, rather than governmental or societal, level. Equality best could be achieved through the perseverance of individual black Americans and the perspicacity of individual white Americans.[99] Willye White, along with the other black women athletes who competed across Europe in the summer of 1961, thus complicated Rudolph's propagandistic power. White instead showed the solidarity that had long spurred the success of black American women athletes, as well as black Americans more broadly.

Through the remainder of the tour, Rudolph remained the star. She thrilled the more than seventy thousand fans in Warsaw, where she again won the 100 meters and anchored the United States to a 400-meter relay win over Poland.[100] At the US team's final meet in London, Rudolph did not race the 100 meters, receiving a well-deserved break to rest the hamstring she pulled during her world record run in Stuttgart.[101] In order not to disappoint the more than twenty-one thousand fans in White City Stadium, she did run the anchor leg in the 400-meter relay. However, because her teammates had established an irrevocable lead, Rudolph did not have to race at her top speed, claiming an eight-yard victory with almost lackadaisical ease.[102] The off-track travel schedule likely contributed to Rudolph's injury, as the US track team's furious trek through Europe featured four meets in eight days. *Sports Illustrated* captured the travails experienced by the American athletes:

> They ate unfamiliar food and slept too little in too many different beds. They spent interminable hours in airports or coiled like pretzels on buses, where their

long legs did not fit. They walked too many miles down the streets of strange towns. Their laundry remained dirty, their stomachs stayed queasy and their wants went unanswered in three foreign languages.[103]

The magazine's Roy Terrell, somewhat cheekily, posited, "Whether, finally, the tour's achievements were worth the effort only the athletes themselves can answer," before insisting that "theirs was a performance to be proud of."[104] His question would not seriously be considered. In contrast, the AAU successfully presented international tours as a preeminent honor. In an October 1961 *Amateur Athlete* editorial, AAU secretary-treasurer Daniel Ferris announced:

> There's no doubt in my mind that an expanded international athletic exchange program would be the greatest stimulant we could have for amateur athletics. The obvious advantages secured from such a program would be the opportunity to give our athletes competition over a longer season, as well as an opportunity to meet in competition the outstanding athletes in other countries.[105]

However, Terrell's comments allude to the significant burden that US sport imposed on its athletes. Their bodies provided the symbolic material for imagining ideal American citizenship. And in an early 1960s where the intersecting concerns of the Cold War and civil rights movement proved ever pressing, a beautiful black woman athlete offered the most powerful material. Bearing the double burden of blackness and femaleness, Wilma Rudolph most evocatively and effectively demonstrated the imagined inclusivity of American democracy. It thus should not be surprising that the AAU and then the US government would request that Rudolph once again symbolically serve her nation. First, in the summer of 1962, Rudolph headlined a subsequent track and field tour to Sweden. She displayed her combination of athleticism and attractiveness, delighting Swedish track enthusiasts in Gothenburg, Hässleholm, Malmö, and Oslo in what popularly was referred to as the "Wilma Rudolph Tour."[106] According to Jo Ann Terry, a fellow Tigerbelle who joined Rudolph in her tour of Sweden, "They just loved her. They had posters up with a big picture of Wilma." Rudolph told the *Afro-American*, "We played to full houses everywhere and I never got so many flowers in all my life."[107] Soon thereafter, the State Department tapped her as an American Sport Specialist, sending her to French West Africa in the spring of 1963.[108]

For the State Department, Rudolph, with her alluring combination of athletic ability and physical attractiveness, was imagined as the perfect candidate to assuage any lingering questions about the content and extent of American democracy, thereby swaying newly autonomous African nations to the American side of the Cold War.[109] Her racial identity encouraged the belief that she would serve as embodied proof against Soviet propaganda that, justifiably, criticized the endurance of American racism when making appeals to the majority black African populace. As Rudolph's trip coincided with Martin Luther King Jr's arrest and imprisonment in Birmingham, as well as the release of his "Letter from Birmingham Jail," she served as a salve for America's inadequacies and hypocrisies, offering an appealing, absolving image.[110] In the eyes of US officials, she fulfilled these expectations during her twenty-seven days abroad.[111] On her return to the States, one such State Department official enthused that she was "a walking flag of the United States of America," an indication of the degree to which she was understood to express the nation's ideals.[112]

Yet, whether serving the nation athletically or diplomatically, Rudolph was so applauded as an icon of American identity because she ultimately shored up the racial, gender, and sexual orders that long had structured US society. Her normative femininity communicated that conforming to racialized gender roles was essential to Americanness. Thus, even as she appeared to show that full and unfettered American citizenship was possible for all Americans, the centrality of racialized gender roles to her image ensured that the Americanness of black Americans always would remain insufficient. Rudolph's image effectively managed the boundaries of American belonging for audiences abroad, as well as at home. Beginning when she returned stateside after the 1961 summer tour, an idealized Rudolph would be used by both mainstream and black America to reconcile and resolve questions and concerns about the definition of Americanness.

WILMA RUDOLPH WINS THE SULLIVAN AWARD

At the close of 1961, the AAU selected Wilma Rudolph as winner of the James E. Sullivan Award, honoring her as the nation's best amateur athlete. Named after one of the founders of the AAU, the Sullivan Award long had served to mark the boundaries of ideal American athleticism, celebrating the amateur athlete "whose ability and character combined have had the greatest influence during the year in advancing the standards of sportsmanship."[113] The history of the award further suggests that it conferred and communicated the imagined boundaries of Americanness.

Until 1954, the AAU members who composed the Sullivan Award tribunal never had deemed a black American athlete in possession of the capacities purportedly required to win the award. That year, Mal Whitfield, the middle-distance runner who had won 800-meter gold at the 1948 and 1952 Olympic Games while also serving in the Air Force during World War II and the Korean War, broke the award's racial barrier. The following year, Harrison Dillard, a gold medalist in the 100-meter sprint in London and 110-meter high hurdles in Helsinki who also had served in World War II, received the honor.[114] Their military backgrounds certified their Americanness, making them worthy of the award. National service and sacrifice, militarily and athletically, appeared necessary for a black American athlete's eligibility for the nation's most vaunted athletic award. In 1960, decathlon gold medalist Rafer Johnson became the third black American voted winner of the award.[115] Johnson also exuded uncontroversial Americanness. Because of his positive experiences in his majority white hometown in inland California and his time at the University of California–Los Angles (UCLA), where he was class president, Johnson possessed an optimistic perspective of American race relations.[116] At the 1960 Olympic Games, Johnson served as the US flag bearer in the opening ceremony parade before demonstrating competitive camaraderie as he defeated Chinese Taipei's CK Yang in a decathlon battle.[117] The combination of his athleticism, achievements, and attitude allowed him to meet the symbolic needs of an early 1960s United States.

Rudolph, who had finished second in 1960, similarly presented an amenable image of American identity, seeming to satisfy the Cold War–civil rights era demands of democracy and equality. AAU President Louis J. Fisher proclaimed that Rudolph "has been one of the greatest ambassadors the United States has ever sent abroad."[118] She advertised an ostensibly inclusive image of America, appearing to have transcended inequities of race, as well as gender, as she was only the third woman winner. At the Sullivan Award luncheon at the New York Athletic Club in early 1962, Rudolph appeared in her feminine finest, outfitted in a fashionable pale pink suit that was accompanied by a chic, white fuzzy hat and elegant costume jewelry. Upon accepting the award, she reservedly remarked, "I'm very proud of this award."[119] In short, she dutifully performed her expected role. However, when *Afro-American* sportswriter Sam Lacy asked for her reaction to winning the award, she shared a more ambitious attitude, stating, "I can't say that I was surprised nor can I say whether I'd have been disappointed." She then clarified, "Actually, I was rather disappointed last year when I didn't win it," insisting, "I thought I had an excellent chance."[120] Yet, this version of an almost cocky Rudolph remained obscured. In the same article in which he included these assertions, Lacy described her as the embodiment of conventional femininity, suggesting that he "views the 21-year-old Tennessee State senior as a soft-spoken young super athlete with a world of poise."[121] He additionally mused, "So thoroughly covered by her sense of humility, the ego that is a prerequisite to greatness in any form of athletic competition, never shows on the surface of Wilma Rudolph."[122] He seemingly chose to ignore Rudolph's words, instead interpreting her in ways that conformed to established cultural narratives. However, as she clearly expressed in her conversation with Lacy, Rudolph did possess an ego. Her success was a product of the self-belief that served as the core of her competitive drive, something she developed and deepened during her athletic career. But this understanding of her did not align with the priorities of mainstream nor black America.

THE WEIGHT OF WILMA RUDOLPH IN BLACK AMERICA

Black America, in particular, attached great importance to the Rudolph ideal. Upon her Sullivan Award win, the black sport press piled on the plaudits, again underscoring her femininity. For instance, the *Afro-American*'s Lula Garrett attempted to account for Rudolph's unique, uncanny appeal, asserting:

> She's pretty, to begin with, with a pert face, sparkling black eyes and a bow of a mouth on which she wears very pale pink lipstick. Her nail polish is pale too and she stands 5 ft. 11 inches tall, and is proud of it. Wears the highest heels to reach still farther skywards. Her voice is soft, actually childish . . . but she has an effective naive manner of saying cute things that win friends and influence people.[123]

Rudolph appeared perfectly to prove that black Americans could not only meet but also exceed expectations of conventional Americanness. As such, any possible evidence of slippage in Rudolph's status, either on the track and off, provoked anxiety. In early 1962, such consternation began to percolate. At the third annual Los Angeles Invitational, Jean Holmes, a West Indian Panamanian freshman at TSU, bested her veteran teammate in the 60-yard dash, shocking the sold-out crowd at the Los Angeles Memorial Sports Arena.[124] However, it was not simply her loss that troubled black sport culture. As put by a *Philadelphia Tribune* headline, she was "Overweight Wilma."[125] "It's hard to believe, but Wilma Rudolph Ward says she's overweight," the *Tribune* reported.[126] *Jet* magazine echoed this assessment, describing her as "overweight and haggard," noting that her condition was due to the "personal appearances that broke into her training routine."[127] The *Chicago Defender* likewise reported, "Obviously suffering from a severe cold, and considerably overweight, Wilma, the recently married Sullivan Award Winner, was slow off the blocks and although she gained on the leader in the late 20 yards she lost by nearly a yard."[128]

Rudolph herself admitted to her poor condition, although she seemed rather unconcerned about her state. "I've been traveling a lot, and I'm not in shape. I haven't been practicing regularly and my legs are sore from the conditioning," she straightforwardly told the *Philadelphia Tribune*.[129] In fact, she predicted that she would face "her toughest competition from Jean Homes."[130] She told the *Afro-American*, "It might well be that I'd have to do 6.9 seconds in order to beat her at 60 (yards) in her present condition. And I don't think I'm that good yet."[131] But her self-aware assessment seemingly was ignored. Instead, *Jet* magazine asked, "What's Wrong with Wilma?," with the question itself suggesting that black America had the right to know about any of her perceived problems.[132] As emphasized, within the black community, young black women were understood as "symbolic material," expected to, in the words of sociologist Maxine Craig, "behave and appear well-groomed" as an "obligation to the race."[133] With her weight gain, Rudolph, previously seen as an irreproachable representative of black Americans' fitness for citizenship, seemed not longer to be fulfilling her obligations. The black press thus did not hesitate indiscriminatingly to access her body, unquestioningly considering her physical being as property of the broader black community. The intense attention to Rudolph's condition exposes the paternalism that continued to permeate black sport culture.

After devoting much coverage to her weight gain, the black sporting press then reported on her recovery from a subsequent appendectomy, even publishing photos of her laid up in the hospital bed.[134] The obsessive coverage of her divorce from William Ward, whom she accused of "cruel and inhuman treatment," further demonstrates the degree to which Rudolph's trials and travails were made available for public consumption.[135] By publicizing her physical and personal intimacies, black sport culture chose not to respect Rudolph's autonomy, thereby reflecting how black sport culture's attitudes about and approach to Rudolph relied on and reinforced the gendered social order of American society.[136] Black America's estimations of Rudolph thus aligned with those of mainstream America; she always was expected to advertise an appealingly democratic, albeit actually delimited, American identity. At the 1962 US–Soviet Union dual in Palo Alto, California, Rudolph would confirm this conservative version of Americanness as she culminated her international athletic career.

RED, WHITE, AND RUDOLPH

Officials of US sport and state invested much significance in the fourth edition of the US–Soviet Union dual meet, viewing it as an opportunity to foster friendship among the rivals' athletes.[137] As made evident by the extensive coverage in the *New York Times*, the AAU and its associates prioritized providing a pleasurable time for the Soviet athletes, an effort to counteract Cold War tensions.[138] However, more important than the experiences of the Soviet athletes was the meaning communicated by the athletes, especially the American athletes. For the event coincided with not only the heights of the Cold War but also the civil rights movement. Although held across the country from the southern locus of direct-action protests, the event occurred in a US sociopolitical environment where the boundaries of American belonging remained contested. As such, black American athletes, especially Wilma Rudolph, possessed propagandistic import.

More than 150,000 packed Stanford Stadium over the two-day affair, witnessing, among other displays of athletic excellence, the believed wonder of Rudolph. The acclaim she earned further encouraged an uncontested and uncontroversial understanding of Americanness. In the 100-meter race, she overcame one of her notoriously slow starts to speed past the Soviet Union's Mariya Itkina and secure the victory. As described by the *Times*'s leading track analyst Joseph Sheehan, she "put on an explosive burst of speed to capture the 100-meter dash by eight feet."[139] As discussed in the introduction, she offered an even more impressive display of come-from-behind heroics in the 400-meter relay, anchoring the Americans to a victory that led *Sports Illustrated* later to proclaim, "But in action or repose, red or red-white-and-blue, black or white, male or female, no one in Palo Alto could match the incomparable Wilma Rudolph Ward for effortless grace and poise."[140] Rudolph thus presented an image of American citizenship that satisfied both mainstream and black America. Yet women's athleticism, especially black women's athleticism, was a radical act, refuting American norms of race and gender. However, in the early 1960s, Rudolph represented the rightness, rather than the radicalness, of the American Way. Her racial and gender identities, in combination with her experiences of struggle and success, seemed to resolve the contradictory demands of the Cold War and civil rights movement.

Notably, Rudolph also appreciated the power of her Palo Alto performance. Although it was not her final competitive effort, she chose to narrate it as such in her autobiography, writing:

> I went out to Palo Alto and read all about the Russian runners in the newspapers. They were this, they were that. Fine. Comes the 100, and I win it easily. I was very satisfied with myself after that race. Coach Temple also had me entered in the relay, and in this event the Russian girls were very good. They were better relay runners, for some reason, than they were sprinters. Anyway, I've got the anchor leg, and I get the baton. This Russian girl is about forty yards ahead of me. I give chase, I start picking up speed, and I start closing on her. She's looking at me out of the corner of her eye, and the look is like, "What is this, I can't believe she's closing so fast." Well, I caught her, passed her, and won the race. That was it. I knew it. The crowd in the stadium was on its feet, giving me a standing ovation, and I knew what time it was. Time to retire, with a sweet taste.[141]

Her editorial selection is significant. Throughout much of her autobiography, Rudolph resisted the overly optimistic interpretations of her story. She shared her struggles of single motherhood and discussed the difficulties she encountered trying to establish a career after her retirement from competitive athletics. She named the array of jobs she shuffled through, from an elementary school teacher in Tennessee and Detroit to a Jobs Corps instructor in Maine and St. Louis to an organizer at the Watts Community Action Committee in Los Angles to an administrative assistant at UCLA to a leader in Mayor Daley's Youth Foundation in Chicago. Reflecting on her continual career dissatisfactions, she wrote, "But I started getting the same old feedback—she was good in track, okay. Now, what else can she do? It was as if they were holding my track success against me."[142] Her working experiences consistently made her feel "used and betrayed." She frustratingly concluded that "people were always expecting me to be a star, but I wasn't making the money to live like one. I felt exploited both as a woman and as a black person, and this bothered me very much."[143] Rudolph's narrative made it clear that she acutely understood the ways in which her racial and gender identities, while making her an inspiring icon of American democracy, conspired to cause her continually to experience the nation's discriminations. At the end of her autobiography, she unhesitatingly asserted, "The fact of the matter is that black women athletes are on the bottom rung of the ladder in American sports."[144] However, the way she chose to tell the close of her competitive athletic career indicates that, for all the ways she intimately experienced the shortcomings of her symbolism, she understood her career as an assertion of her Americanness. She exercised editorial control to claim her autonomy.

Yet, despite more than a decade of black American women track stars passing the baton and, in turn, putting pressure on the raced and gendered boundaries of American identity, the alternative Americanness actually embodied by Rudolph and other black American track women would remain unexplored. Even as the athletic excellence of black women track stars, most especially that of Rudolph, raised questions about the content and extent of Americanness, these questions would be answered in rather conservative ways. Like the wax used to make and mold the statue of Rudolph displayed in Madame Tussauds, mainstream and black American sport cultures made and molded, and remade and remolded, the meanings of black women athletes, interpreting their efforts in ways that enforced, rather than eroded, the boundaries of American belonging.

CONCLUSION
THE PRECARITY OF THE BATON PASS
RACE, GENDER, AND THE ENDURING BARRIERS
TO AMERICAN BELONGING

At the 1961 National AAU Indoor Championship, Helen Shipley, a white seventeen-year-old from Newton, Massachusetts, ran the fastest half-mile in US women's history, bettering the existing AAU mark by fifteen seconds. Of all women's track events, the half-mile race had long provoked the most anxiety. Since the collapse of competitors at the end of the 800-meter race at the 1928 Olympic Games, the distance was considered too long for women, a too-demanding tax of their physical capacities.[1] This intransigence did not begin to fade until the late 1950s. In 1958, the AAU again started holding 880-meter and 880-yard races, as the International Amateur Athletic Federation had begun to petition the IOC to add the distance to the women's Olympic program.[2] Considering this history of hesitancy, it was remarkable that the teenage Shipley's win inspired such excitement.

The *New York Times* declared, "A 17-year-old Massachusetts girl, running the first race of her career, stole the attention today at the Amateur Athletic Union women's indoor track and field championships."[3] Described as "the 120-pound, 5-foot-5-inch freckled miss" and "a brunette with hazel eyes," the paper praised her performance, noting, "She roared out front by fifteen yards on the first lap and stayed there. When the challengers spurted on the final round she moved right out, too. She won by at least ten yards."[4] *Amateur Athlete* likewise expressed enthusiasm for the success of Shipley, taking delight in the fact that she explained her performance by insisting that she "just loved to run."[5]

All the more remarkably, Shipley outshone Wilma Rudolph. It was at this 1961 title meet that Rudolph struggled, suffering from illness and exhaustion. These circumstances led voices in the AAU to propose, "Miss Rudolph's defeats and Miss Shipley's success could properly be taken as signs of the increasing competition in women's track and field in the United States." Even though Rudolph still set a 220-yard record at the meet, *Amateur Athlete* suggested the event might evince "the rise and fall of Wilma Rudolph."[6] The interpretations of the unexpected emergence of Shipley and the uneven efforts of Rudolph not only expose the AAU's still simmering desire for a "whiter" women's track and field, but also introduce how Rudolph actually made a whiter women's track and field more possible. While praised and promoted, Rudolph also was imagined as making possible a new era of women's track, one presumably dominated by white women and supported by black women. *Amateur Athlete's* summation reveals as much, as the official magazine of the AAU posited, "While Helen Shipley is indeed a unique story, there must be literally thousands of other girls like her around the United States—girls who 'just love to run' and trudge lonely miles because of it. Maybe somebody will 'discover' these other women track and field stars before the next Olympiad."[7]

As documented, the world of American women's track and field, always controlled by white men and women, had prioritized fostering the abilities and achievements of young white women. From Evelyne Hall to Frances Kaszubski to Roxy Andersen, the white women leaders of the AAU and USOC had sought to cultivate a women's track cohort that resembled younger versions of themselves. Along the way, they willingly accommodated black women athletes, realizing their successes could bolster the sport. Wilma Rudolph appeared to validate and culminate their strategy. Although a black woman, Rudolph's brand of feminine athletic excellence provided permission for white women not only to participate in the sport but also to begin to be praised for doing so. Just like young Helen Shipley. US women's track culture embraced the opportunity introduced by Rudolph and her image. In the years immediately following Rudolph's 1960 Roman triumph, US women's track and field expanded its institutional capacity, an effort that implicitly aimed also to adjust the identity of the sport and its athletes. Although the ultimate outcomes were uneven, the post-Rome moment represented a period of vigorous action within the sport that indicates the influence of Rudolph.

The AAU began to more aggressively and enthusiastically advertise an array of women's track programs. *Amateur Athlete* announced meets and profiled programs from across the nation, all of which featured primarily white athletes.[8] Soon after Shipley inspired excitement, women's track culture directed attention to Billie Pat Daniels, the former mentee of Willye White who now was a student at Brigham Young University and competed for the San Mateo Girls' Athletic Association. Daniels won the 1961 National AAU Women's Pentathlon Championship, leading the AAU to declare her "New Queen of the Pentathlon."[9] Even more than the half-mile, the five-event pentathlon requires significant exertion, resulting in it also having "unfeminine" connotations. The enthusiasm about Daniels's international potential further suggests a social shift, with American sport culture providing aspiring white women athletes a greater amount of space to attain athletic success in a broader range of track and field activities.[10] As additional evidence, Janell Smith, a fifteen-year-old sprinter from Fredonia, Kansas, reportedly stole the show at the 1962 National AAU Championship, receiving much interest for finishing second to Edith McGuire, a rising sprint star at TSU. Described as a "cheerleader" who "not only plays the snare drum but is secretary of the school band," the blonde Smith ostensibly embodied the ideal American track woman.[11] Soon thereafter, members of the USOC and AAU, in coordination with the American Association for Health, Physical Education, and Recreation, formed a Women's Advisory Board to the USOC, which subsequently planned National Institutes on Girls' Sports in order to "increase the depth of experiences and to expand opportunities for girls and women in sport."[12] Or, to find more Smiths, Daniels, and Shipleys.

Even as black women athletes, especially Wilma Rudolph, had provided US sport and society with propagandistic value by offering an ostensibly equitable image of American identity, Smith and other young white women still remained the ideal. That the AAU always had chosen to understand Rudolph through a color-blind, gendered lens further indicates the ways in which her potential influence was envisioned. For instance, in announcing her 1961 Sullivan Award win, the AAU described her as "only the third woman to win the coveted award," failing also to mention she represented only the fourth black American to win.[13] Within the world of women's sport, racial identity was imagined as irrelevant. Of course, it was not. The ability of Rudolph and other young black women athletes to represent American identity was dependent on the racialization of the sport of women's track and field. Because the sport widely was understood as "black," their visibility as icons of Americanness maintained the racialized gender difference that organized US society. Rudolph, with her seemingly self-evident femininity, somewhat troubled this racialized boundary. While her feminine identity made her a more powerful, popular icon, it also introduced the potential of feminine black women to destabilize the racialized gender hierarchy that prevailed in the United States. Creating cultural space for attractive, young white women to achieve athletically counteracted this subtle threat. All the more, in a mid-1960s American society increasingly preoccupied with social and political ruptures, white American women athletes offered reassurance.

So, rather ironically, the efforts of black women athletes bent the boundaries of American belonging in ways that ultimately opened up more opportunities for white women. A decade of dedicated baton passing by black American women allowed white American women to grab the stick, situating themselves as exemplars of ideal American identity. A *Sports Illustrated* article about the 1964 USA-USSR track and field dual and subsequent 1964 US Women's Olympic Track and Field Trials titled "At Last the Girls Are Ours" encapsulates these shifting dynamics. The article opens with Ed Temple exclaiming, "I've heard those television people before. It was always 'the girls.' But when they started beating the Russians in Los Angeles, you know what that announcer called them? He called them 'our girls.'"[14] Temple was celebrating what the iconicity of Wilma Rudolph seemed to have certified—black American track women were, finally and fully, American. However, an examination of the remainder of the article suggests that the title actually references the arrival and acceptance of talented white American track women. For example, the aforementioned Janell Smith was hyped as "a saucy little 17-year old blonde" who "gives every indication that the U.S. is about to win some medals in the longer races," while RaNae Bair, a javelin thrower described as "a tall, slender, sandy blonde from San Diego," reportedly encouraged an Olympic Trials official to muse, "That, sir, is pure beauty." The article concluded by confirming, "That, sir, is one of our girls."[15]

The leading example of "our girls" was Flamin' Mamie's Bouffant Belles of the Texas Track Club, a team of primarily blonde and buxom "southern belles" from Abilene, Texas. As described by *Sports Illustrated*'s Gilbert Rogin in the spring of 1964, "The Texas Track Club is celebrated on two counts—its athletic achievements and the uncommon beauty of its girls, who compete in dazzling uniforms, elaborate makeup and majestic hairdos."[16] Margaret Ellison, coach of the Bouffant Belles, was not shy about her intention, declaring, "I'm trying to change the stereotyped image of the track girl."[17] Rogin appeared to judge her effort a success, arguing that "the Texas Track Club has done more to promote women's track in the US than if its members had, say, won the national AAU championships."[18] *Sports Illustrated* editor Sidney L. James echoed this estimation, suggesting that the magazine made the trio of sprinting southern belles—Janis Rinehart, Paula Walter, and Jeanne Ellison—the first women track athletes to appear on the cover of the magazine "because the Texans' mixture of grace and drive deserves to be known to a few more million people."[19]

Many readers agreed. A fellow Texan named Eddie Smith insisted, "Let the Russian amazons have the Olympics. Dames like 'Flamin' Mamie's Bouffant Belles' can just stand in the starting blocks and they'll get my vote for first every time. Wow!"[20] From Brookline, Massachusetts, Eddie Steinberg shared a rather sexist quip, "As a patriotic American in an Olympic-year, I would like to volunteer my services as team trainer."[21] However, some readers perceptively recalled Wilma Rudolph and her excellence, with their words serving as evidence of her influence. It was Rudolph who first demonstrated that athletic ability and utmost femininity were compatible. Bill Elsen, a reader from Nashville, Tennessee, wrote, "I don't believe the Olympics have yet produced any medal winners with bouffant hairdos, and I hope the Texas gals will provide a first in that regard, but they won't be the first glamour gals in the Games. A Tennessee belle named Wilma Rudolph beat them to it."[22] Nevertheless, the blinding white femininity of the Texas Track Club allowed them to earn a kind of acclaim impossible for Rudolph. In contrast to a black woman athlete who communicated democracy and equality, white women athletes provided a clear, comforting representation of traditional gender norms.

Approximately one year later, *Sports Illustrated* again promoted the prospects of Janell Smith, along with those of another young white woman runner, Marie Mulder. In April 1965, the magazine praised these "Quick Young Ladies of Quality," underscoring their girlish femininity while highlighting their participation on an AAU team that competed in London and Berlin.[23] The next month, the pair would be featured on the cover. This editorial decision further substantiated the shifting ideology about women's sport that Rudolph and other black women athletes, although having never appeared on the cover of the magazine, inaugurated. In the accompanying article, sportswriter John Underwood explicated this shift, writing, "Reasons are fast accumulating to make the colleges reshape their thinking about girls' running." Of Smith and Mulder, he noted, "They are teenagers from towns 1,400 miles apart and from starkly variant backgrounds, but girls full of expectancy and promise; girls who can run like boys with hardly an inhibition to clutter their way, and who can make the switch to the dance floor without missing a beat. Run like boys? Run better in most cases."[24] He thus concluded that they stood as "excellent examples of the present and future of American women's track and field."[25] Again, readers shared similar opinions. Sue Tharnish of Nebraska cheered, "I know you couldn't have chosen more appropriate representatives for the new class of middle-distance runners. Girls like Marie Mulder and Janell Smith will definitely increase the lagging interest in the middle distances. These feminine runners are typical of the new faces appearing in girls' track today."[26] These media-driven efforts to alter the imagery of women's track and field also were accompanied by an array of scientific and medical studies, offering supposedly assuring evidence that validated white women's more vigorous engagement with the sport.[27]

Despite these celebrated displays of athletic white womanhood, the reality of American women's track and field did not demonstrably change. In her autobiography, Wyomia Tyus offered a blunt assessment of Margaret Ellison, or Flamin' Mamie, who served as head coach for the women's track and field team that competed in Moscow in the summer of 1963. Tyus writes, "Naturally, we knew not to do anything Mamie told us to do. We had seen her before at meets with her skintight outfits and her bouffant hair. She would come out to the track—heels *this* high—and you knew she couldn't coach. She couldn't tell us anything besides how to put on eye shadow, tease our hair, and wear skimpy clothing."[28] In other words, displays of white feminine athleticism could not overcome the gap in athletic ability. Due to the well-developed track and field programs at TSU and Tuskegee, black women had much better training and, thus, were much better athletes. Even as more white women would compete, and would get recognition for competing, the sport remained dominated by black women athletes.

However, Rudolph's influence on the racial dynamics of American women's athleticism would be reflected in women's sport more broadly. Because blackness was the believed antithesis of femininity, Rudolph's racial identity allowed her to powerfully communicate the viability of an athletic yet feminine identity. Her position thus provided permission for white women athletes in a wider spectrum of sports likewise to insist upon the compatibility of athleticism and femininity. In the postwar period, white women primarily received public celebration as athletes when competing in figure skating and swimming, sports understood as unquestionably appropriate because they were defined by feminine flair or youthful vigor.[29] Otherwise, even the performatively feminine women who played in the All-American Girls' Baseball League, in the words of historian Susan K. Cahn, "heighten[ed] the cultural dissonance between 'masculine' athleticism and 'feminine' womanhood," indicating the uncertainty caused by white women's athleticism.[30] But Wilma Rudolph changed the equation.

Beginning in the 1960s, white women became visible as more aggressive, aspiring athletes. Not only did Billie Jean King begin to lead the effort for women's equality in tennis, but an increasing number of white women began to run marathons, launching an almost two-decade movement to establish a women's Olympic marathon. Because of Rudolph, supporters of women's distance running and women's tennis took for granted the belief that elite, competitive women athletes were feminine.[31] This ideological alteration opened a space for the American iconicity of white women athletes, especially as second-wave feminism remained understood as a rather amusing, unthreatening novelty. By the mid-1970s, as the burbling backlash against feminism had begun to combine with wider frustrations with identity-based movements, the likes of tennis sweetheart Chris Evert and distance running darling Mary Decker, along with the feminized fitness figures of Farrah Fawcett and Jane Fonda, became prominent, potent symbols of American women's athleticism, unquestionably feminine athletic icons who did not threaten traditional gender norms.[32] The implementation of sex testing at the Olympic Games serves as further evidence of the effort to enshrine and exalt the white woman athlete.[33] As argued by sport studies scholar Lindsay Parks Pieper, "Sex testing/gender verification thereby outlined a specific category of 'woman' for sport, one which required female athletes to demonstrate conventional 'Western' femininity."[34]

Wilma Rudolph thus propelled the modern popularization of the "feminine bargain," establishing femininity as a prerequisite for women athletes.[35] This development adversely effected black women athletes. In a cultural landscape that not only featured an ever-increasing number of appropriately feminine white women athletes but also remembered the unimpeachable femininity of Rudolph, black women who competed in track and field, as well as other sports, struggled to show themselves to be sufficiently feminine, especially since their femininity already was understood as always in question. The fate of the Wyomia Tyus illuminates this conundrum. At the 1964 Olympic Games in Tokyo, Tyus unexpectedly triumphed in the 100-meter sprint, besting her favored teammate, Edith McGuire, to establish herself as the heir to Rudolph's throne. Four years later, at the 1968 Mexico City Games, Tyus exceeded the achievements of her much-praised predecessor. She became the first athlete, regardless of gender, race, or nationality, to successfully defend her 100-meter gold medal, setting a new world and Olympic record in the process. Yet, her display of American athletic excellence earned her little acclaim.[36]

Not only did Tyus not possess the captivating femininity of Rudolph, but the Temple and Tigerbelle brand of black athletic womanhood also had lost its ideological luster. Political and cultural conditions no longer called for the stabilizing national imagery offered by black women track stars. The fracturing of the civil rights movement, emergence of second-wave feminism, and increasing agitation against the Vietnam War superseded the Cold War–civil rights context that had made a heteronormative black woman athlete an effective representative of Americanness.[37] The needs of the American nation had begun to exceed the safe, satisfying symbolism black American women track stars were understood to communicate. Furthermore, as part of the civil rights movement's shift away from an emphasis on assimilation and toward assertions of Black Power, black athletes who followed the activist model of Muhammad Ali, such as 1968 200-meter medalists Tommie Smith and John Carlos, had increasing cultural purchase. The exclusion of women athletes from the Olympic Project for Human Rights, the boycott-turned-protest movement captained by San Diego State University track and field coach and sociologist Harry Edwards, also expresses the increasingly masculinist ethos of black cultural politics, especially in the space of sport.[38]

So, among the fury and furor of 1968, Tyus and her achievement did not resonate, even though she did engage in her own form of protest. For the 400-meter relay, which Tyus and her three black American teammates won in an Olympic and world-record time, she wore black shorts, rather than the standard white running shorts. "As part of my contribution to the protest for human rights, I had worn black running shorts for the relay, rather than the regular white running shorts that were issued to us—although I'm not sure anyone noticed," she writes in her autobiography.[39] As a young black woman athlete who almost always abided by the Temple Way, perfectly performing black women's athletic respectability, she did not embody the aspirations or anxieties of mainstream or black American sport cultures. And thus, she was easily overlooked, regardless of the potential relevancy of her athletic and activist actions. As Tyus puts it, "Mr. Temple felt that, because of the whole movement and what Tommie and Carlos did on the victory stand, no one ever really look at all that I had done: back-to-back gold medals in the 100 and three gold medals total and breaking all kinds of records. But if it was that, it wasn't only that. It was also because I'm not only Black but a woman." She continues, "It was bigger than that. At the time, they were not about to bathe a Black woman in glory. It would give us too much power, wouldn't it? Because it would have been a moment."[40]

Tyus's assessment is not quite right. Her analysis ignores the celebrated status of her predecessor, as Wilma Rudolph certainly had been bathed in glory and allowed to have her moment. But yes, Rudolph's moment of power was fleeting. In only a few years' time, the understood representational power of a black American woman athlete had altered, sharply and significantly. Beginning with Alice Coachman, black women athletes had required the world to take notice. They challenged the boundaries of American belonging, contesting the raced and gendered associations of Americanness through their international athletic efforts. Mainstream and black American sport cultures then accommodated this challenge, increasingly presenting black American track women, especially Rudolph, as safe representatives of the nation's possibilities. Now, changed sociopolitical circumstances conspired to make Tyus irrelevant to the imagistic needs of the nation. This trajectory suggests the precariousness of black women athletes' belonging. Marked by race and gender, they always were almost citizens, shifting inside and outside the boundaries of idealized Americanness depending on the social, political, or cultural developments of the day. However, as Tyus aptly asserts, "If you make history, there's no way they can not put you in it. It may not be the way I want, but every time they talk about the 100 meters, they have to mention my name. Maybe softly. Maybe just once. But they have to. They can't leave you out of history you've made."[41]

Following Tyus, black American track women would continue to pass the baton, allowing them again to find possibility amid precarity. In the early 1980s, a conservative turn in US politics and culture reopened a space for black women track stars to project an ostensibly inclusive image of Americanness. The reinvigoration of the Cold War under the Ronald Reagan administration, in combination with the rise of a stringently individualist, supposedly color-blind

American culture, again endowed black women athletes with communicative power. Yet, as had been the case in the late 1950s and early 1960s, this power was premised on the ways in which such women athletes were understood as protecting, rather than threatening, the status quo racial, gender, and sexual hierarchies of US society. Like Wilma Rudolph before them, both Jackie Joyner-Kersee and Florence Griffith Joyner possessed an appealing charisma that ultimately confirmed racialized gender perceptions. But even as Joyner-Kersee and Griffith Joyner reinserted black women athletes at the forefront of the imagery of American athleticism and identity, they remained subject to race- and gender-based discriminations.[42]

Throughout the late twentieth century and into the twenty-first century, the Rudolph model has prevailed. As bearers of the double burden, black American women athletes only enter the popular consciousness when needed to meet the political and social demands of the historical moment. Their Americanness is affirmed when playing a particular part in the nation's democratic diorama.[43] They must bolster, not threaten, the racialized and gendered foundations of America's believed democracy. That Serena Williams has earned more (but far from completely) uncontested acclaim as an exemplary American since she embraced motherhood again affirms that the Americanness of black American women athletes remains contingent on circumstances that situate such women as less threatening icons.[44]

Black American women athletes thus are barometers of American belonging, indexing the ways in which barriers of race and gender, as well as class and sexuality, are constituted and reconstituted in ways that allow for the inspiring performance, but incomplete practice, of US democracy. The meanings ascribed to the trials and triumphs they achieved as they have metaphorically passed the baton demonstrate how white heteronormativity operates hegemonically, working to protect the race and gender inequities that have long been intrinsic to American identity. Nonetheless, black women athletes retain an "insurgent power."[45] By taking to the track, field, court, gym, or other sporting space as representatives of the United States, they expose these enduring inequalities, using sport's emotive and unscripted power to exceed the expectations ascribed to them due to their racial and gender identities. Their athletic efforts are expressions of the possibility of an unbounded Americanness.

NOTES

INTRODUCTION

1. Tex Maule, "Whirling Success for the U.S.," *Sports Illustrated*, July 30, 1962, 14.

2. "2 Relay Marks Set: U.S. Men and Soviet Women Lead—Miss Rudolph Excels," *New York Times*, July 16, 1961, S1; Roy Terrell, "The High Meet the Mighty," *Sports Illustrated*, July 24, 1961, 17.

3. Brittney C. Cooper, *Beyond Respectability: The Intellectual Thought of Race Women* (Urbana: University of Illinois Press, 2017), 6.

4. For analyses of sport's nationalistic symbolism, as well as the role of black male athletes in this symbolism, see S. W. Pope, *Patriotic Games: Sporting Traditions in the American Imagination, 1876–1926* (New York: Oxford University Press, 1997); Mark Dyreson, *Making the American Team: Sport, Culture, and the Olympic Experience* (Urbana: University of Illinois Press, 1998), and *Crafting Patriotism for Global Dominance: America at the Olympics* (New York: Routledge, 2009); Russell Crawford, "Consensus All-American: Sport and the Promotion of the American Way of Life during the Cold War, 1946–1965," PhD diss., University of Nebraska–Lincoln, 2004; Damion Thomas, *Globetrotting: African American Athletes and Cold War Politics* (Urbana: University of Illinois Press, 2012).

5. For analyses of the sport prohibitions imposed on young white women during the postwar period, see Susan K. Cahn, *Coming On Strong: Gender and Sexuality in Women's Sport* (New York: Free Press, 1994; 2nd ed., Urbana: University of Illinois Press, 2015), 83–109, 140–184; Mary Jo Festle, *Playing Nice: Politics and Apologies in Women's Sports* (New York: Columbia University Press, 1996), 75–104; Martha Verbrugge, *Active Bodies: A History of Women's Physical Education in Twentieth-Century America* (New York: Oxford University Press, 2012), 102–152; Jaime Schultz, *Qualifying Times: Points of Change in U.S. Women's Sport* (Urbana: University of Illinois Press, 2014), 73–102.

6. For analyses of the women's athletic ideology that long had prevailed in black American sport culture, see Cahn, *Coming on Strong*, 110–139; Festle, *Playing Nice*, 53–74; Verbrugge, *Active Bodies*, 77–152; Yevonne Smith, "Women of Color in Society and Sport," *Quest* 44 (1992): 228–250; Patricia Vertinsky and Gwendolyn Captain, "More Myth than History: American Culture and Representations of the Black Female's Athletic Ability," *Journal of Sport History* 25, no. 3 (Fall 1998): 532–561; Rita Liberti, "'We Were Ladies, We Just Played Basketball Like Boys': African American Womanhood and Competitive Basketball at Bennett College, 1928–1942," *Journal of Sport History* 26, no. 3 (Fall 1999): 567–584.

7. Glenda Gilmore, *Gender and Jim Crow: Women and the Politics of White Supremacy in North Carolina, 1896–1920* (Chapel Hill: University of North Carolina Press, 1996), 2.

8. Cooper, *Beyond Respectability*, 10.

9. Nicole R. Fleetwood, *Troubling Vision: Performance, Visuality, and Blackness* (Chicago: University of Chicago Press, 2011), 6.

CHAPTER 1. RAISING THE BAR

1. Sam Lacy, "Tuskegee Girls Win Nat'l AAU Track and Field Championship in Landslide," *Afro-American*, July 15, 1944, 18.

2. Joseph M. Sheehan, "U.S. Track Team Takes All Events to Crush Canada," *New York Times*, August 4, 1946, 81.

3. Daniel A. Nathan, "Baseball As the National Pastime: A Fiction Whose Time Is Past," *The International Journal of the History of Sport* 31, nos. 1–2 (January 2014): 91–108; Damion Thomas, "Let the Games Begin: Sport, U.S. Race Relations, and Cold War Politics," *The International Journal of the History of Sport* 24, no. 2 (2007): 157–171; Louis Moore, *We Will Win the Day: The Civil Rights Movement, the Black Athlete, and the Quest for Equality* (Santa Barbara, CA: Praeger, 2017), 2–11.

4. Jules Tygiel, *Baseball's Great Experiment: Jackie Robinson and His Legacy* (New York: Oxford University Press, 1983).

5. For perspectives on the political, social, and cultural dynamism of the postwar United States, see Taylor Branch, *Parting the Waters: America in the King Years, 1954–63* (New York: Simon and Schuster, 1989); Rickie Solinger, *Wake Up Little Susie: Single Pregnancy and Race before Roe v. Wade* (New York: Routledge, 1992); Joanne Jay Meyerowitz, ed., *Not June Cleaver: Women and Gender in Postwar America, 1945–1960* (Philadelphia: Temple University Press, 1999); Susan Jeanne Douglas, *Where the Girls Are: Growing Up Female with Mass Media* (New York: Times Books, 1995); Mary Dudziak, *Cold War Civil Rights: Race and the Image of American Democracy* (Princeton, NJ: Princeton University Press, 2000); Ruth Feldstein, *Motherhood in Black and White: Race and Sex in American Liberalism, 1930–1965* (Ithaca, NY: Cornell University Press, 2000); Gary Gerstle, *American Crucible: Race and Nation in the Twentieth Century* (Princeton, NJ: Princeton University Press, 2001); Derrick Bell, *Silent Covenants: Brown v. Board of Education and the Unfilled Hopes for Racial Reform* (New York: Oxford University Press, 2004); Elaine Tyler May, *Homeward Bound: American Families in the Cold War Era* (New York: Basic Books, 2008); David K. Johnson, *The Lavender*

Scare: The Persecution of Gays and Lesbians in the Federal Government (Chicago: University of Chicago Press, 2009); Beth Bailey, *Sex in the Heartland* (Cambridge, MA: Harvard University Press, 2009); Dayo F. Gore, *Radicalism at the Crossroads: African American Women Activists in the Cold War* (New York: New York University Press, 2011); K. A. Cuordileone, *Manhood and American Political Culture in the Cold War* (New York: Rutledge, 2012).

6. For a thorough account of Coachman's early years and influences, see Jennifer Lansbury, *A Spectacular Leap: Black Women Athletes in Twentieth-Century America* (Fayetteville: University of Arkansas Press, 2014), 43–60.

7. Maxine Craig, *Ain't I a Beauty Queen? Black Women, Beauty, and the Politics of Race* (New York: Oxford University Press, 2002), 156.

8. Craig, *Ain't I a Beauty Queen?*, 35.

9. Craig, *Ain't I a Beauty Queen?*, 36.

10. Verbrugge, *Active Bodies*, 137.

11. Throughout this book, I define "femininity" as white-defined femininity, meaning the performance of the spectrum of traits believed to be possessed by white women. In short, I understand femininity as a racialized gender ideology and performance.

12. For more information on Walsh, see Toby C. Rider and Sarah Teetzel, "The Strange Tale of Stella Walsh's Olympic Eligibility," in *Intersections and Intersectionalities in Olympic and Paralympic Studies*, ed. Janice Forsyth, Christine O'Bonsawin, and Michael Heine (London: International Centre for Olympic Studies, 2014): 18–23; Matt Tulis, "Who Was Stella Walsh?: The Story of the Intersex Olympian," *SB Nation*, June 27, 2013, http://www.sbnation.com/longform/2013/6/27/4466724/stella-walsh-profile-intersex-olympian; Sheldon Anderson, *The Forgotten Legacy of Stella Walsh: The Greatest Female Athlete of Her Time* (Lanham, MD: Rowman & Littlefield, 2017).

13. Lacy, "Tuskegee Girls Win," 18.

14. Sam Lacy, "'Coachman Best' Says Walsh," *Afro-American*, July 15, 1944, 18.

15. Pope, *Patriotic Games*; Dyreson, *Making the American Team;* Dyreson, *Crafting Patriotism for Global Dominance*.

16. Cahn, *Coming on Strong*, 110–139.

17. May, *Homeward Bound*.

18. Sam Lacy, "Looking 'Em Over," *Afro-American*, July 15, 1944, 15.

19. Cindy Himes Gissendanner, "African American Women Olympians: The Impact of Race, Gender, and Class Ideologies, 1932–1968," *Research Quarterly for Exercise and Sport* 67, no. 2 (June 1996): 173–174.

20. Avery Brundage, "Saluting Track and Field; On Millrose 40th Anniversary," (speech, New York, Madison Square Garden, 1 February 1947), Avery Brundage Collection, 1908–82, University of Illinois, Record Series 21/251/5 (hereafter noted as Brundage Collection).

21. Elizabeth Borgwardt, *A New Deal for the World: America's Vision for Human Rights* (Cambridge, MA: Harvard University Press, 2005).

22. "Name Alice Coachman to U.S. Team for Canada Invasion," *Afro-American*, July 27, 1946, 17; "Crack U.S. Cinder Aces in Canada for All-Star Meet," *Afro-American*, August 3, 1946, 16.

23. "Famed Woman Star Receives Bid from AAU," *New York Amsterdam News*, July 27, 1946, 11.

24. "Famed Woman Star"; "Name Alice Coachman to U.S. Team."

25. "Alice Coachman Gains Three All-America Places," *Afro-American*, January 19, 1946, 22.

26. "Tuskegee Girls Captures 10th National A.A.U. Track Title," *Philadelphia Tribune*, August 6, 1946, 10; "'Skegee Wins A.A.U. Crown," *Chicago Defender*, August 10, 1946, 11.

27. "U.S. Athletes Selected," *New York Times*, July 19, 1946, 17; "Crack U.S. Cinder Aces."

28. Sheehan, "U.S. Track Team Takes All Events."

29. "Colored Athletes Believed Out of Nat'l AAU Track Games," *Afro-American*, January 12, 1946, 18; "Pioneer Track Club's Coach Sees 'Lily White' Meet If Texas Plans Go Through," *Philadelphia Tribune*, January 12, 1946, 11; "Pioneer Club Bolsters Squad: To Pass Up National Meet in San Antonio," *Chicago Defender*, January 12, 1946, 7; "Sentiment Grows against AAU Texas Track Meet," *Afro-American*, January 19, 1946, 22; "No AAU Games in Texas," *New York Amsterdam News*, February 9, 1946, 10; "Crack Athletes Head for AAU Texas Games in Special Car," *Afro-American*, June 29, 1946, 19.

30. Sam Lacy, "Tan Athletes Take 11 of 18 Events in Texas Meet," *Afro-American*, July 6, 1946, 16.

31. Kimberly L. Phillips, *War! What Is It Good For? Black Freedom Struggles and the U.S. Military from World War II to Iraq* (Chapel Hill, NC: University of North Carolina Press, 2012), 1–127.

32. "Miss Walsh Keeps 200-Meter Crown," *New York Times*, June 29, 1947, S6; U. J. Andrews, "Tuskegee Thinclads Chalk Up 107 Points to Retain Women's National AAU Crown," *Atlanta Daily World*, July 2, 1947, 5; "Tuskegee Women Win 2 National Track Titles," *Chicago Defender*, July 5, 1947, 11.

33. Andrews, "Tuskegee Thinclads Chalk Up 107 Points."

34. "Tuskegee Institute Girls Triumph in Senior and Junior A.A.U. Track," *New York Times*, June 30, 1947, 23.

35. "Tuskegee Lassies Eye '48 U.S. Olympic Team," *Philadelphia Tribune*, December 20, 1947, 8.

36. The black sport press frequently questioned and criticized Ferris's racial beliefs. His pattern of decisions as AAU secretary-treasurer also indicated racial insensitivity; see "A.A.U. under Fire in Selecting Texas as Track Meet Site," *Philadelphia Tribune*, January 19, 1946, 11; Joe Bostic, "The Scoreboard: An Open Letter to the International Amateur Federation; the National AAU, Dan Ferris and the Honorable Dean Acheson," *New York Amsterdam News*, July 1, 1950, 31; Russ J. Cowans, "Russ' Corner," *Chicago Defender*, July 8, 1950, 16; Alvin Moses, "Beating the Gun: Dan Ferris, Our Old Opponent," *Philadelphia Tribune*, July 11, 1950, 11; "Spikes Dan Ferris' Denial That Jim Crow Blocked Negroes' Trip," *New York Amsterdam News*, July 1, 1950, 29.

37. "United States Women's Team at Lowest Ebb," *St. Louis Post-Dispatch*, November 26, 1946, 15.

38. Carol Mauer, "Follow The Girls . . . with Carol Mauer," *Montreal Gazette*, August 23, 1947, 7; "Ewell Takes Two Titles in Canada," *Afro-American*, September 13, 1946, 13.

39. George L. Gardner, "Untitled," press release, undated, Brundage Collection, Record Series 17/170/9.

40. Catherine D. Meyer, "Women's Track & Field: Report of Committee Chairman," in *Report of the United States Olympic Committee: Games of the XIVth Olympiad, London, England, July 29 to August 14, 1948; Vth Olympic Winter Games; St. Moritz, Switzerland; January 30 to February 8, 1948*, ed. Asa Bushnell (New York: United States Olympic Association, 1949), 106–107.

41. Meyer, "Women's Track & Field."

42. Meyer, "Women's Track & Field."

43. "Mrs. Kaszubski Annexes Shot Put, Discus Throw in Olympic Tests," *New York Times*, July 13, 1948, 24.

44. "Mrs. Kaszubski Annexes Shot Put."

45. "Mrs. Kaszubski Annexes Shot Put."

46. "Mrs. Kaszubski Annexes Shot Put."

47. "Capture Nine Out of Eleven Berths in Providence," *Norfolk New Journal and Guide*, July 24, 1948, E14.

48. Russ Cowans, "Dr. Carver's Discovery Is Must with 'Skegee Lassies," *Norfolk New Journal and Guide*, July 31, 1948, 21.

49. Kathy Lee Peiss, *Hope in a Jar: The Making of America's Beauty Culture* (New York: Metropolitan Books, 1998).

50. "Photo Standalone 22—No Title," *Chicago Defender*, July 24, 1948, 10.

51. Brundage, "Saluting Track and Field; On Millrose 40th Anniversary," Brundage Collection, Record Series 21/251/5.

52. Laura A. Belmonte, *Selling the American Way: U.S. Propaganda and the Cold War* (Philadelphia: University of Pennsylvania Press, 2010), 179.

53. H. Jamison Starts, "Supplies and Equipment Committee," in Bushnell, *Report of the United States Olympic Committee*, 266.

54. "Olympic Women's Track and Field Championships," in Bushnell, *Report of the United States Olympic Committee*, 110.

55. IOC Archives / Olympic Games of London 1948—women's scrapbook, press clippings, 1948.

56. Mollie Panter-Downes, "Letter from the Olympics," *New Yorker*, August 14, 1948, 66.

57. "Women's Results," *Track & Field News*, August 1948, 7; Arthur Daley, "Sports of the Times: Not Quite Misogyny," *New York Times*, December 28, 1948, 27; "Reigning Sensations in European Track: Mrs. Blankers-Koen," *Amateur Athlete*, February 1949, 8; "An Olympic Champion Pacing the Field," *New York Times*, May 17, 1948, 32; May, *Homeward Bound*.

58. Fanny Blankers-Koen, *Olympedia*, http://www.olympedia.org/athletes/73711, last modified 2020.

59. "Olympic Women's Track and Field Championships," in Bushnell, *Report of the United States Olympic Committee*, 110–111.

60. Allison Danzig, "U.S. Boy, 17, Wins Decathlon in Erie Setting at Olympics," *New York Times*, August 7, 1948, 1; "1948 Summer Olympics, Athletics: 200 metres, Women," *Olympedia*, http://www.olympedia.org/results/58783, last modified 2020. Note: "Stole" is an accurate description. Subsequent video analysis determined Strickland finished third and Patterson fourth. However, Patterson's medal was not revoked, and Strickland was not awarded a medal.

61. Danzig, "U.S. Boy, 17, Wins Decathlon."

62. Danzig, "U.S. Boy, 17, Wins Decathlon."

63. Ollie Stewart, "Writer Describes the Drama, Excitement and Pathos of Famed Olympic Games," *Afro-American*, August 14, 1948, 8.

64. Edwin Roth, "This Memorable VIV Olympiad," *Weekly Sporting Review*, undated in IOC Archives / Olympic Games of London 1948—press clippings, 1948.

65. Karen Rosen, "Recalling: Alice Coachman," Team USA, http://www.teamusa.org/News/2012/January/01/London-Re-Calling-Home/London-ReCalling-Series-Alice-Coachman, last modified January 1, 2012.

66. Rosen, "Recalling: Alice Coachman."

67. Roth, "This Memorable VIV Olympiad."

68. IOC Archives / Olympic Games of London 1948—press clippings, 1948.

69. Richard Goldstein, "Alice Coachman, 90, Dies; First Black Woman to Win Olympic Gold," *New York Times*, July 14, 2014, https://www.nytimes.com/2014/07/15/sports/alice-coachman-90-dies-groundbreaking-medalist.html.

70. The invisibility of Don Barksdale as a racial pioneer likewise shows the uncertainty about race and American identity that characterized the 1948 American Olympic experience; see Chad Carlson, "Basketball's Forgotten Experiment: Don Barksdale and the Legacy of the United States Olympic Basketball Team," *International Journal of the History of Sport* 27, no. 8 (2010): 1330–1359.

71. Allison Danzig, "83,000 at Olympics," *New York Times*, August 8, 1948, S1.

72. "Olympic Women's Track and Field Championships," in Bushnell, *Report of the United States Olympic Committee,* 110.

73. "Alice Coachman Sets New Olympic Record in High Jump," *Atlanta Daily World*, August 8, 1948, 7.

74. Ollie Stewart, "Coachman Is Only Woman Victor for U.S.," *Afro-American*, August 14, 1948, 9.

75. Russ Cowans, "Alice Coachman Only U.S. Girl Winner in Olympic Track Meet," *Chicago Defender*, August 14, 1948, 1.

76. "Mal Whitfield Draws Toughest Assignment," *New York Amsterdam News*, July 31, 1948, 15; "Dillard, Whitfield Olympic Stars," *New York Amsterdam News*, August 7, 1948, 14; Ollie Stewart, "Dillard, Whitfield Win: Tan Aces Cop 3 World Titles," *Afro-American*, August 7, 1948, 1; Stewart, "Writer Describes the Drama"; Jack Clowser, "Dillard's Big Moment . . . ," *Afro-American*, August 20, 1949, A4.

77. "The Courier Salutes," *Pittsburgh Courier*, August 28, 1948, 3.

78. Revella Clay, "Olympic Champ Called Versatile," *Afro-American*, November 6, 1948, 11.

79. Rubye Weaver Arnold, "Reporter Scribes Career Story of Miss Coachman," *Atlanta Daily World*, September 25, 1948, 1.

80. "Gala Festivities to Mark Alice Coachman Day Here," *Atlanta Daily World*, September 12, 1948, 7.

81. Ozeil F. Woolcock, "Miss Coachman Greeted by Women Contingents," *Atlanta Daily World*, September 25, 1948, 1.

82. "Celebration for Miss Alice Coachman to Highlight Dedication of Herndon Stadium," *Atlanta Daily World*, September 21, 1948, 5.

83. "Alice Coachman Hangs Up Spikes," *Pittsburgh Courier*, November 5, 1949, 4.

84. "Women Athletes Return: Alice Coachman Ends Track Competition," *Norfolk New Journal and Guide*, September 4, 1948, 19.

85. Paul Newberry, "Alice Coachman: First Black Woman to Win Olympic Gold," *Philadelphia Tribune*, June 4, 1996, 7C.

86. Rosen, "Recalling: Alice Coachman."

87. William C. Rhoden, "Good Things Happening for One Who Decided to Wait," *New York Times*, April 27, 1995, B14.

88. Howie Evans, "Alice Coachman Davis: Super Lady," *New York Amsterdam News*, June 2, 1979, 58.

89. Rosen, "Recalling: Alice Coachman."

90. "Untitled Photo Spread" in Bushnell, *Report of the United States Olympic Committee*, 67.

91. Jay Weiner, "A Place in History, Not Just a Footnote," *Minneapolis Star Tribune*, July 29, 1996, 4S.

92. Evans, "Alice Coachman Davis."

93. Evans, "Alice Coachman Davis."

94. Evans, "Alice Coachman Davis."

95. James Hicks, "No Officials of State at Coachman Arrival," *Afro-American*, September 4, 1948, 1.

96. Claiborne Carson, *In Struggle: SNCC and the Black Awakening of the 1960s* (Cambridge, MA: Harvard University Press, 1995), 56–65.

97. "Albany Pays Tribute to Alice Coachman," *Atlanta Constitution*, September 2, 1948, 22.

98. "But Georgia Still Upheld the 'White Supremacy' Lie," *Afro-American*, September 11, 1948, A1.

99. Marion E. Jackson, "Sports of the World," *Atlanta Daily World*, September 3, 1948, 7.

100. "Albany Pays Tribute to Alice Coachman."

101. "Georgia Town 'Erases' Color Line to Honor Negro Olympic Star," *Chicago Defender*, September 11, 1948, 1.

102. "Georgia Honors Negro Girl Winner of Olympic Medal," *Washington Post*, August 12, 1948, 16; "Georgia Town to Honor Girl Olympic Ace," *Philadelphia Inquirer*, August 12, 1948, 26; "Georgia Town Slates Parade for Negro Games Champion," *Oakland Tribune*, August 15, 1948, 25.

103. "A Brave Effort," *Chicago Defender*, September 18, 1948, 14.

104. Jackson, "Sports of the World," September 3, 1948.

105. "Negro Aces Visit Truman," *New York Times*, October 23, 1948, 11.

106. "This Gave Her a Thrill, Too," *Afro-American*, January 15, 1949, 8.

107. "Dillard, Hurdle Champ, Eyes 1948 Olympic Title: Expect Noted Athlete to Cop World Honors," *Chicago Defender*, April 3, 1948, 13; Clowser, "Dillard's Big Moment"; Joseph M. Sheehan, "Whitfield Gained the Spotlight in Final Olympic Track Tryouts," *New York Times*, July 12, 1948, 16; "Ewell Ordered to Report for Military Duty," *Afro-American*, June 14, 1941, 20.

108. Richard Gergel, *Unexampled Courage: The Blinding of Sgt. Isaac Woodard and the Awakening of President Harry S. Truman and Judge J. Waites Waring* (New York: Farrar, Strauss and Giroux, 2019).

109. Allison Danzig, "Patton Wins 200-Meter Title and Thompson Paces American Shot-Put Sweep," *New York Times*, August 4, 1948, 25; Danzig, "U.S. Boy, 17, Wins Decathlon."

110. For further discussion of the politics of race in the Truman administration, see Thomas Borstelmann, *The Cold War and the Color Line* (Cambridge, MA: Harvard University Press, 2001), 45–84.

CHAPTER 2. SPRINTS OF CITIZENSHIP

1. "U.S. Girls Set Relay Mark," *Amateur Athlete*, August 1952, 7; "The Women's Events," in Sulo Kolkka, ed., *The Official Report of the Organising Committee for the Games of the XV Olympiad, Helsinki 1952* (Porvoo, Finland: Werner Söderström Osakeyhtio, 1955), 264; Allison Danzig, "Zatopek Breaks Marathon Record to Win Third Olympic Gold Medal," *New York Times*, July 28, 1952, 1.

2. Melvyn P. Leffler, "The Emergence of an American Grand Strategy, 1945–1952," in *The Cambridge History of the Cold War*, ed. Melvyn P. Leffler and Odd Arne Westad (New York: Cambridge University Press, 2010), 67–89; Laura McEnaney, "Cold War Mobilization and Domestic Politics: The United States," in Leffler and Westad, *Cambridge History of the Cold War*, 420–441.

3. Crawford, "Consensus All-American."

4. Thomas, *Globetrotting*; L. Moore, *We Will Win the Day*, 107–136; Louis Moore, "Doby Does It! Larry Doby, Race, and American Democracy in Post–World War II America," *Journal of Sport History* 42, no. 3 (Fall 2015): 363–370.

5. Mark Dyreson, "Globalizing the Nation-Making Process: Modern Sport in World History," *International Journal of the History of Sport* 20, no. 1 (2003): 91–106.

6. In this chapter, I borrow Laura Belmonte's idea of the American Way to capture the vision of the nation and its values that the institutions of US sport sought to promote through international competition. "Freedom, tolerance, and individuality" formed the core of the American Way, even as the American Way most often was actualized through policies and practices that privileged whiteness, capitalism, middle-classness, and heterosexuality. Belmonte, *Selling the American Way*, 65.

7. For analytical perspectives of sport, national identity, and politics, see Pope, *Patriotic Games*; Dyreson, *Making the American Team*: Allen Guttmann, *The Olym-*

pics: A History of the Modern Games (Urbana: University of Illinois Press, 2002); C. L. R. James, *Beyond a Boundary* (Durham, NC: Duke University Press, 2003); Alan Tomlinson and Christopher Young, eds., *National Identity and Global Sports Events: Culture, Politics, and Spectacle in the Olympics and Football World Cup* (Albany: State University of New York Press, 2006); Dyreson, *Crafting Patriotism for Global Dominance.*

8. "Misses May Miss Pan-Olympics," *Afro-American*, August 19, 1950, 17.

9. Curtis Ray Emery, "The History of the Pan American Games," Ph.D. dissertation, Louisiana State University, 1964.

10. Avery Brundage, "Pan American Games," in Bushnell, *Report of the United States Olympic Committee*, 354.

11. "First Pan-American Games," Brundage Collection, Record Series 19/223/16.

12. Toby C. Rider, *Cold War Games: Propaganda, the Olympics, and U.S. Foreign Policy* (Urbana: University of Illinois Press, 2016), 4.

13. Rider, *Cold War Games*, 7.

14. Gilbert M. Joseph, Catherine C. LeGrand, and Ricardo D. Salvatore, eds., *Close Encounters of Empire: Writing the Cultural History of U.S.-Latin America Relations* (Durham, NC: Duke University Press, 1998).

15. "1/29/51 Fundraising Letter," Brundage Collection, Record Series 19/224/4.

16. "State Dept. Lauds U.S. Pan-Am and Olympic Participation," *Amateur Athlete*, February 1951, 8.

17. Brenda Elsey, "Cultural Ambassadorship and the Pan-American Games of the 1950s," *International Journal of the History of Sport* 33, nos. 1–2 (March 2016): 109.

18. "Misses May Miss Pan-Olympics."

19. "Misses May Miss Pan-Olympics."

20. A. S. "Doc" Young, "Morgan College Relay Team Gets Big to Compete in Coast Relays," *Chicago Defender*, May 13, 1950, 18.

21. "U.S.C. Relay Team Clips World Mark," *New York Times*, May 22, 1949, S3.

22. Catherine D. Meyer, "Will U.S. Girls Rate Places on Pan-American and Olympic Teams?," *Amateur Athlete*, April 1949, 16.

23. Meyer, "Will U.S. Girls Rate Places."

24. Meyer, "Will U.S. Girls Rate Places."

25. "U.S.C. Relay Team Clips World Mark."

26. A. S. "Doc" Young, "Morgan College Relay Team Gets Bid."

27. "Jean Patton Sought," *Bakersfield Californian*, May 2, 1950, 20; "Tennessee State Woman Sprinter to Arrive," *Los Angeles Times*, May 15, 1950, 67.

28. "Miss Robinson Sets Track Mark," *Amateur Athlete*, September 1949, 11.

29. "Patton Is Crowned Gals' Sprint Champ," *Afro-American*, February 23, 1950, A16.

30. "Tenn. State Women Break Tuskegee's 21-Year Reign," *Afro-American*, May 20, 1950, A17.

31. "Jean Patton, Andy Stanfield Triumph at Coliseum Relays," *Atlanta Daily World*, May 23, 1950, 5.

32. Chester L. Washington, "Jean Patton, Whitfield Win L.A. Coliseum Races," *Pittsburgh Courier*, May 27, 1950, 24.

33. "Patton Whips Aussie Star in LA Relays," *Nashville Tennessean*, May 20, 1950, 9.

34. Evelyne Hall, "Women's Track & Field Needs Promotion," *Amateur Athlete*, September 1950, 22.

35. Joseph M. Sheehan, "U.S. Team Seeking $150,000 for Trip," *New York Times*, January 23, 1951, 31.

36. "Contributions through 'Businessmen's Committee,'" Brundage Collection, Record Series 19/224/1.

37. Letter, Evelyne Hall to Avery Brundage, 3 January 1951, Brundage Collection, Record Series 19/224/2.

38. In my research, I have found no evidence that explains further how funds were raised. Brenda Elsey, in her research on 1950s Pan-American Games, also provides no notation or explanation in her article. Elsey, "Cultural Ambassadorship," 109.

39. Festle, *Playing Nice*, 3–104; Cahn, *Coming on Strong*, 140–184.

40. Schultz, *Qualifying Times*, 86.

41. "8 Tuskegee Women Star in National Indoor Meet," *Afro-American*, March 26, 1949, 9.

42. "National Women's Track Champs at Odessa, Tex.," *Amateur Athlete*, June 1949, 19.

43. "Tuskegee Girls Track Team Best in Nation," *Atlanta Daily World*, April 26, 1950, 5.

44. "Tuskegee Girls Track Team Best."

45. "Tuskegee Girls Retain Title in National AAU," *Chicago Defender*, September 2, 1950, 17; "Dixie Meet Won by Tuskegee," *New York Amsterdam News*, September 2, 1950, 24. Of note, Lawler also is the mother of future American track stars Carl and Carol Lewis.

46. "Tuskegee Women Keep Track Title," *New York Times*, August 28, 1950, 22.

47. "Ninth National Crown for Nancy Phillips," *Amateur Athlete*, April 1950, 8.

48. Avery Brundage to the Chairmen of Olympic Sport Committees, "Untitled Memo on Transportation Arrangements," undated, Brundage Collection, Record Series 19/223/17; "Tuskegee Aces Off for Pan American Games," *Atlanta Daily World*, February 21, 1951, 5.

49. Raanan Rein, "Turning the Country into an 'Immense and Clamorous Stadium': Perón, the New Argentina, and the 1951 Pan-American Games," *International Journal of the History of Sport* 33, nos. 1–2 (2016): 29–43.

50. For evidence of US officials' reactions to the Peróns' influence over the Pan-American Games, see Milton Bracker, "Perons Make Hay of Olympic Meet," *New York Times*, February 24, 1951, 6; Arthur Daley, "Sports of the Times: At Home and Abroad," *New York Times*, February 25, 1951, 44; Virginia Lee Warren, "U.S. Aide at Games Chides Argentines," *New York Times*, March 5, 1951, 14; "Charge FBI Use of U.S. Athletes in Buenos Aires," unidentified newspaper, March 21, 1951, Record Series 19/223/8, Brundage Collection.

51. Elsey, "Cultural Ambassadorship," 111.

52. Elsey, "Cultural Ambassadorship."

53. "U.S. Athletes Set Four Marks, Take Five Events in Pan-American Games," *New York Times*, March 6, 1951, 33.

54. "Whitfield Cops 2d Pan-Am Title," *Philadelphia Tribune*, March 6, 1951, 11.

55. "El Gráfico," no. 1649, 16 March 1951, in IOC Archives/Pan American Games of Buenos Aires 1951—Publications, 1951.

56. Elsey, "Cultural Ambassadorship," 111.

57. Emery, "History of the Pan-American Games," 213; "Pan American Games," gbrathletics, the best historical British athletics stats site, http://www.gbrathletics .com/ic/pag.htm, last modified 2007.

58. Elsey, "Cultural Ambassadorship," 112.

59. Evelyne Hall Adams, interviewed by George A. Hodak, Oceanside, CA, October 1987, Olympian Oral Histories, Amateur Athletic Foundation of Los Angeles, LA84 Foundation Digital Library, https://digital.la84.org/digital/collection/p17103coll11/ id/41/rec/2.

60. "Tuskegee's Pan-Am Champs Come Home," *Philadelphia Tribune*, March 27, 1951, 10.

61. "Discus, Shot-Put Go to Fuchs in Chile," *New York Times*, March 19, 1951, 38.

62. "Tuskegee's Pan-Am Champs Come Home."

63. "Tuskegee's Pan-Am Champs Come Home."

64. "Discus, Shot-Put Go to Fuchs."

65. "Fleet Jean Patton Finds UN Doesn't Move As Fast As She," *Chicago Defender*, April 28, 1951, 13.

66. "Fleet Jean Patton Finds UN Doesn't Move."

67. "Fleet Jean Patton Finds UN Doesn't Move."

68. "Fleet Jean Patton Finds UN Doesn't Move."

69. "Fleet Jean Patton Finds UN Doesn't Move."

70. Lula Jones Garrett, "Gadabouting in the U.S.A.," *Afro-American*, April 7, 1951, 11.

71. "Tuskegee's Pan-Am Champs Come Home."

72. Chuck Davis, "CHUCK-a-luck," *Chicago Defender*, April 7, 1951, 18.

73. Thaddeus Russell, "The Color of Discipline," *American Quarterly* 60, no. 1 (March 2008): 103, 116.

74. May, *Homeward Bound*.

75. "Tan Trio In Pan Olympic Games," *Afro-American*, January 27, 1951, 18; "Whitfield Cops 2d Pan-Am Title."

76. "Fleet Jean Patton Finds UN Doesn't Move."

77. "Jean Patton Received by Tennessee Friends," *New York Amsterdam News*, March 31, 1951, 27.

78. "Nashville Honors Ace Jean Patton," *Chicago Defender*, May 12, 1951, 17.

79. "Nashville Honors Ace Jean Patton."

80. "Nashville Honors Ace Jean Patton."

81. For various perspectives of sport's function as a form of international and domestic propaganda during the Cold War, see Thomas Domer, "Sport in Cold War America, 1953–1963: The Diplomatic and Political Use of Sport in the Eisenhower

and Kennedy Administrations," PhD diss., Marquette University, 1976; Crawford, "Consensus All-American"; Thomas, *Globetrotting*; Rider, *Cold War Games*; Erin Elizabeth Redihan, *The Olympics and the Cold War, 1948–1968: Sport as Battleground in the U.S.-Soviet Rivalry* (Jefferson, NC: McFarland, 2017).

82. "Want a Trip to Finland?," *Amateur Athlete*, December 1951, 11.

83. Roxy Atkins Andersen, "Why European Superiority?," *Amateur Athlete*, December 1951, 10.

84. Roxy Andersen, "Meet the Opposition," *Amateur Athlete*, August 1952, 15.

85. Belmonte, *Selling the American Way*, 154.

86. Belmonte, *Selling the American Way*, 157, 164.

87. Belmonte, *Selling the American Way*, 158.

88. Penny Von Eschen, *Satchmo Blows Up: Jazz Ambassadors Play the Cold War* (Cambridge, MA: Harvard University Press, 2009); Thomas, *Globetrotting*.

89. Thomas, *Globetrotting*, 4.

90. Thomas, *Globetrotting*, 43.

91. Damion Thomas, "Around the World: Problematizing the Harlem Globetrotters as Cold War Warriors," *Sport in Society* 14, no. 6 (2011): 778; Thomas, *Globetrotting*, 41–74.

92. Von Eschen, *Satchmo Blows Up*, 20–22.

93. Sam Lacy, "From A to Z," *Afro-American*, July 12, 1952, 15.

94. Louise Mead Tricard, *American Women's Track and Field: A History, 1895 through 1980*, vol. 1 (Jefferson, NC: McFarland, 1996), 312–337.

95. Sam Lacy, "'Sweet Georgia Brown': McNabb Hurt, Hardy Cops AAU Track Triple," *Afro-American*, July 5, 1952, 18; Lacy, "From A to Z," July 12, 1952, 15.

96. "Nine Women Named to U.S. Squad after Harrisburg Track Tryouts," *New York Times*, July 5, 1952, 11.

97. "Nine Women Named to U.S. Squad."

98. "Nine Women Named to U.S. Squad."

99. For examples of the ways in which political, social, and cultural concerns were foisted onto young people, see Regina Kunzel, "Pulp Fictions and Problem Girls: Reading and Rewriting Single Pregnancy in the Postwar United States," *American Historical Review* 100, no. 5 (1995): 1465–1487; Regina Kunzel, "White Neurosis, Black Pathology: Constructing Out-of-Wedlock Pregnancy in the Wartime and Postwar United States," in *Not June Cleaver: Women and Gender in Postwar America, 1945–1960*, ed. Joanne Jay Meyerowitz (Philadelphia: Temple University Press, 1999); Judith Kafka, "Disciplining Youth, Disciplining Women: Motherhood, Delinquency, and Race in Postwar American Schooling," *Education Studies: Journal of the American Educational Studies Association* 44, no. 3 (2008): 197–221; Ramona Caponegro, "Where the 'Bad' Are (Contained): Representations of the 1950s Female Juvenile Delinquent in Children's Literature and *Ladies' Home Journal*," *Children's Literature Association Quarterly* 34, no. 4 (2009): 312–329; Rebecca Jo Plant, *Mom: The Transformation of Motherhood in Modern America* (Chicago: University of Chicago Press, 2010).

100. Meyer, "Will U.S. Girls Rate Places."

101. Elmer D. Mitchell, "Educational Implications of the Recent Olympic Games," *Amateur Athlete*, August 1949, 10; "83 Kiwanis Clubs Sponsor Physical Fitness Tests," *Amateur Athlete*, February 1951, 9; "Physical Fitness Tests," *Amateur Athlete*, July 1951, 10; "AAU Playground Chairman Calls for Program Planning," *Amateur Athlete*, August 1951, 27; Seymour Lieberman, "Junior Olympics," *Amateur Athlete*, May 1952, 12; Seymour Lieberman, "Junior Olympics," *Amateur Athlete*, August 1952, 14.

102. "They'll Represent U.S. at Helsinki," *Afro-American*, July 19, 1952, 15.

103. Fulvio Regli, "Women," *Track & Field News*, August 1952, 21.

104. "U.S. Girls Set Relay Mark."

105. Ollie Stewart, "Ace Olympic Runners Had 2 Spangled Banner Days," *Afro-American*, August 2, 1952, 17.

106. Allison Danzig, "U.S. Olympian Sets Steeplechase Mark," *New York Times*, July 26, 1952, 1.

107. "U.S. Girls Set Relay Mark."

108. Regli, "Women."

109. Danzig, "U.S. Olympian Sets Steeplechase Mark."

110. Regli, "Women."

111. Regli, "Women."

112. Allison Danzig, "2 Americans, Russian, Czech Set Records as Olympic Meet Begins," *New York Times*, July 21, 1952, 1.

113. Danzig, "2 Americans, Russian, Czech Set Records."

114. Regli, "Women."

115. "U.S. Girls Set Relay Mark."

116. "Women Give Soviet Edge," *New York Times*, July 26, 1952, 16.

117. "Women Give Soviet Edge."

118. Daniel J. Ferris, "Let's Have More Co-Ed Sports," *Amateur Athlete*, October 1952, 17.

119. "Wins Indoor Dash Titile; Gets Warm Welcome," *Chicago Defender*, February 24, 1951, 18; Marion E. Jackson, "Sports of the World," *Atlanta Daily World*, February 16, 1951, 7.

120. Lacy, "From A to Z," July 12, 1952.

121. Danzig, "Zatopek Breaks Marathon Record."

122. "U.S. Girls Set Relay Mark."

123. "Women's Events," in Kolkka, *Official Report of the Organising Committee*, 264.

124. "Women's Events," in Kolkka, *Official Report of the Organising Committee*.

125. "Miscellaneous Committee," *New York Amsterdam News*, July 26, 1952, 25.

126. "2 Olympic Marks Broken, 5 World Titles Annexed," *Afro-American*, August 2, 1952, 1.

127. Dudziak, *Cold War Civil Rights*.

128. Along with delimiting the civil rights movement, the discourse of communism was used to enhance the supposed deviancy of gay and lesbian Americans; see Johnson, *Lavender Scare*.

129. Penny Von Eschen, *Race against Empire: Black Americans and Anticolonialism, 1937–1957* (Ithaca, NY: Cornell University Press, 1997); Brenda Gayle Plummer, *Rising Wind: Black Americans and U.S. Foreign Affairs, 1935–1960* (Chapel Hill: University of North Carolina Press, 1996); Brenda Gayle Plummer, *Window on Freedom: Race, Civil Rights, and Foreign Affairs, 1945–1988* (Chapel Hill: University of North Carolina Press, 2003); Brenda Gayle Plummer, *In Search of Power: African Americans in the Era of Decolonization, 1956–1974* (New York: Cambridge University Press, 2013).

130. Thomas, *Globetrotting*, 13–40.

131. Thomas, *Globetrotting*; L. Moore, *We Will Win the Day.*

132. Thomas, "Let the Games Begin."

133. Sam Lacy, "From A to Z," *Afro-American*, January 26, 1952, 15.

134. Sam Lacy, "From A to Z," *Afro-American*, August 2, 1952, 16.

135. "Women's Four of Olympics Surprise Entry," *Philadelphia Tribune*, August 2, 1952, 11.

136. Fay Young, "Fay Says: Four Happy Girls," *Chicago Defender*, August 9, 1952, 17.

137. Al Moses, "Beating the Gun: Summer Reflections," *Philadelphia Tribune*, August 12, 1952, 11.

138. Craig, *Ain't I a Beauty Queen?*, 110.

139. Alexander Feinberg, "Olympic Athletes Get Warm Send-Off," *New York Times*, July 8, 1952, 1.

140. Harrison E. Salisbury, "Russians Recount, Then Recant; Concede Tie to U.S. in Olympics," *New York Times*, August 7, 1952, 16.

141. Allison Danzig, "4 Olympic Titles Won by U.S.; Soviet Leads," *New York Times*, July 22, 1952, 1; Joseph M. Sheehan, "Sports of the Times: Not Fastest, but First," *New York Times*, July 25, 1952, 23; Allison Danzig, "U.S. Takes 3 More Track Titles but Russia Keeps Olympic Lead," *New York Times*, July 23, 1952, 1; Allison Danzig, "U.S. Sweeps Olympic Hurdle Race But Trails Russia by 102 1/2 Points," *New York Times*, July 25, 1952, 1; Allison Danzig, "World Record Set," *New York Times*, July 27, 1952, S1.

CHAPTER 3. PASSING THE BATON TOWARD BELONGING

1. Fay Young, "Fay Says: The Brown Girls," *Chicago Defender*, December 15, 1956, 17.

2. Mae Faggs Starr, "Mae Faggs Starr," in *Better than the Best: Black Athletes Speak, 1920–2007*, ed. John C. Walter and Malina Iida (Seattle: University of Washington Press, 2010), 54–55.

3. Tracey M. Salisbury, "First to the Finish: The Tennessee State Tigerbelles, 1944–1994," Ph.D. diss., University of North Carolina at Greensboro, 2009, 104.

4. Starr, "Mae Faggs Starr," 55.

5. Edward Stanley Temple, interviewed by Cat Ariail, University Library, Tennessee State University, June 9, 2014 (hereafter designated as Temple interview).

6. For perspectives of the Cold War, the civil rights movement, and black athletes, see Dudziak, *Cold War Civil Rights*; Thomas, *Globetrotting*; L. Moore, *We Will Win the Day*; Ashley Brown, "American Women Tennis Players in Diplomatic Goodwill Tours, 1941–59," *Journal of Sport History* 42, no. 3 (Spring 2016): 289–309.

7. T. M. Salisbury, "First to the Finish," 90–99.

8. Aimee Meredith Cox, *Shapeshifters: Black Girls and the Choreography of Citizenship* (Durham, NC: Duke University Press, 2015), viiii-ix.

9. Temple joined the TSU coaching staff in 1950, assisting with both the men's and women's track teams under head coach Clyde Kincaide. In 1953, Kincaide decided to coach only the men's squad, leaving Temple as head coach of the women's team. Salisbury, "First to the Finish," 79–137.

10. T. M. Salisbury, "First to the Finish," 91.

11. For more information on Temple's coaching philosophy, see Ed Temple with B'Lou Carter, *Only the Pure in Heart Survive* (Nashville, TN: Broadman Press, 1980), 46–51.

12. Salisbury, "First to the Finish," 93.

13. Wyomia Tyus with Elizabeth Terzakis, *Tigerbelle: The Wyomia Tyus Story* (Brooklyn, NY: Akashic Books, 2018), 57.

14. Craig, *Ain't I a Beauty Queen?*, 129.

15. T. M. Salisbury, "First to the Finish," 92.

16. Frank Litsky, "Ed Temple, Track Coach Who Produced Olympians and National Titles, Dies at 89," *New York Times*, September 23, 2016, http://www.nytimes.com/2016/09/24/sports/ed-temple-pioneering-olympic-track-coach-dies-at-89.html?_r=0.

17. Tyus, *Tigerbelle*, 65.

18. Claude Harrison, "People in Sports," *Philadelphia Tribune*, February 19, 1957, 10.

19. Tyus, *Tigerbelle*, 41–43.

20. Tyus, *Tigerbelle*, 175.

21. For perspectives on women's citizenship in the 1950s, see Belmonte, *Selling the American Way*; May, *Homeward Bound*.

22. Roxy Andersen, "Battle of the Sexes," *Amateur Athlete,* July 1954, 11.

23. Frances Kaszubski, "The Modern Cinderella," *Amateur Athlete*, September 1954, 21.

24. Dudziak, *Cold War Civil Rights*, 15.

25. Russell, "Color of Discipline."

26. C. Todd White, *Pre-Gay L.A.: A Social History of the Movement for Homosexual Rights* (Urbana: University of Illinois Press, 2009).

27. Mary L. Dudziak, "Brown as a Cold War Case," *Journal of American History* 91, no. 1 (June 2004): 32–42.

28. For perspectives on the ways in which sentiments of anticommunism governed the sporting press in the United States, see John Massaro, "Press Box Propaganda? The Cold War and *Sports Illustrated*, 1956," *Journal of American Culture* 26 no. 3 (2003): 361–370; Rider, *Cold War Games*, 112–117.

29. Peter Brandwein, "Three American College Marks among 12 Cut at Drake Relays over Week-End; Santee of Kansas Named Meet Star," *New York Times*, April 28, 1952, 25; "Santee's Mile Mark Stirs Track Circles," *New York Times*, June 7, 1953, S1; "Marks Are Broken by Santee, O'Brien," *New York Times*, June 6, 1953, 13; "Santee

Runs 1,500 Meters in 3:44.2, Fastest Ever by an American," *New York Times*, July 24, 1953, 21; "Santee Again Helps Kansas Beat American Sprint Medley Record," *New York Times*, April 24, 1954, 22; Louis Effrat, "Santee Takes Mile Run from Dwyer in Olympic Carnival before 10,300," *New York Times*, October 21, 1955, 33; Joseph M. Sheehan, "Santee Triumphs in 4:07.9 Mile Run for A.A.U. Record," *New York Times*, February 20, 1955, S1; "Santee Takes Mile in 4:04.6, A Second over Indoor Record," *New York Times*, March 25, 1955, 20; "Santee Runs Mile in 4:05.5 on Coast," *New York Times*, May 21, 1955, 13; "Santee Triumphs with a 4:06.9 Mile," *New York Times*, March 17, 1956, 15; "Jackrabbit from Texas: Bobby Joe Morrow," *New York Times*, November 28, 1956, 58; Bert Nelson, "Kuts, Morrow, Danielsen Are Top Stars in Great Field," *Track & Field News,* December 1956, 1; Paul O'Neil, "Sportsman of 1956," *Sports Illustrated*, January 7, 1957, 6–13; Daniel J. Ferris, "U.S. Stars Dominate Track and Field at Melbourne with 15 Golds," *Amateur Athlete*, January 1957, 8–9.

30. Kurt Edward Kemper, *College Football and American Culture in the Cold War Era* (Urbana: University of Illinois Press, 2009); Jeffrey Montez de Oca, *Discipline and Indulgence: College Football, Media, and the American Way of Life during the Cold War* (New Brunswick, NJ: Rutgers University Press, 2013); Stephen H. Norwood, "The Philadelphia Eagles, the Crisis of Post–World War II Masculinity, and the Rise of Pro Football, 1946–60," in *Philly Sports: Teams, Games, and Athletes from Rocky's Town*, ed. Ryan A. Swanson and David K. Wiggins (Fayetteville: University of Arkansas Press, 2016), 71–90; Stephen H. Norwood, "The New York Giants and Cold War Manhood: Pro Football in the Age of the Marlboro Man and the ICBM," in *New York Sports: Glamour and Grit in the Empire City*, ed. Stephen H. Norwood and David K. Wiggins (Fayetteville: University of Arkansas Press, 2018); 81–106; Randy Roberts and Johnny Smith, *A Season in the Sun: The Rise of Mickey Mantle* (New York: Basic Books, 2018).

31. For a thorough analysis of constructions of raced and sexed masculine identities in the Cold War era, see Cuordileone, *Manhood and American Political Culture*.

32. Thomas, "Let The Games Begin"; L. Moore, "Doby Does It."

33. Thomas, *Globetrotting*, 103–131.

34. Rachel Devlin, *A Girl Stands at the Door: The Generation of Young Women Who Desegregated America's Schools* (New York: Basic Books, 2018).

35. Jo Ann Gibson Robinson, *Montgomery Bus Boycott: Women Who Started It* (Knoxville: University of Tennessee Press, 1987).

36. Cahn, *Coming on Strong*, 110–139.

37. Beyond the fact that competing as representatives of the US national team worked to protect them from overtly harsh insinuations about their sexuality, I have not uncovered a critical mass of coverage that aimed to delegitimize black women track stars through suspicions about their sexuality. Numerous scholars have identified black women athletes as subject to accusations of lesbianism and mannishness. In discussing the implicit "mannish" appearance of black women athletes, historian Susan Cahn draws on broader histories of black women that analyze the negative stereotypes affixed to them. Her examination of black women's track and field participants focuses on the exceptional femininity of Wilma Rudolph, with

the supposed unfeminineness of Rudolph's contemporaries unsubstantiated by evidence. Cahn instead emphasizes articles that accentuated the femininity of white female athletes, especially swimmers, interpreting the attention to them as implicit rebukes of overly athletic black female athletes. While Cahn is not misguided, it is also important to recognize the effectiveness of black female athletes' feminine presentation, which served as a preemptive prophylactic against direct criticisms. In the specific context of international track and field, negative depictions were the exception and, therefore, not central to the understandings of black women track athletes. In contrast, black tennis star Althea Gibson, by competing as an individual in a traditionally upper-class, white, and more feminine sport, did encounter more explicit suspicions of mannishness. In particular, her aggressive and athletic style of play was presented as evidence of her lack of femininity. Both Cahn and Jennifer Lansbury substantiate their analyses of Gibson with extensive media sources from white and black newspapers that specifically stereotype her. The research of Cindy Himes Gissendanner and Lansbury also does not document accusations of mannishness against black American track women; instead, this research focuses on their cultivation of femininity to guard against racism and sexism. Cahn, *Coming on Strong*, 110–130, 181; Gissendanner, "African American Women Olympians"; Lansbury, *Spectacular Leap*, 64–90, 110–134.

38. "Women Track and Field Tryouts for Pan-Am," *Amateur Athlete*, February 1955, 14.

39. Frances T. Kaszubski, "Women U.S. Indoor Track and Field," *Amateur Athlete*, April 1955, 12.

40. Kaszubski, "Women U.S. Indoor Track and Field."

41. Kaszubski, "Women U.S. Indoor Track and Field."

42. "Three U.S. Aces Win in Mexico City, Brazilian Tops World Record," *New York Times*, March 17, 1955, 82.

43. "Pitt Runner Set 800-Meter Mark," *New York Times*, March 16, 1955, 44.

44. "Barbara Jones Sparks Tan Pan-Am. Stars," *Chicago Defender*, March 26, 1955, 10.

45. Cahn, *Coming on Strong*, 115–116.

46. "Lou Jones Sets New World 400 Record; Arnold Sowell Wins 800," *Afro-American*, March 26, 1955, 16; "Athletes vs. Altitude," *Sports Illustrated*, March 28, 1955, 33; Arthur Daley, "An Attitude on Altitude," *New York Times*, April 5, 1955, 36.

47. "Barbara Jones Sparks Tan Pan-Am. Stars."

48. "Miranda Defeats Santee in Upset for 1,500 Crown," *New York Times*, March 20, 1955, S1.

49. "U.S. Team Wins 3 More Track Titles to Increase Pan-American Games Lead; Miss M'Daniel High Jump Victor," *New York Times*, March 18, 1955, 37.

50. "U.S. First As Meet in Mexico Closes," *New York Times*, March 27, 1955, S1.

51. Hugo Aguilar quoted in Earl Morris, "Morris Proud of Negro Track Stars in Pan-American Games," *Philadelphia Tribune*, April 5, 1955, 11.

52. Morris, "Morris Proud of Negro Track Stars."

53. Morris, "Morris Proud of Negro Track Stars."

54. "Women Track Stars Off for Mexico," *Afro-American*, March 12, 1955, 16.

55. Alvin "Chick" Webb, "Tan Female Flashes In Pan Am's Games," *New York Amsterdam News*, February 19, 1955, 34.

56. "Tan Yanks Star in Pan American Track Games," *Philadelphia Tribune*, March 22, 1955, 11; "Barbara Jones Sparks Tan Pan-Am. Stars."

57. Sylvester Cummings, "Are We Beginning a New Golden Age: Tremendous Strides Made," *Philadelphia Tribune*, June 25, 1955, A4.

58. "Barbara Jones Sparks Tan Pan-Am. Stars."

59. "Barbara Jones Sparks Tan Pan-Am. Stars."

60. Lee D. Jenkins, "Barbara Jones, Nation's Fastest Female, Proves Feminine, Too," *Chicago Defender*, September 20, 1958, 12.

61. Russ J. Cowans, "Russ' Corner: The Greatest Month," *Chicago Defender*, April 2, 1955, 10.

62. Cummings, "Are We Beginning a New Golden Age."

63. "Women's Track on Upswing in the U.S.," *Philadelphia Tribune*, August 7, 1956, 11.

64. Marion E. Jackson, "Sports of the World," *Atlanta Daily World*, August 20, 1956, 5.

65. Sam Lacy, "First Gold Medal Winners in 22 Years," *Afro-American*, April 19, 1958, A1.

66. Lacy, "First Gold Medal Winners."

67. "Best Musician with Dons," *Chicago Defender*, March 21, 1956, 20.

68. Claude Harrison, "Tennessee State Univ. Retains Jr. and Sr. AAU Track Titles," *Philadelphia Tribune*, August 21, 1956, 8; Malcolm Poindexter, "Mae Faggs Paces Tennessee Club to Second Straight AAU Title," *Chicago Defender*, September 1, 1956, 17.

69. Fay Young, "Australia Bound," *Chicago Defender*, September 8, 1956, 17.

70. "'My Dream Team' Says Tennessee State Coach," *Afro-American*, September 1, 1956, 15.

71. "'My Dream Team.'"

72. "'My Dream Team.'"

73. "Photo Standalone 1—They're Best by U.S. Test," *Chicago Defender*, August 27, 1955, 1.

74. "Six Tenn. Girls, Matron Win Olympic Berths," *Afro-American*, September 1, 1956, 15.

75. Starr, "Mae Faggs Starr," 52.

76. Temple, *Only the Pure in Heat Survive*, 36.

77. T. M. Salisbury, "First to the Finish," 88.

78. Fay Young, "Wrong Attitude," *Chicago Defender*, May 23, 1953, 22.

79. F. Young, "Wrong Attitude."

80. F. Young, "Wrong Attitude."

81. F. Young, "Wrong Attitude."

82. F. Young, "Wrong Attitude."

83. F. Young, "Wrong Attitude."

84. F. Young, "Wrong Attitude."

85. Cox, *Shapeshifters*, viiii–ix.

86. Tyus, *Tigerbelle*, 176.

87. Temple interview.

88. T. M. Salisbury, "First to the Finish," 135.

89. Tyus, *Tigerbelle*, 62.

90. Frances Kaszubski, "Girls'-Women's Team Title to Tenn. State," *Amateur Athlete*, July 1955, 22; T. M. Salisbury, "First to the Finish," 96–97; Tricard, *American Women's Track and Field* 1:350–351.

91. "Tennessee State Wins AAU Outdoor Track Championship," *Chicago Defender*, July 2, 1955, 11.

92. Mary Snow, "The Girls at Ponca City," *Sports Illustrated*, July 4, 1955, 17.

93. Snow, "Girls at Ponca City."

94. T. M. Salisbury, "First to the Finish," 97.

95. Fay Young, "Some 'Figgers,'" *Chicago Defender*, July 9, 1955, 11.

96. Mrs. Frances Kaszubski, "Fancy Facts on Women's Track," *Amateur Athlete*, October 1956, 11.

97. Kaszubski, "Fancy Facts on Women's Track."

98. "6 Men, 2 Girl Track Stars Tour Africa," *Amateur Athlete*, April 1956, 28; To Board of Governors from Daniel J. Ferris, "Digest of Minutes of Executive and Foreign Relations Committee Meeting Held at the New York Athletic Club on Sunday, February 19, 1956 at 9:00 A.M.," Brundage Collection 1/3/17. In the fall of 1955, Althea Gibson became the first black woman athlete to be sent abroad, traveling to East Asia with white tennis beauty Karol Fagores and two white male tennis players. For further analysis of this goodwill initiative, see A. Brown, "American Women Tennis Players."

99. "Minutes of Joint Meeting of A.A.U. Executive and Foreign Relations Committee held at the New York Athletic Club on Sunday, February 21st at 9:27 A.M.," page 5, Brundage Collection 4/25/7.

100. *Accra Daily Graphic*, quoted in "U.S. Track Athletes Hailed in Africa," *Amateur Athlete*, June 1956, 15.

101. "U.S. Track Athletes Hailed in Africa."

102. Roxy Andersen, "They Knew We Were There!," *Amateur Athlete*, January 1957, 11.

103. "The Women," *Sports Illustrated*, November 19, 1956, 59.

104. Allison Danzig, "3 Records Broken: Miss McDaniel, U.S., Aussie Relay Team Set World Marks," *New York Times*, December 2, 1956, S1.

105. Danzig, "3 Records Broken."

106. Danzig, "3 Records Broken."

107. Robert Alden, "Highlights, Sidelights Provide Memorable Days at Melbourne," *New York Times*, December 3, 1956, 53.

108. "Jackrabbit from Texas"; Nelson, "Kuts, Morrow, Danielsen"; O'Neil, "Sportsman of 1956"; Ferris, "U.S. Stars Dominate Track and Field."

109. "Davis in Hurdles, Morrow in 100, Connolly in Hammer Throw Win for U.S.," *New York Times*, November 24, 1956, 23; "Danielsen Sets Javelin Record," *New York Times*, November 27, 1956, 55; "Campbell and Johnson Near One, Two Finish for U.S. in Olympic Decathlon," *New York Times*, November 30, 1956, 38.

110. "Miss McDaniel Brings Honor to Nation," *Atlanta Daily World*, December 12, 1956, 8.

111. "Miss McDaniel Brings Honor."

112. "Miss McDaniel Brings Honor."

113. Marion E. Jackson, "City Fetes Two Olympic Stars," *Atlanta Daily World*, December 21, 1956, 1.

114. Jackson, "City Fetes Two Olympic Stars."

115. Jackson, "City Fetes Two Olympic Stars."

116. Jackson, "City Fetes Two Olympic Stars."

117. Mabel Crooks, "Gala Welcome Tendered to Tennessee's 'Fabulous Six,'" *Afro-American*, December 22, 1956, 14.

118. Wilma Rudolph with Bud Greenspan, *Wilma* (New York: Signet, 1977), 82–83.

119. Rudolph, *Wilma*, 84.

120. Rudolph, *Wilma*, 81.

121. Starr, "Mae Faggs Starr," 54.

122. Rudolph, *Wilma*, 82.

123. "All the Comforts of Home in Olympic Games Village," XVIth Olympiad News Release, undated, Brundage Collection 17/179/3.

124. "All the Comforts of Home."

125. For perspectives of the intentionally welcoming atmosphere constructed by Australia during the 1956 Olympic Games, see Graeme Davison, "Welcoming the World: The 1956 Olympic Games and the Representation of Melbourne," *Australian Historical Studies* 28, no. 109 (October 1997): 64–76; Rachel Buchanan, "The Home Front: Hostess, Housewife and Home in Olympic Melbourne, 1956," *Journal of Australian Studies* 26, no. 72 (2002): 201–209; John Hughson, "The Friendly Games—The 'Official' IOC Film of the 1956 Melbourne Olympics as Historical Record," *Historical Journal of Film, Radio, and Television* 30, no. 4 (December 2010): 529–542; John Hughson, "An Invitation to 'Modern' Melbourne: The Historical Significance of Richard Beck's Olympic Poster Design," *Journal of Design History* 25, no. 3 (2012): 268–284.

126. Crooks, "Gala Welcome Tendered."

127. Crooks, "Gala Welcome Tendered."

128. Robert Lipsyte, "A Sports Sisterhood, Measured in Olympiads," *New York Times*, October 17, 1999, 1.

129. Lorraine Harrell, "Willye White," *Chicago Tribune*, March 10, 1991, 3.

130. Harrell, "Willye White."

131. "Lee Calhoun, Villanova's Charley Jenkins Win Olympic Gold Medals," *Philadelphia Tribune*, December 1, 1956, 13.

132. Crooks, "Gala Welcome Tendered."

133. Rudolph, *Wilma*, 93.

134. Harrell, "Willye White."

135. Rudolph, *Wilma*, 91.
136. Rudolph, *Wilma*, 90.
137. Rudolph, *Wilma*, 96.
138. Rudolph, *Wilma*,
139. Rudolph, *Wilma*, 97.
140. Rudolph, *Wilma*, 98–99.
141. Harrell, "Willye White."
142. Robert Lipsyte, "A Practical Woman with Dreams Intact," *New York Times*, October 3, 1993, A3.
143. Julie Deardoff, "Ex-Olympian White Still Running Hard—To Help Others," *Chicago Tribune*, February 1, 1994, 1.
144. Harrell, "Willye White."
145. Rudolph, *Wilma*, 97.
146. "1956 Summer Olympics, Athletics: Long Jump, Women," *Olympedia*, http://www.olympedia.org/results/59570, last modified 2020.

CHAPTER 4. WINNING AS AMERICAN WOMEN

1. "Tenn. Girls Cop 4th Track Crown," *Afro-American*, March 29, 1958, 13; Samuel Haynes, "Tenn. State Women Set 4 New Records," *Afro-American*, July 12, 1958, 13.
2. Thomas, *Globetrotting*, 108. For additional information on Whitfield's extensive ambassadorial role, see Kevin B. Witherspoon, "'An Outstanding Representative of America': Mal Whitfield and America's Black Sports Ambassadors in Africa," in *Defending the American Way of Life: Sport, Culture, and the Cold War*, ed. Toby C. Rider and Kevin B. Witherspoon (Fayetteville: University of Arkansas Press, 2018), 129–140.
3. "U.S. Track Squad Awaits Russia Meet," *Amateur Athlete*, August 1958, 5.
4. Belmonte, *Selling the American Way*, 139.
5. Robert Musel, "U.S. Track Stars Upset Russians," *Chicago Defender*, July 28, 1958, 23; "U.S. Captures Summit Meet from Russians," *Chicago Defender*, July 29, 1958, 24.
6. Temple, *Only the Pure in Heart Survive*, 114.
7. Kevin B. Witherspoon, "America's Team: The US Women's National Basketball Team Confronts the Soviets, 1958–1969," in Rider and Witherspoon, *Defending the American Way of Life*, 99–100.
8. "Track and Field," in 71st Annual Convention Program, Amateur Athletic Union of the United States, December 4, 5, 6, 7, 1958, La Salle Hotel, Chicago, Brundage Collection 1/4/1.
9. Max Frankel, "100,000 to See U.S.-Russian Track Meet Today," *New York Times*, July 27, 1958, S1.
10. Claude Harrison, "Tennessee State's Eddie Temple to Coach U.S. Women's Track Team Vying in Russia," *Philadelphia Tribune*, July 12, 1958, 12.
11. Pincus Sober, "U.S. Track and Field Teams Compete in Moscow, Warsaw, Budapest, Athens," *Amateur Athlete*, September 1958, 5.
12. Max Frankel, "U.S. Leads Russia after First Day of Dual Track and Field Meet in Moscow," *New York Times*, July 28, 1958, 17.

13. Frankel, "U.S. Leads Russia after First Day."

14. Temple interview.

15. "Foreign Relations Committee Report" in "71st Annual Convention Program, Amateur Athletic Union of the United States, December 4, 5, 6, 7, 1958, La Salle Hotel, Chicago, Brundage Collection, Record Series 1/4/1.

16. Musel, "U.S. Track Stars Upset Russians," 23.

17. Musel, "U.S. Track Stars Upset Russians."

18. Lindsay Parks Pieper, "'Wolves in Skirts?': Sex Testing in Cold War Women's Sport," in Rider and Witherspoon, *Defending the American Way of Life*, 91.

19. After the meet in Moscow, the US team then participated in events in Poland, Greece, and Hungary. "U.S. Tan Stars Show Track Ware to Poles," *Chicago Defender*, August 9, 1958, 24; "Pace U.S. Track Win over Poles," *Afro-American*, August 9, 1958, 13; "U.S. Track Squad Triumphs in 14 of 15 Events in Greece," *New York Times*, August 10, 1958, S3; "Tan Americans Cop 11 Titles in Budapest Meet," *Afro-American*, August 16, 1958, 14.

20. Michael D. Davis, *Black American Women in Olympic Track and Field: A Complete Illustrated Reference* (Jefferson, NC: McFarland, 1992), 23–37.

21. Young, "Fay Says: The Brown Girls."

22. "Mrs. Brown Betters Two Track Records," *New York Times*, August 26, 1956, S1.

23. "Mrs. Brown Betters Two Track Records."

24. Frankel, "100,000 to See U.S.-Russian Track Meet Today."

25. Frankel, "100,000 to See U.S.-Russian Track Meet Today."

26. Peggy Pascoe, *What Comes Naturally: Miscegenation Law and the Making of Race in America* (New York: Oxford University Press, 2009), 163–246.

27. Rita Liberti and Maureen M. Smith, *(Re)presenting Wilma Rudolph* (Syracuse, NY: Syracuse University Press, 2015), 42–70.

28. Liberti and Smith, *(Re)presenting Wilma Rudolph*, 60.

29. Elie Abel, "U.S. and Czech Olympic Stars Seek to Wed," *New York Times*, March 3, 1957, 1.

30. "Discus Star Urges Zapotocky to Let Her Wed U.S. Athlete," *New York Times*, March 7, 1957, 31; Sydney Gruson, "U.S. Champion Leaves Prague Today, Still Uncertain He Can Wed Czech Star," *New York Times*, March 8, 1957, 4; "Connolly to 'Fight' to Wed Czech Girl," *New York Times*, March 10, 1957, 20; "Czechs Bow to Love: U.S. Boy Gets Girl," *New York Times*, March 22, 1957, 1; "Connolly's Fiancée Applies for U.S. Visa," *New York Times*, March 23, 1957, 10; "All Prague Agog as Athletes Wed," *New York Times*, March 28, 1957, 33; Edith Evans Asbury, "Newly Wed Olympic Winners Arrive," *New York Times*, April 25, 1957, 1.

31. "Olympians' Wedding Set Today in Prague," *New York Times*, March 27, 1957, 5. For further analysis of the Connollys' love story and its propagandistic implications, see Mark Dyreson, "The Californization of Olympian Love: Olga Fikotová and Harold Connolly's Cold War Romance," *Journal of Sport History* vol. 46, no. 1 (Spring 2019): 36–61.

32. "Women's Title Track Meet to Be Held at Shaker Heights," *Amateur Athlete*, August 1957, 15.

33. Ed Chay, "Women Set Five Records at Track Meet," *Amateur Athlete*, September 1957, 13.

34. In *(Re)Presenting Wilma Rudolph*, Liberti and Smith argue that Brown and Chris von Saltza, the young white swimmer who won four medals at the 1960 Olympic Games, influenced understandings of Wilma Rudolph: "We contend that the meanings generated by and around Rudolph's, Brown's, and von Saltza's multiple identities create a much more dynamic, complex narrative. In looking beyond binaries then, we consider the multiple intersections in play as they are represented in media accounts of the three athletes. The athletes' identities are constructed in opposition, yet are simultaneously interdependent upon each other. Read collectively, representations that feature Rudolph, Brown, and von Saltza open up a discursive space in which to explore the construction and contestation of multiple subjectivities. Ultimately, we contend that these discourses reinforce rather than subvert or even de-stabilize dominant racialized, gendered, sized, nationalized, and other arrangements of difference throughout the late 1950s and early 1960s" (43). This analysis is not incorrect; however, such an ideological concept operated earlier, through the bodies of Brown, Connolly, and the Tigerbelles.

35. "Tan Americans Cop 11 Titles," 14.

36. "Foreign Relations Committee Report"; Edward J. Shields, "U.S. Tan Stars Show Track Ware to Poles," *Chicago Defender*, August 9, 1958, 24; "Pace U.S. Track Win over Poles," 13.

37. "Foreign Relations Committee Report."

38. Kunzel, "White Neurosis, Black Pathology," 314–324.

39. Craig, *Ain't I a Beauty Queen?*, 162.

40. Narratives and analyses of Rudolph that mostly ignore her early pregnancy include Gissendanner, "African American Women Olympians," 176; T. M. Salisbury, "First to the Finish," 151; Liberti and Smith, *(Re)Presenting Wilma Rudolph*, 124–125, 145; Aram Goudsouzian, "Wilma Rudolph (1940–1994): Running for Freedom," in *Tennessee Women: Their Lives and Times*, ed. Sarah Wilkerson Freeman and Beverly Greene Bond (Athens: University of Georgia Press, 2009), 312.

41. Rudolph, *Wilma*, 109.

42. Rudolph, *Wilma*, 111.

43. Rudolph, *Wilma*, 114.

44. Rudolph, *Wilma*, 115.

45. Rudolph, *Wilma*, 118.

46. "Tenn. Girls Take 8 Track Titles," *Afro-American*, January 31, 1959, 13.

47. Rudolph, *Wilma*, 119.

48. "Mrs. Brown, Miss Daniels Pace A.A.U. Track," *New York Times*, June 29, 1959, 38.

49. Claude Harrison, "Young Lady on the Move," *Philadelphia Tribune*, July 14, 1959, 10.

50. "Negro Trackmen Won Six First in Philly," *New York Amsterdam News*, July 25, 1959, 23.

51. Sam Lacy, "Tan Stars Annex 15 Gold Medals in Pan-Am Track," *Afro-American*, September 12, 1959, 14.

52. "Wilma Rudolph Stars as Tennessee State Wins Indoor Track," *Amateur Athlete*, May 1960, 11.

53. "Wilma Rudolph Sets 2 Records," *New York Times*, April 17, 1960, S7.

54. Earl Clanton, "Tennessee State Gals Eye 6th Straight Track Title," *Afro-American*, July 9, 1960, 14.

55. "American Woman Sets Sprint Mark," *New York Times*, July 11, 1960, 37; "Wilma Rudolph Scores as Tenn. Takes 6th Title," *Chicago Defender*, July 11, 1960, 27; "U.S. Women's Olympic Prospects Look Good," *Chicago Defender*, July 12, 1960, 27.

56. "Records Fall in AAU Meet," *Amateur Athlete*, August 1960, 8.

57. "The Lucky Thirteen," *Amateur Athlete*, August 1960, 9.

58. "The Gals Are Better," *Afro-American*, August 6, 1960, A5.

59. "The Gals Are Better."

60. "Rudolph Seen Double Winner at Rome," *Philadelphia Tribune*, June 30, 1960, 13.

61. Craig, *Ain't I a Woman?*, 6.

62. Earl Clanton III, "Morale Boosts Women's Squad," *Chicago Defender*, August 27, 1960, 23.

63. Rudolph, *Wilma*, 126.

64. Rudolph, *Wilma*, 127.

65. Rudolph, *Wilma*.

66. Rudolph, *Wilma*, 128.

67. Rudolph, *Wilma*.

68. Rudolph, *Wilma*, 130.

69. Rudolph, *Wilma*.

70. Rudolph, *Wilma*.

71. Rudolph, *Wilma*, 131.

72. Rudolph, *Wilma*, 133.

73. Rudolph, *Wilma*.

74. Rudolph, *Wilma*, 135.

75. Rudolph, *Wilma*.

76. Rudolph, *Wilma*.

77. Rudolph, *Wilma*, 136.

78. "Tiger Belles Crack 400 Meter Relay Standard," *Chicago Defender*, September 8, 1960, A27.

79. "Tiger Belles Crack 400 Meter Relay Standard"; Allison Danzig, "Norton Runs out of Passing Zone," *New York Times*, September 9, 1960, 20.

80. "Tiger Belles Crack 400 Meter Relay Standard."

81. Rudolph, *Wilma*, 136.

82. Rudolph, *Wilma*.

83. Rudolph, *Wilma*.

CHAPTER 5. "OLYMPIAN QUINTESSENCE"

1. "The Frozen Face of Fame," *Sports Illustrated*, June 26, 1961, 20–21.
2. "The Frozen Face of Fame."
3. "Notes from Olympic Sidelines: U.S. Spectators Win Song Title," *New York Times*, September 6, 1960, 45.
4. "Double Sprint Champion Hurries Only on Track," *New York Times*, September 6, 1960, 44.
5. Robert L. Teague, "Everyone Has Wilma Rudolph on the Run," *New York Times*, February 4, 1961, 11.
6. "A Grand Olympiad," *Sports Illustrated*, September 19, 1960, 14; Tex Maule, "The Most Exciting Five Minutes," *Sports Illustrated*, September 19, 1960, 25.
7. "Others Worthy of Honor," *Sports Illustrated*, January 9, 1961, 34.
8. Craig, *Ain't I a Beauty Queen?*, 32.
9. Liberti and Smith, *(Re)Presenting Wilma Rudolph*, 48.
10. Liberti and Smith, *(Re)presenting Wilma Rudolph*, 49.
11. Tex Maule, "Citius! Altius! Fortis!," *Sports Illustrated*, September 12, 1960, 22.
12. Robert M. Lipsyte, "Wilma Rudolph Pauses Briefly for Medal, Visits and Plaudits," *New York Times*, September 27, 1960, 46.
13. "Miss Rudolph Named Top Athlete," *New York Times*, January 29, 1961, S2.
14. Maule, "Most Exciting Five Minutes," 25.
15. Teague, "Everyone Has Wilma Rudolph on the Run."
16. Lipsyte, "Wilma Rudolph Pauses Briefly," 46; Peter Simmons, "'Nooga Chit Chat: Miss Rudolph Feted, Given Keys to City," *Afro-American*, January 28, 1961, 17; "Governor to Greet Olympic Queen," *Afro-American*, September 17, 1960, 1; "City, Alumni Honor Tenn. State Olympians," *New York Amsterdam News*, October 1, 1960, 26; "Christian Street 'Y' to Cite 1960 Olympic Champion," *Philadelphia Tribune*, November 19, 1960, 12; "'Y' Emblem Club Honor Wilma Rudolph Friday," *Philadelphia Tribune*, November 29, 1960, 12; "11th Annual Emblem Club Award for Wilma," *Philadelphia Tribune*, December 6, 1960, 10; "Philadelphia Fetes Wilma Rudolph," *Chicago Defender*, January 3, 1961, 22; Malcolm Poindexter, "Cotillion Honor Wilma Rudolph, Joan Crawford," *Philadelphia Tribune*, January 3, 1961, 1.
17. "Words of the Week," *Jet*, August 10, 1961, 30.
18. James H. Meriwether, *Proudly We Can Be Africans, 1935–1961* (Chapel Hill: University of North Carolina Press, 2002), 181–246.
19. For a critical analysis of the film, see Melinda Schwenk, "'Negro Stars' and the USIA's Portrait of Democracy," *Race, Gender & Class* 8, no. 4 (October 2001): 116–139.
20. "President Is Host to Wilma Rudolph," *New York Times*, April 15, 1961, 12.
21. Simmons, "'Nooga Chit Chat."
22. Lula Garrett, "'60's Top Ten," *Afro-American*, December 31, 1961, 12.
23. Thomasina Norford, "On the Town," *New York Amsterdam News*, December 17, 1960, 12.
24. "Wilma Getting Taste of Fame," *Chicago Defender*, September 12, 1960, 23; Marion E. Jackson, "Sports of the World," *Atlanta Daily World*, September 24, 1960, 7.

25. Marion E. Jackson, "Sports of the World," *Atlanta Daily World*, October 18, 1960, 5; "Off the Main Stem," *Philadelphia Tribune*, January 3, 1961, 9; Claude Harrison, "Wilma Will Quit Running in 1962; No Marriage Plans," *Philadelphia Tribune*, December 6, 1960, 10; Les Matthews, "Sports Whirl," *New York Amsterdam News*, February 11, 1961, 23.

26. Claude Harrison, "Sports Roundup: Wilma Rudolph Denies an Olympic Romance with Ray Norton Existed," *Philadelphia Tribune*, October 8, 1960, 12.

27. "Uptown Lowdown: Name Dropping," *New York Amsterdam News*, December 3, 1960, 9.

28. "New York Beat," *Jet*, February 16, 1961, 63.

29. "Wilma Rudolph Becomes Wife," *Chicago Defender*, November 29, 1961, 22; "It's Mrs. Ward for Wilma Now," *Afro-American*, December 9, 1961, 6; "Wilma Meets In-Laws; Spending Xmas Holidays," *Chicago Defender*, December 18, 1961, 23.

30. For a critical analysis of women's complicated role in the classical civil rights movement, see Cooper, *Beyond Respectability*, 115–139.

31. "Freedom Riders Marry, Settle in Mississippi," *Jet*, January 11, 1962, 23.

32. Linda T. Wynn, "Diane Judith Nash (1938-): A Mission for Equality, Justice, and Social Change," in Freeman and Bond, *Tennessee Women*, 281–304.

33. "Wilma to Be Honored," *Clarksville Leaf-Chronicle*, September 12, 1960, 1; "An Honor Well Deserved," *Clarksville Leaf-Chronicle*, September 13, 1960, 4; W. W. Barksdale, "Proclamation," *Clarksville Leaf-Chronicle*, October 4, 1960, 7; "Wilma Rudolph Honored," *Clarksville Leaf-Chronicle*, October 4, 1960, 4; "Wilma Hopes to Justify Faith of Those Who Believe in Her," *Clarksville Leaf-Chronicle*, October 5, 1960, 1; "A Program Well Handled," *Clarksville Leaf-Chronicle*, October 6, 1960, 4; for further analysis of the hometown celebration held for Rudolph, see Liberti and Smith, *(Re) Presenting Wilma Rudolph*, 18–41.

34. Rudolph, *Wilma*, 143.

35. "Wilma Accepts Bid to 'Freedom' Rally," *Afro-American*, November 12, 1960, 14.

36. "Freedom Fund Fete Draws Crowd of 1,030," *New York Amsterdam News*, December 3, 1960, 3.

37. "Negro Progress in 1960," *Ebony*, January 1961, 81–82.

38. Marion E. Jackson, "Sports of the World," *Atlanta Daily World*, January 31, 1961, 5.

39. Craig, *Ain't I a Beauty Queen?*, 70.

40. "Athlete in Protest," *New York Times*, May 30, 1963, 32.

41. "Hometown Cafe Nixes Wilma's Key," *Afro-American*, June 8, 1963, 9.

42. Rudolph, *Wilma*, 146.

43. "Olympic Girl Champ Dreads Coming Home," *New York Amsterdam News*, September 10, 1960, 1.

44. "Olympic Girl Champ Dreads Coming Home."

45. Gwilym Brown, "Olympians Indoors," *Sports Illustrated*, January 16, 1961, 42.

46. Claude Harrison, "Wilma, Tennessee State Teammates to Run in Three N.Y. Track Meets," *Philadelphia Tribune*, January 7, 1961, 10.

47. For a detailed account of Rudolph at the 1961 Los Angeles Invitational, see Liberti and Smith, *(Re)Presenting Wilma Rudolph*, 49–54.

48. James Murray, "A Big Night for Wilma," *Sports Illustrated*, January 30, 1961, 48.

49. Murray, "A Big Night for Wilma."

50. Murray, "A Big Night for Wilma," 49.

51. Claude E. Harrison Jr., "Wilma, Tennessee State Teammates to Run in Three NY Track Meets," *Philadelphia Tribune*, January 7, 1961, 10.

52. "Wilma Rudolph, Ralph Boston, and Bragg Top Millrose Track Field Tonight," *New York Times*, February 3, 1961, 19.

53. Brown, "Olympians Indoors," 42.

54. Joseph M. Sheehan, "One World Indoor Record Set and Two Tied in Millrose Track at Garden," *New York Times*, February 4, 1961, 11.

55. George Barner, "Jaspers Share Honors with Stars," *New York Amsterdam News*, February 11, 1961, 23.

56. "Wilma Rudolph Mason-Dixon Featured Star," *Chicago Defender*, February 11, 1961, 24.

57. "Sprint Mark Set by Miss Rudolph," *New York Times*, February 19, 1961, 179.

58. "Wilma Rudolph Clips 220 Mark with 0:25 in Indoor Title Trials," *New York Times*, March 11, 1961, 16; "Wilma Breaks All 220 Marks," *Afro-American*, March 18, 1961, 13.

59. "Girl, 17, Smashes 880 Indoor Mark," *New York Times*, March 12, 1961, S1.

60. "N.Y. Girl Set Record; Wilma Ill," *New York Amsterdam News*, March 18, 1961, 26.

61. "N.Y. Girl Set Record."

62. "Girl, 17, Smashes 880 Indoor Mark."

63. "Wilma Rudolph Is Ill," *New York Times*, March 14, 1961, 39; "Wilma Enters Hospital," *Philadelphia Tribune*, March 18, 1961, 9.

64. Marion E. Jackson, "Sports of the World," *Atlanta Daily World*, March 23, 1961, 7.

65. Jackson, "Sports of the World," March 23, 1961.

66. Temple, *Only The Pure in Heart Survive*, 84–85.

67. "Scorecard," *Sports Illustrated*, February 13, 1961, 8.

68. Claude E. Harrison Jr., "Smoky Garden May Force Wilma to Quit Indoor Track," *Philadelphia Tribune*, February 7, 1961, 11.

69. Rudolph, *Wilma*, 147–148.

70. Rudolph, *Wilma*, 147.

71. Rudolph, *Wilma*.

72. "Wilma Rudolph Becomes Wife"; "It's Mrs. Ward for Wilma Now"; "Wilma Married," *Philadelphia Tribune*, December 2, 1961, 13.

73. "Wilma's Secret's Out; She's Married," *New York Amsterdam News*, December 2, 1961, 14.

74. "Words of the Week," *Jet*, December 14, 1961, 30.

75. Sam Lacy, "Wilma Tells AFRO She Wants 4 Girls," *Afro-American*, January 20, 1962, 1.

76. "Wilma to Be Relays First," *New York Amsterdam News*, April 15, 1961, 31; "Boston, Thomas, Wilma at Drake," *Philadelphia Tribune*, April 29, 1961, 10.

77. "U.S.-U.S.S.R. Track Meet at Moscow Tops List of International Events," *Amateur Athlete*, January 1961, 11.

78. "U.S.-U.S.S.R. Track Meet at Moscow Tops List."

79. "Wilma Rudolph Takes A.A.U. 100," *New York Times*, July 3, 1961, 11.

80. Claude E. Harrison Jr., "Wilma Not in Shape, but She Wins," *Philadelphia Tribune*, July 8, 1961, 10.

81. Harrison, "Wilma Not in Shape."

82. Tex Maule, "Power versus Perfection: The US-Europe Track Meets," *Sports Illustrated*, July 17, 1961, 16.

83. "Wilma Rudolph Takes A.A.U. 100."

84. Ruth Feldstein, *How It Feels to Be Free: Black Women Entertainers and the Civil Rights Movement* (New York: Oxford University Press, 2013), 182.

85. "2 Relay Marks Set," S1.

86. Terrell, "High Meet the Mighty," 13.

87. "2 Relay Marks Set."

88. Terrell, "High Meet the Mighty," 17.

89. Terrell, "High Meet the Mighty."

90. Terrell, "High Meet the Mighty."

91. Terrell, "High Meet the Mighty."

92. Robert Daley, "U.S. Trackmen Rout West Germany; Miss Rudolph Sets Record," *New York Times*, July 20, 1961, 20.

93. "West German Women Rout Americans in Track; Men's Meet to Start Today," *New York Times*, July 18, 1961, 22.

94. "Wilma Credits Willie White with Help in World Mark," *Afro-American*, September 29, 1962, 10.

95. Lipsyte, "Sports Sisterhood, Measured in Olympiads."

96. Lipsyte, "Sports Sisterhood, Measured in Olympiads."

97. Lipsyte, "Practical Woman with Dreams Intact."

98. Harrell, "Willye White"; T. M. Salisbury, "First to the Finish," 92.

99. Feldstein, *Motherhood in Black and White*, 40–85.

100. Robert Daley, "U.S. Leads Poles in Track, 68–49," *New York Times*, July 30, 1961, S1.

101. "Wilma Sets World Record in '100,'" *Afro-American*, July 29, 1961, 14.

102. Fred Tupper, "Budd Loses in 220," *New York Times*, July 23, 1961, S1.

103. Roy Terrell, "Very Good, Very Tired and Winners All the Way," *Sports Illustrated*, July 31, 1961, 12.

104. Terrell, "Very Good, Very Tired."

105. Daniel J. Ferris, "The Greatest Stimulant for Sports," *Amateur Athlete*, October 1961, 5.

106. "Atterberry Victor in 2 Swedish Races," *New York Times*, August 21, 1962, 40; "Hayes, Wilma Score for US," *Afro-American*, August 25, 1962, 9; "8 Firsts Go to US in Swedish Track," *New York Times*, August 31, 1962, 15; "Wilma Wins in Oslo," *Philadelphia Tribune*, September 8, 1962, 12.

107. "Wilma, Back from Latest Triumphs Abroad, Ready to Resume Studies," *Afro-American*, September 22, 1962, 9.

108. For a closer analysis of Rudolph's American Sports Specialist experience, see Cat Ariail, "One of the Greatest Ambassadors That the United States Has Ever Sent Abroad": Wilma Rudolph, American Athletic Icon for the Cold War and the Civil Rights Movement," in *Defending the American Way of Life: Sport, Culture, and the Cold War*, 141–154.

109. Borstelmann, *Cold War and the Color Line*, 135–221.

110. In his research on black Peace Corps volunteers, Jonathan Zimmerman emphasizes the multiple meanings black Africans ascribed to black American volunteers, evincing the ways in which they did not automatically absorb the intended messages of the US government. Jonathan Zimmerman, "Beyond Double Consciousness: Black Peace Corps Volunteers in Africa, 1961–1971," *Journal of American History* 82, no. 3 (1995): 999–1028.

111. "American Specialists Program 1963," Bureau of Educational and Cultural Affairs Historical Collection, Special Collections, University of Arkansas Library, Fayetteville (hereafter noted as CU Collection); "Wilma Rudolph to Attend African Friendship Meet," *Chicago Defender*, April 4, 1963, 26; "Wilma Rudolph Off to Senegal," *New York Times*, April 13, 1963, 33; "Senegal in Salute to Wilma Rudolph," *New York Times*, April 14, 1963, 168; "Wilma Rudolph to Tour Ghana," *New York Times*, April 24, 1963, 55; "Wilma Rudolph Cited on Trip for 'Goodwill,'" *Chicago Defender*, May 6, 1963, 24; Kwaku Adjisan, "Wilma Would Help Train Ghana Track Prospect," *Afro-American*, May 18, 1963, 7; "Rudolph Says She's 'Itchy' to Run Again," *Afro-American*, August 24, 1963, 10; Nicholas Rodis, "The State Department's Athletes Give a New Look to Foreign Policy," *Amateur Athlete*, August 1964, 18, 36.

112. Wilma Rudolph interviewed by Tony Merrill, August 13, 1963, CU Collection, Group 19, Series 2, Subseries 1, Box 351, Tape 2.

113. Undated brochure on James E. Sullivan, Box 10, Sullivan, James E. Award 1904, 1930–31, 1935, 1946–50, Record Series 1/10/14, Brundage Collection.

114. Joseph M. Sheehan, "Whitfield Is First Negro to Gain the Sullivan Trophy," *New York Times*, December 31, 1954, 19; Joseph M. Sheehan, "Sullivan Award Goes to Dillard," *New York Times*, January 1, 1956, S1.

115. "Johnson Gains Sullivan Award," *New York Times*, January 1, 1961, S1.

116. Coles Phinizy, "Another Giant from the Valley," *Sports Illustrated*, July 16, 1956, 41–43; "Record Wrecker: Rafer Lewis Johnson," *New York Times*, July 29, 1958, 27; Harrison, "People in Sports," 10; Bob Sweizer, "Rafer Johnson, the World's Best Athlete Also Is Top Student," *Afro-American*, April 11, 1959, A1.

117. "Rafer Johnson Carries Colors; Mates Approve," *Philadelphia Tribune*, August 30, 1960, 12; Allison Danzig, "Decathlon Taken by Rafer Johnson," *New York Times*, September 7, 1960, 50.

118. "Wilma Rudolph Gets Sullivan Sportsmanship Award," *New York Times*, February 26, 1962, 34.

119. "Wilma Rudolph Gets Sullivan."

120. Sam Lacy, "From Wilma to Ernie in Same Day," *Afro-American*, January 27, 1962, 13.

121. Lacy, "From Wilma to Ernie."

122. Lacy, "From Wilma to Ernie."

123. Lula Garrett, "Gadabouting U.S.A.," *Afro-American*, January 20, 1962, 12.

124. "Wilma Rudolph Beaten on Coast," *New York Times*, January 21, 1962, 163; "Beatty Lauds Jazy, Runner-Up, for 'Smart' Mile at Los Angeles," *New York Times*, January 22, 1962, 39.

125. "Overweight Wilma Races Sat. Night," *Philadelphia Tribune*, January 20, 1962, 13.

126. "Overweight Wilma Races Sat. Night."

127. "Wilma Loses 1962 Track Debut, Praises Winner," *Jet*, February 8, 1962, 55.

128. Tommy Picou, "Tommy's Corner," *Chicago Defender*, January 23, 1962, 22.

129. "Overweight Wilma Races Sat. Night."

130. "Overweight Wilma Races Sat. Night."

131. Sam Lacy, "Wilma Foresaw Defeat in Debut," *Afro-American*, January 27, 1962, 13.

132. "What's Wrong with Wilma?," *Jet*, June 28, 1962, 53.

133. Craig, *Ain't I a Beauty Queen?*, 129, 35.

134. "Olympic Star Undergoes Surgery," *Chicago Defender*, February 9, 1963, 1; "Disrupted Track Plans," *Jet*, February 21, 1963, 55.

135. "Wilma Admits Marriage on Rocks," *Afro-American*, February 9, 1963, 1; "Files Suit for Divorce; Says Mate Was 'Cruel,'" *Afro-American*, February 9, 1963, 1; "Wilma Files for Divorce," *New York Amsterdam News*, February 9, 1963, 18; "Wilma Sticking to 'No Comment,'" *Afro-American*, February 16, 1963, 1; "Wilma Rudolph Seeks Divorce, Gets Italian Award," *Jet*, February 14, 1963, 14.

136. "Trouble Continues to Dog Wilma, Who's Never Had an Easy Life," *Chicago Defender*, February 21, 1963, 24.

137. For a thorough analysis of the event and its implications, see Chris Elzey, "A Friendly Competition: The 1962 US-USSR Track Meet at the Farm," in *San Francisco Bay Area Sports*, ed. Rita Liberti and Maureen M. Smith (Fayetteville: University of Arkansas Press, 2017): 165–183.

138. Joseph M. Sheehan, "Soviet Team of 59 Arrives for Meet," *New York Times*, July 14, 1962, 35; Joseph M. Sheehan, "Soviet Team at Home Away from Home," *New York Times*, July 16, 1962, 39; Joseph M. Sheehan, "Americans Figure to Win 14 Events," *New York Times*, July 21, 1962, 33.

139. Joseph M. Sheehan, "World Mark Set," *New York Times*, July 22, 1962, 123.

140. Maule, "Whirling Success for the U.S.," 14.

141. Rudolph, *Wilma*, 152–153.

142. Rudolph, *Wilma*, 164.

143. Rudolph, *Wilma*, 163.

144. Rudolph, *Wilma*, 167.

CONCLUSION

1. Colleen English, "'Not a Very Edifying Spectacle': The Controversial Women's 800-Meter Race in the 1928 Olympics," *Sport in American History*, October 8, 2015, https://ussporthistory.com/2015/10/08/not-a-very-edifying-spectacle-the-controversial-womens-800-meter-race-in-the-1928-olympics/.

2. Sydney Skilton, "Women in Olympics," *Amateur Athlete*, February 1957, 22.

3. "Girl, 17, Smashes 880 Indoor Mark."

4. "Girl, 17, Smashes 880 Indoor Mark."

5. "Miss Shipley 'Just Loves to Run,'" *Amateur Athlete*, April 1961, 10.

6. "Miss Shipley 'Just Loves to Run,'" 11.

7. "Miss Shipley 'Just Loves to Run.'"

8. "Women's Track Meet in Mass.," *Amateur Athlete*, January 1961, 35; "The First of the Fitness Fairs," *Amateur Athlete*, June 1961, 9; "Youth Movement at San Mateo," *Amateur Athlete*, June 1961, 16; Marilyn K. Sanicky, "Girls Age Group Track," *Amateur Athlete*, November 1961, 18; "Hanford Groups Hold Huge Meet," *Amateur Athlete*, June 1962, 20–21; "Girls Jam Ohio State for Track Meet, Clinic," *Amateur Athlete*, June 1962, 28; Frances T. Kaszubski, "The Jinx of Colorado State," *Amateur Athlete*, April 1963, 24–25; Frances T. Kaszubski, "Lake Erie Association Has Booming Program," *Amateur Athlete*, June 1963, 22–23: Mrs. Frances T. Kaszubski, "Women's Track and Field Merger in California," *Amateur Athlete*, August 1963, 28.

9. "New Queen of the Pentathlon," *Amateur Athlete*, November 1961, 19.

10. "Billie Pat Becomes Miss Pentathlon," *Amateur Athlete*, August 1963, 15.

11. Mrs. Frances T. Kaszubski, "Janell Smith: The Cinderella Girl," *Amateur Athlete*, August 1962, 28.

12. Sara Staff Jernigan, "First 'Sports Institute for Girls' Set," *Amateur Athlete*, July 1963, 24.

13. "Wilma Wins Sullivan Award," *Amateur Athlete*, January 1962, 5.

14. "At Last the Girls Are Ours," *Sports Illustrated*, August 17, 1964, 68.

15. "At Last the Girls Are Ours," 69.

16. Gilbert Rogin, "Flamin' Mamie's Bouffant Belles," *Sports Illustrated*, April 20, 1964, 30.

17. Rogin, "Flamin' Mamie's Bouffant Belles," 31.

18. Rogin, "Flamin' Mamie's Bouffant Belles," 30.

19. Sidney L. James, "Letter from the Publisher," *Sports Illustrated*, April 20, 1964, 4.

20. "19th Hole: The Readers Take Over," *Sports Illustrated*, May 4, 1964, 114.

21. "19th Hole: The Readers Take Over," May 4, 1964.

22. "19th Hole: The Readers Take Over," May 4, 1964.

23. John Lovesey, "Quick Young Ladies of Quality," *Sports Illustrated*, April 19, 1965, 108.

24. John Underwood, "This Is the Way the Girls Go," *Sports Illustrated*, May 10, 1965, 35.

25. Underwood, "This Is the Way the Girls Go."

26. "The 19th Hole: The Readers Take Over," *Sports Illustrated*, May 24, 1965, 98.

27. Ernst Jokl, M.D., "The Athletic Status of Women," *Amateur Athlete*, May 1962, 14–15, 23; Mrs. Frances Kaszubski, "In Defense of Women Athletes—Part I," *Amateur Athlete*, September 1962, 6–7; Mrs. Frances Kaszubski, "In Defense of Women Athletes—Part II," *Amateur Athlete*, October 1962, 16, 27; Ernst Jokl, M.D., "The Athletic Success of Young Girls," *Amateur Athlete*, January 1963, 20–21.

28. Tyus, *Tigerbelle*, 53.

29. Cahn, *Coming on Strong*, 111, 129–130; Schultz, *Qualifying Times*, 73–102; Mary Louise Adams, "From Mixed-Sex Sport to Sport for Girls: The Feminization of Figure Skating," *Sport in History* 30, no. 2 (June 2010): 218–241; Maureen M. Smith and Matthew R. Holder, "Pioneers in the Pool: The Santa Clara Swim Club Mermaids of the 1950s and 1960s," in Liberti and Smith, *San Francisco Bay Area Sports*, 143–164; Susan Brownell, "Figure Skating in Southern California: From Frontier to Epicenter," in *LA Sports: Play, Games, and Community in the City of Angels*, ed. Wayne Wilson and David K. Wiggins (Fayetteville: University of Arkansas Press, 2018), 71–92.

30. Cahn, *Coming on Strong*, 141.

31. Susan Ware, *Game, Set, Match: Billie Jean King and the Revolution in Women's Sports* (Chapel Hill: University of North Carolina Press, 2011); Annemarie Jutel, "'Thou Dost Run in Flotation': Femininity, Reassurance, and the Emergence of the Women's Marathon," *International Journal of the History of Sport* 20, no. 3 (September 2003): 17–36; Jaime Schultz, "Going the Distance: The Road to the 1984 Olympic Women's Marathon," *International Journal of the History of Sport* 32, no. 1 (January 2015): 72–88.

32. For perspectives of the sociopolitical environment of the 1970s and the emerging reaction to second-wave feminism, see Bruce J. Schulman, *The Seventies: The Great Shift in American Culture, Society, and Politics* (New York: Simon and Schuster, 2001); Bruce J. Schulman and Julian E. Zelizer, *Rightward Bound: Making America Conservative in the 1970s* (Cambridge, MA: Harvard University Press, 2008); Susan Faludi, *Backlash: The Undeclared War against Women* (New York: Crown, 1991). For perspectives of the increased attention given to feminized white American women athletes, see Larry Keith, "Happiness Is Six Hours a Day with Your Eye on the Ball," *Sports Illustrated*, July 26, 1971, 58–61; Curry Kirkpatrick, "Say Hello to the Girl Next Door," *Sports Illustrated*, August 30, 1976, 78–88; "Jogging for Joy," *People*, July 4, 1977, https://people.com/archive/cover-story-jogging-for-joy-vol-8-no-1/; Kenny Moore, "It Was Just Another Mary Chase," *Sports Illustrated*, July 26, 1982, 20–21; Craig Neff, "A Double Decker for Mary," *Sports Illustrated*, August 8, 1983, 28–29; Craig Neff, "Mary, Mary, Still Contrary," *Sports Illustrated*, January 28, 1985, 50–52; Nancy E. Spencer, "'America's Sweetheart' and 'Czech-Mate': A Discursive Analysis of the Evert-Navratilova Rivalry," *Journal of Sport & Social Issues* 27, no. 1 (February 2003): 18–37; Louise Mansfield, "'Sexercise': Working Out Heterosexuality in Jane Fonda's Fitness Books," *Leisure Studies* 30, no. 2 (April 2011): 237–255; Mary Jo Festle, "Friendly Rivals: Martina Navratilova and Chris Evert," in *Rivals: Legendary Matchups That Made Sports History*, ed. David K. Wiggins and Pierre R. Rodgers (Fayetteville:

University of Arkansas Press, 2012), 109–131; Matthew P. Llewellyn, Toby C. Rider, and John Gleaves, "The Golden Games: The 1984 Los Angeles Olympics," in Wilson and Wiggins, *LA Sports*, 213.

33. Schultz, *Qualifying Times*, 103–122; Kathryn E. Henne, *Testing for Athlete Citizenship: Regulating Doping and Sex in Sport* (New Brunswick, NJ: Rutgers University Press, 2015), 87–114; Lindsay Parks Pieper, *Sex Testing: Gender Policing in Women's Sports* (Urbana: University of Illinois Press, 2016), 1–88.

34. Lindsay Parks Pieper, "Sex Testing and the Maintenance of Western Femininity in International Sport," *International Journal of the History of Sport* 30, no. 13 (2014): 1558.

35. Festle, *Playing Nice*, 100.

36. For a sample of period, retrospective, and scholarly accounts of Tyus, see "Olympic Win Would Put Wyomia in Special Class," *Afro-American*, October 12, 1968, 24; "Wyomia Tyus Becomes 1st Woman to Repeat in Olympic 100 Meter," *Philadelphia Tribune*, October 19, 1968, 20; Howie Evans, "Olympian Tyus, a Hall of Fame," *New York Amsterdam News*, May 16, 1987, 52; Wyomia Tyus, "Wyomia Tyus," in Walter and Iida, *Better than the Best*; Connie Aitcheson, "Wyomia Tyus," *Sports Illustrated*, July 14, 2008, https://www.si.com/vault/1969/12/31/105711795/wyomia-tyus#; Lansbury, *Spectacular Leap*, 135–162.

37. Alexander Bloom and Wini Breines, eds., *Takin' It to the Streets: A Sixties Reader* (New York: Oxford University Press, 2015).

38. For scholarly perspectives of sport in 1968 that reflect the absence of attention to black American women athletes, see Amy Bass, *Not the Triumph But the Struggle: The 1968 Olympics and the Making of the Black Athlete* (Minneapolis: University of Minnesota Press, 2002); Douglas Hartmann, *Race, Culture and the Revolt of the Black Athlete: The 1968 Olympic Protests and Their Aftermath* (Chicago: University of Chicago Press, 2003). For perspectives for how the events of 1968 altered the US government's perception of the propagandistic power of black athletes, especially as goodwill ambassadors, see Kevin B. Witherspoon, "Going 'to the Fountainhead': Black American Athletes as Cultural Ambassadors in Africa, 1970–1971," *International Journal of the History of Sport* 30, no. 13 (2013): 1508–1522.

39. Tyus, *Tigerbelle*, 128.

40. Tyus, *Tigerbelle*, 129.

41. Tyus, *Tigerbelle*, 136.

42. For period and scholarly perspectives of Joyner-Kersee and Griffith Joyner, see Kenny Moore, "On Top of the World," *Sports Illustrated*, September 14, 1987, 18–23; Barbara Lloyd, "Joyner-Kersee Is on Course for Even Greater Conquests," *New York Times*, February 22, 1988, C1; Frank Litsky, "Griffith Joyner Keeps Going," *New York Times*, July 18, 1988, A1; Kenny Moore, "Get Up and Go," *Sports Illustrated*, July 25, 1988, 14–21; Kenny Moore, "Heart and Seoul," *Sports Illustrated*, August 1, 1988, 16–24; Diana Nyad, "This Year's Top Female Athlete Is . . . ," *New York Times*, October 2, 1988, S15; Michael Janofsky, "Florence Griffith Joyner Has Some Great Expectations," *New York Times*, October 8, 1990, C2; Charlie Nobles, "Griffith Joyner

Enjoys the Long Route," *New York Times*, January 19, 1992, S6; Michael Janofsky, "Joyner-Kersee Leaps onto Center Stage," *New York Times*, May 25, 1992, 27; William C. Rhoden, "You Can Indeed Go Home Again," *New York Times*, July 11, 1994, C9; Jere Longman, "A Queen Retires the Way She Ruled: With Class," *New York Times*, July 21, 1998, C5; William C. Rhoden, "Taking One Last Leap on Two Steady Feet," *New York Times*, July 26, 1998, S10; Jere Longman, "Florence Griffith Joyner, 38, Champion Sprinter, Is Dead," *New York Times*, September 22, 1998, C23; Samantha Stevenson, "2,000 Recall Griffith Joyner, Track Star with Commitment," *New York Times*, September 27, 1998, 42; Tim Layden, "Florence Griffith Joyner (1959–98)," *Sports Illustrated*, September 28, 1998, https://www.si.com/vault/1998/09/28/249599/florence-griffith-joyner-1959–98; Lansbury, *Spectacular Leap*, 163–189; Yvonne D. Sims, "Florence Griffith Joyner: Sexual Politician in a Unitard," in *A Locker Room of Her Own: Celebrity, Sexuality, and Female Athletes*, ed. David C. Ogden and Joel Nathan Rosen (Oxford, MS: University Press of Mississippi, 2013), 146–161.

43. C. L. Cole and Michael D. Giardina, "Embodying American Democracy: Performing the Female Sporting Icon," in *A Companion to Sport*, ed. David L. Andrews and Ben Carrington (West Sussex, UK: Wiley Blackwell, 2013), 532–547; Eileen Narcotta-Welp, "A Black Fly in White Milk: The 1999 Women's World Cup, Briana Scurry, and the Politics of Inclusion," *Journal of Sport History* 42, no. 3 (Fall 2015): 382–393.

44. Rob Haskell, "Serena Williams on Motherhood, Marriage, and Making Her Comeback," *Vogue*, January 10, 2018, https://www.vogue.com/article/serena-williams-vogue-cover-interview-february-2018.

45. Daphne Brooks, *Bodies in Dissent: Spectacular Performances of Race and Freedom, 1850–1910* (Durham, NC: Duke University Press, 2006), 8.

BIBLIOGRAPHY

ARCHIVAL MATERIALS

Avery Brundage Collection, 1908–1982. University of Illinois.
Bureau of Educational and Cultural Affairs Collection. University of Arkansas Library.
International Olympic Committee Archives. Olympic Studies Centre, Lausanne.

NEWSPAPERS

Afro-American, 1941–68
Atlanta Constitution, 1948
Atlanta Daily World, 1947–56
Bakersfield Californian, 1950
Chicago Defender, 1946–63
Chicago Tribune, 1991–94
Clarksville (TN) Leaf Chronicle, 1960
Los Angeles Times, 1950
Minneapolis Star Tribune, 1996
Montreal Gazette, 1947
New York Amsterdam News, 1946–63, 1979, 1987
New York Times, 1946–63, 1988–99, 2014–16
Norfolk New Journal and Guide, 1948
Oakland Tribune, 1948
Philadelphia Inquirer, 1948
Philadelphia Tribune, 1946–62, 1968, 1996
Pittsburgh Courier, 1948–50

St. Louis Post-Dispatch, 1946
Tennessean, 1950
Washington Post, 1948

OTHER SOURCES

"1948 Summer Olympics, Athletics: 200 metres, Women." *Olympedia*, http://www .olympedia.org/results/58783, last modified 2020.

"1956 Summer Olympics, Athletics: Long Jump, Women." *Olympedia*, http://www .olympedia.org/results/59570, last modified 2020.

"AAU Playground Chairman Calls for Program Planning." *Amateur Athlete*, August 1951, 27.

Adams, Mary Louise. "From Mixed-Sex Sport to Sport for Girls: The Feminization of Figure Skating." *Sport in History* 30, no. 2 (June 2010): 218–241.

Aitcheson, Connie. "Wyomia Tyus." *Sports Illustrated*, July 14, 2008. https://www .si.com/vault/1969/12/31/105711795/wyomia-tyus#.

Andersen, Roxy. "Battle of the Sexes." *Amateur Athlete*, July 1954, 11.

———. "Meet the Opposition." *Amateur Athlete*, August 1952, 15.

———. "They Knew We Were There!" *Amateur Athlete*, January 1957, 11.

———. "Why European Superiority?" *Amateur Athlete*, December 1951, 10.

Anderson, Sheldon. *The Forgotten Legacy of Stella Walsh: The Greatest Female Athlete of Her Time*. Lanham, MD: Rowman & Littlefield, 2017.

Ariail, Cat. "'One of the Greatest Ambassadors That the United States Has Ever Sent Abroad': Wilma Rudolph, American Athletic Icon for the Cold War and the Civil Rights Movement." In Rider and Witherspoon, *Defending the American Way of Life*, 141–154.

"Athletes vs. Altitude." *Sports Illustrated*, March 28, 1955, 33.

"At Last the Girls Are Ours." *Sports Illustrated*, August 17, 1964, 68.

Bailey, Beth. *Sex in the Heartland*. Cambridge, MA: Harvard University Press, 2009.

Bass, Amy. *Not the Triumph but the Struggle: The 1968 Olympics and the Making of the Black Athlete*. Minneapolis: University of Minnesota Press, 2002.

Bell, Derrick. *Silent Covenants:* Brown v. Board of Education *and the Unfulfilled Hopes for Racial Reform*. New York: Oxford University Press, 2004.

Belmonte, Laura. *Selling the American Way: U.S. Propaganda and the Cold War*. Philadelphia: University of Pennsylvania Press, 2010.

"Billie Pat Becomes Miss Pentathlon." *Amateur Athlete*, August 1963, 15.

Bloom, Alexander, and Wini Breines, eds. *Takin' It to the Streets: A Sixties Reader*. New York: Oxford University Press, 2015.

Borgwardt, Elizabeth, *A New Deal for the World: America's Vision for Human Rights*. Cambridge, MA: Harvard University Press, 2005.

Borstelmann, Thomas. *The Cold War and the Color Line: American Race Relations in the Global Arena*. Cambridge, MA: Harvard University Press, 2001.

Branch, Taylor. *Parting the Waters: America in the King Years, 1954–63*. New York: Simon and Schuster, 1989.

Brooks, Daphne. *Bodies in Dissent: Spectacular Performances of Race and Freedom, 1850–1910.* Durham, NC: Duke University Press, 2006.

Brown, Ashley. "American Women Tennis Players in Diplomatic Goodwill Tours, 1941–59." *Journal of Sport History* 42, no. 3 (Spring 2016): 289–309.

Brown, Gwilym. "Olympians Indoors." *Sports Illustrated*, January 16, 1961, 42.

Brownell, Susan. "Figure Skating in Southern California: From Frontier to Epicenter." In *LA Sports: Play, Games, and Community in the City of Angels*, edited by Wayne Wilson and David K. Wiggins, 71–92. Fayetteville: University of Arkansas Press, 2018.

Brundage, Avery. "Pan American Games." In Bushnell, *Report of the United States Olympic Committee*.

Buchanan, Rachel. "The Home Front: Hostess, Housewife and Home in Olympic Melbourne, 1956." *Journal of Australian Studies* 26, no. 72 (2002): 201–209.

Bushnell, Asa S. *Report of the United States Olympic Committee: Games of the XIVth Olympiad; London, England; July 29 to August 14, 1948; Vth Olympic Winter Games; St. Moritz, Switzerland; January 30 to February 8, 1948.* New York: United States Olympic Association, 1949.

Cahn, Susan K. *Coming on Strong: Gender and Sexuality in Twentieth-Century Women's Sport.* New York: Free Press, 1994; 2nd ed., Urbana: University of Illinois Press, 2015.

Caponegro, Ramona. "Where the 'Bad' Are (Contained): Representations of the 1950s Female Juvenile Delinquent in Children's Literature and *Ladies' Home Journal*." *Children's Literature Association Quarterly* 34, no. 4 (2009): 312–329.

Carlson, Chad. "Basketball's Forgotten Experiment: Don Barksdale and the Legacy of the United States Olympic Basketball Team." *International Journal of the History of Sport* 27, no. 8 (2010): 1330–1359.

Carson, Claiborne. *In Struggle: SNCC and the Black Awakening of the 1960s.* Cambridge, MA: Harvard University Press, 1995.

Chay, Ed. "Women Set Five Records at Track Meet." *Amateur Athlete*, September 1957, 13.

Cole, C. L., and Michael D. Giardina. "Embodying American Democracy: Performing the Female Sporting Icon." In *A Companion to Sport*, edited by David L. Andrews and Ben Carrington, 532–547. West Sussex, UK: Wiley Blackwell, 2013.

Cooper, Brittney C. *Beyond Respectability: The Intellectual Thought of Race Women.* Urbana: University of Illinois Press, 2017.

Cox, Aimee Meredith. *Shapeshifters: Black Girls and the Choreography of Citizenship.* Durham, NC: Duke University Press, 2015.

Craig, Maxine. *Ain't I a Beauty Queen? Black Women, Beauty, and the Politics of Race.* New York: Oxford University Press, 2002.

Crawford, Russell. "Consensus All-American: Sport and the Promotion of the American Way of Life during the Cold War, 1946–1965." Ph.D. diss., University of Nebraska–Lincoln, 2004.

Cuordileone, K. A. *Manhood and American Political Culture in the Cold War.* New York: Routledge, 2012.

Davis, Michael D. *Black American Women in Olympic Track and Field: A Complete Illustrated Reference*. Jefferson, NC: McFarland, 1992.

Davison, Graeme. "Welcoming the World: The 1956 Olympic Games and the Representation of Melbourne." *Australian Historical Studies* 28, no. 109 (October 1997): 64–76.

Devlin, Rachel. *A Girl Stands at the Door: The Generation of Young Women Who Desegregated America's Schools*. New York: Basic Books, 2018.

"Disrupted Track Plans." *Jet*, February 21, 1963, 55.

Domer, Thomas. "Sport in Cold War America, 1953–1963: The Diplomatic and Political Use of Sport in the Eisenhower and Kennedy Administrations." Ph.D. diss., Marquette University, 1976.

Douglas, Susan Jeanne. *Where the Girls Are: Growing Up Female with Mass Media*. New York: Times Books, 1995.

Dudziak, Mary L. "Brown as a Cold War Case." *Journal of American History* 91, no. 1 (June 2004): 32–42.

———. *Cold War Civil Rights: Race and the Image of American Democracy*. Princeton, NJ: Princeton University Press, 2000.

Dyreson, Mark. "The Californization of Olympian Love: Olga Fikotová and Harold Connolly's Cold War Romance." *Journal of Sport History* 46, no. 1 (Spring 2019): 36–61.

———. *Crafting Patriotism for Global Dominance: America at the Olympics*. New York: Routledge, 2009.

———. "Globalizing the Nation-Making Process: Modern Sport in World History." *International Journal of the History of Sport* 20, no. 1 (2003): 91–106.

———. *Making the American Team: Sport, Culture, and the Olympic Experience*. Urbana: University of Illinois Press, 1998.

"83 Kiwanis Clubs Sponsor Physical Fitness Tests." *Amateur Athlete*, February 1951, 9.

Elsey, Brenda. "Cultural Ambassadorship and the Pan-American Games of the 1950s." *The International Journal of the History of Sport* 33, nos. 1–2 (March 2016): 105–126.

Elzey, Chris. "A Friendly Competition: The 1962 US-USSR Track Meet at the Farm." In *San Francisco Bay Area Sports*, edited by Rita Liberti and Maureen M. Smith, 165–183. Fayetteville: University of Arkansas Press, 2017.

Emery, Curtis Ray. "The History of the Pan American Games." Ph.D. diss., Louisiana State University, 1964.

English, Colleen. "'Not a Very Edifying Spectacle': The Controversial Women's 800-Meter Race in the 1928 Olympics." *Sport in American History*, October 8, 2015. https://ussporthistory.com/2015/10/08/not-a-very-edifying-spectacle-the-controversial-womens-800-meter-race-in-the-1928-olympics/.

Faludi, Susan. *Backlash: The Undeclared War against Women*. New York: Crown, 1991.

"Fanny Blankers-Koen." *Olympedia*, http://www.olympedia.org/athletes/73711, last modified 2020.

Feldstein, Ruth. *How It Feels to Be Free: Black Women Entertainers and the Civil Rights Movement*. New York: Oxford University Press, 2013.

———. *Motherhood in Black and White: Race and Sex in American Liberalism, 1930–1965*. Ithaca, NY: Cornell University Press, 2000.

Ferris, Daniel J. "The Greatest Stimulant for Sports." *Amateur Athlete*, October 1961, 5.

———. "Let's Have More Co-Ed Sports." *Amateur Athlete*, October 1952, 17.

———. "U.S. Stars Dominate Track and Field at Melbourne with 15 Golds." *Amateur Athlete*, January 1957, 8–9.

Festle, Mary Jo. "Friendly Rivals: Martina Navratilova and Chris Evert." In *Rivals: Legendary Matchups That Made Sports History*, edited by David K. Wiggins and Pierre R. Rodgers, 109–131. Fayetteville: University of Arkansas Press, 2012.

———. *Playing Nice: Politics and Apologies in Women's Sport.* New York: Columbia University Press, 1996.

"The First of the Fitness Fairs." *Amateur Athlete*, June 1961, 9.

Fleetwood, Nicole R. *Troubling Vision: Performance, Visuality, and Blackness.* Chicago: University of Chicago Press, 2011.

"Freedom Riders Marry, Settle in Mississippi." *Jet*, January 11, 1962, 23.

Freeman, Sarah Wilkerson, and Beverly Greene Bond, eds. *Tennessee Women: Their Lives and Times.* Athens: University of Georgia Press, 2009.

"The Frozen Face of Fame." *Sports Illustrated*, June 26, 1961, 20–21.

Gergel, Richard. *Unexampled Courage: The Blinding of Sgt. Isaac Woodard and the Awakening of President Harry S. Truman and Judge J. Waites Waring.* New York: Farrar, Strauss and Giroux, 2019.

Gerstle, Gary. *American Crucible: Race and Nation in the Twentieth Century.* Princeton, NJ: Princeton University Press, 2001.

Gilmore, Glenda. *Gender and Jim Crow: Women and the Politics of White Supremacy in North Carolina, 1896–1920.* Chapel Hill: University of North Carolina Press, 1996.

"Girls Jam Ohio State for Track Meet, Clinic." *Amateur Athlete*, June 1962, 28.

Gissendanner, Cindy Himes. "African American Women Olympians: The Impact of Race, Gender, and Class Ideologies, 1932–1968." *Research Quarterly for Exercise and Sport* 67, no. 2 (June 1996): 173–174.

Gore, Dayo. *Radicalism at the Crossroads: African American Women Activists in the Cold War.* New York: New York University Press, 2011.

Goudsouzian, Aram. "Wilma Rudolph (1940–1994): Running for Freedom." In Freeman and Bond, *Tennessee Women*, 305–332.

"A Grand Olympiad." *Sports Illustrated*, September 19, 1960, 14.

Guttmann, Allen. *The Olympics: A History of the Modern Games.* Urbana: University of Illinois Press, 2002.

Hall, Evelyne. "Women's Track & Field Needs Promotion." *Amateur Athlete*, September 1950, 22.

"Hanford Groups Hold Huge Meet." *Amateur Athlete*, June 1962, 20–21.

Hartmann, Douglas. *Race, Culture and the Revolt of the Black Athlete: The 1968 Olympic Protests and Their Aftermath.* Chicago: University of Chicago Press, 2003.

Haskell, Rob. "Serena Williams on Motherhood, Marriage, and Making Her Comeback." *Vogue.* January 10, 2018. https://www.vogue.com/article/serena-williams-vogue-cover-interview-february-2018.

Henne, Kathryn. *Testing for Athlete Citizenship: Regulating Doping and Sex in Sport.* Rutgers, NJ: Rutgers University Press, 2015.

Hughson, John. "The Friendly Games—The 'Official' IOC Film of the 1956 Melbourne Olympics as Historical Record." *Historical Journal of Film, Radio, and Television* 30, no. 4 (December 2010): 529–542.

———. "An Invitation to 'Modern' Melbourne: The Historical Significance of Richard Beck's Olympic Poster Design." *Journal of Design History* 25, no. 3 (2012): 268–284.

James, C. L. R. *Beyond a Boundary*. Durham, NC: Duke University Press, 2003.

James, Sidney L. "Letter from the Publisher." *Sports Illustrated*, April 20, 1964, 4.

Jernigan, Sara Staff. "First 'Sports Institute for Girls' Set." *Amateur Athlete*, July 1963, 24.

"Jogging for Joy." *People*, July 4, 1977. https://people.com/archive/cover-story-jogging -for-joy-vol-8-no-1/.

Johnson, David K. *The Lavender Scare: The Persecution of Gays and Lesbians in the Federal Government*. Chicago: University of Chicago Press, 2009.

Jokl, Ernst. "The Athletic Status of Women." *Amateur Athlete*, May 1962, 14–15, 23.

———. "The Athletic Success of Young Girls." *Amateur Athlete*, January 1963, 20–21.

Joseph, Gilbert M., Catherine C. LeGrand, and Ricardo D. Salvatore, eds. *Close Encounters of Empire: Writing the Cultural History of U.S.-Latin America Relations*. Durham, NC: Duke University Press, 1998.

Jutel, Annemarie. "'Thou Dost Run in Flotation': Femininity, Reassurance, and the Emergence of the Women's Marathon." *International Journal of the History of Sport* 20, no. 3 (September 2003): 17–36.

Kafka, Judith. "Disciplining Youth, Disciplining Women: Motherhood, Delinquency, and Race in Postwar American Schooling." *Education Studies: Journal of the American Educational Studies Association* 44, no. 3 (2008): 197–221.

Kaszubski, Frances T. "Fancy Facts on Women's Track." *Amateur Athlete*, October 1956, 11.

———. "Girls'-Women's Team Title to Tenn. State." *Amateur Athlete*, July 1955, 22.

———. "In Defense of Women Athletes—Part I." *Amateur Athlete*, September 1962, 6–7.

———. "In Defense of Women Athletes—Part II." *Amateur Athlete*, October 1962, 16, 27.

———. "Janell Smith: The Cinderella Girl." *Amateur Athlete*, August 1962, 28.

———. "The Jinx of Colorado State." *Amateur Athlete*, April 1963, 24–25.

———. "Lake Erie Association Has Booming Program." *Amateur Athlete*, June 1963, 22–23.

———. "The Modern Cinderella." *Amateur Athlete*, September 1954, 21.

———. "Women's Track and Field Merger in California." *Amateur Athlete*, August 1963, 28.

———. "Women U.S. Indoor Track and Field." *Amateur Athlete*, April 1955, 12.

Keith, Larry. "Happiness Is Six Hours a Day with Your Eye on the Ball." *Sports Illustrated*, July 26, 1971, 58–61.

Kemper, Kurt Edward. *College Football and American Culture in the Cold War Era*. Urbana: University of Illinois Press, 2009.

Kirkpatrick, Curry. "Say Hello to the Girl Next Door." *Sports Illustrated*, August 30, 1976, 78–88.

Kolkka, Sulo, ed. *The Official Report of the Organising Committee for the Games of the XV Olympiad, Helsinki 1952*. Porvoo, Finland: Werner Söderström Osakeyhtio, 1955.

Kunzel, Regina. "Pulp Fictions and Problem Girls: Reading and Rewriting Single Pregnancy in the Postwar United States." *American Historical Review* 100, no. 5 (1995): 1465–1487.

———. "White Neurosis, Black Pathology: Constructing Out-of-Wedlock Pregnancy in the Wartime and Postwar United States." In Meyerowitz, *Not June Cleaver*.

Lansbury, Jennifer. *A Spectacular Leap: Black Women Athletes in Twentieth-Century America*. Fayetteville: University of Arkansas Press, 2014.

Layden, Tim. "Florence Griffith Joyner (1959–98)." *Sports Illustrated*, September 28, 1998. https://www.si.com/vault/1998/09/28/249599/florence-griffith-joyner-1959-98.

Leffler, Melvyn P. "The Emergence of an American Grand Strategy, 1945–1952." In Leffler and Westad, *Cambridge History of the Cold War*, 67–89.

Leffler, Melvyn P., and Odd Arne Westad, eds. *The Cambridge History of the Cold War*. New York: Cambridge University Press, 2010.

Liberti, Rita. "'We Were Ladies, We Just Played Basketball Like Boys': African American Womanhood and Competitive Basketball at Bennett College, 1928–1942." *Journal of Sport History* 26, no. 3 (Fall 1999): 567–584.

Liberti, Rita, and Maureen M. Smith. *(Re)presenting Wilma Rudolph*. Syracuse, NY: Syracuse University Press, 2015.

Lieberman, Seymour. "Junior Olympics." *Amateur Athlete*, May 1952, 12.

———. "Junior Olympics." *Amateur Athlete*, August 1952, 14.

Llewellyn, Matthew P., Toby C. Rider, and John Gleaves, "The Golden Games: The 1984 Los Angeles Olympics." In *LA Sports: Play, Games, and Community in the City of Angels*, edited by Wayne Wilson and David K. Wiggins, 201–218. Fayetteville: University of Arkansas Press, 2018.

Lovesey, John. "Quick Young Ladies of Quality." *Sports Illustrated*, April 19, 1965, 108.

"The Lucky Thirteen." *Amateur Athlete*, August 1960, 9.

Mansfield, Louise. "'Sexercise': Working Out Heterosexuality in Jane Fonda's Fitness Books." *Leisure Studies* 30, no. 2 (April 2011): 237–255.

Massaro, John. "Press Box Propaganda? The Cold War and *Sports Illustrated*, 1956." *Journal of American Culture* 26 no. 3 (2003): 361–370.

Maule, Tex. "Citius! Altius! Fortis!" *Sports Illustrated*, September 12, 1960, 22.

———. "The Most Exciting Five Minutes." *Sports Illustrated*, September 19, 1960, 25.

———. "Power versus Perfection: The US-Europe Track Meets." *Sports Illustrated*, July 17, 1961, 16.

———. "Whirling Success for the U.S." *Sports Illustrated*, July 30, 1962, 14.

May, Elaine Tyler. *Homeward Bound: American Families in the Cold War Era*. New York: Basic Books, 2008.

McEnaney, Laura. "Cold War Mobilization and Domestic Politics: The United States." In Leffler and Westad, *Cambridge History of the Cold War*, 420–441.

Meriwether, James H. *Proudly We Can Be Africans, 1935–1961*. Chapel Hill: University of North Carolina Press, 2002.

Meyer, Catherine D. "Will U.S. Girls Rate Places on Pan-American and Olympic Teams?" *Amateur Athlete*, April 1949, 16.

———. "Women's Track & Field: Report of Committee Chairman." In Bushnell, *Report of the United States Olympic Committee*.

Meyerowitz, Joanne Jay, ed. *Not June Cleaver: Women and Gender in Postwar America, 1945–1960*. Philadelphia: Temple University Press, 1999.

"Miss Robinson Sets Track Mark." *Amateur Athlete*, September 1949, 11.

"Miss Shipley 'Just Loves to Run.'" *Amateur Athlete*, April 1961, 10.

Mitchell, Elmer D. "Educational Implications of the Recent Olympic Games." *Amateur Athlete*, August 1949, 10.

Montez de Oca, Jeffrey. *Discipline and Indulgence: College Football, Media, and the American Way of Life during the Cold War*. New Brunswick, NJ: Rutgers University Press, 2013.

Moore, Kenny. "Get Up and Go." *Sports Illustrated*, July 25, 1988, 14–21.

———. "Heart and Seoul." *Sports Illustrated*, August 1, 1988, 16–24.

———. "It Was Just Another Mary Chase." *Sports Illustrated*, July 26, 1982, 20–21.

———. "On Top of the World." *Sports Illustrated*, September 14, 1987, 18–23.

Moore, Louis. "Doby Does It! Larry Doby, Race, and American Democracy in Post–World War II America." *Journal of Sport History* 42, no. 3 (Fall 2015): 363–370.

———. *We Will Win the Day: The Civil Rights Movement, the Black Athlete, and the Quest for Equality*. Santa Barbara, CA: Praeger, 2017.

Murray, James. "A Big Night for Wilma." *Sports Illustrated*, January 30, 1961, 48.

Narcotta-Welp, Eileen. "A Black Fly in White Milk: The 1999 Women's World Cup, Briana Scurry, and the Politics of Inclusion." *Journal of Sport History* 42, no. 3 (Fall 2015): 382–393.

Nathan, Daniel A. "Baseball As the National Pastime: A Fiction Whose Time Is Past." *International Journal of the History of Sport* 31, nos. 1–2 (January 2014): 91–108.

"National Women's Track Champs at Odessa, Tex." *Amateur Athlete*, June 1949, 19.

Neff, Craig. "A Double Decker for Mary." *Sports Illustrated*, August 8, 1983, 28–29.

———. "Mary, Mary, Still Contrary." *Sports Illustrated*, January 28, 1985, 50–52.

"Negro Progress in 1960." *Ebony*, January 1961, 81–82.

Nelson, Bert. "Kuts, Morrow, Danielsen Are Top Stars in Great Field." *Track & Field News,* December 1956, 1.

"New Queen of the Pentathlon." *Amateur Athlete*, November 1961, 19.

"New York Beat." *Jet*, February 16, 1961, 63.

"19th Hole: The Readers Take Over." *Sports Illustrated*, May 4, 1964, 114.

"The 19th Hole: The Readers Take Over." *Sports Illustrated*, May 24, 1965, 98.

"Ninth National Crown for Nancy Phillips." *Amateur Athlete*, April 1950, 8.

Norwood, Stephen H. "The New York Giants and Cold War Manhood: Pro Football in the Age of the Marlboro Man and the ICBM." In *New York Sports: Glamour and Grit in the Empire City*, edited by Stephen H. Norwood and David K. Wiggins, 81–106. Fayetteville: University of Arkansas Press, 2018.

———. "The Philadelphia Eagles, the Crisis of Post–World War II Masculinity, and the Rise of Pro Football, 1946–60." In *Philly Sports: Teams, Games, and Athletes from Rocky's Town*, edited by Ryan A. Swanson and David K. Wiggins, 71–90. Fayetteville: University of Arkansas Press, 2016.

Ogden, David C., Joel Nathan Rosen, Roberta J. Newman, and Jack Lule, eds. *A Locker Room of Her Own: Celebrity, Sexuality, and Female Athletes*. Oxford: University Press of Mississippi, 2013.

O'Neil, Paul. "Sportsman of 1956." *Sports Illustrated*, January 7, 1957, 6–13.

"Others Worthy of Honor." *Sports Illustrated*, January 9, 1961, 34.

"Pan American Games." Gbrathletics, the best historical British athletics stats site. http://gbrathletics.com/ic/pag.htm. Last modified 2007.

Panter-Downes, Mollie. "Letter from the Olympics." *New Yorker*, August 14, 1948, 66.

Pascoe, Peggy. *What Comes Naturally: Miscegenation Law and the Making of Race in America*. New York: Oxford University Press, 2009.

Peiss, Kathy Lee. *Hope in a Jar: The Making of America's Beauty Culture*. New York: Metropolitan Books, 1998.

Phillips, Kimberly L. *War! What Is It Good For? Black Freedom Struggle and the U.S. Military from World War II to Iraq*. Chapel Hill: University of North Carolina Press, 2012.

Phinizy, Coles. "Another Giant From the Valley." *Sports Illustrated*, July 16, 1956, 41–43.

"Physical Fitness Tests." *Amateur Athlete*, July 1951, 10.

Pieper, Lindsay Parks. *Sex Testing: Gender Policing in Women's Sports*. Urbana: University of Illinois Press, 2016.

———. "Sex Testing and the Maintenance of Western Femininity in International Sport." *International Journal of the History of Sport* 30, no. 13 (2014): 1557–1576.

———. "'Wolves in Skirts?': Sex Testing in Cold War Women's Sport." In Rider and Witherspoon, *Defending the American Way of Life*, 85–98.

Plant, Rebecca Jo. *Mom: The Transformation of Motherhood and Modern America*. Chicago: University of Chicago Press, 2010.

Plummer, Brenda Gayle. *In Search of Power: African Americans in the Era of Decolonization, 1956–1974*. New York: Cambridge University Press, 2013.

———. *Rising Wind: Black Americans and U.S. Foreign Affairs, 1935–1960*. Chapel Hill: University of North Carolina Press, 1996.

———. *Window on Freedom: Race, Civil Rights, and Foreign Affairs, 1945–1988*. Chapel Hill: University of North Carolina Press, 2003.

Pope, S. W. *Patriotic Games: Sporting Traditions in the American Imagination, 1876–1962*. New York: Oxford University Press, 1997.

"Records Fall in AAU Meet." *Amateur Athlete*, August 1960, 8.

Redihan, Erin Elizabeth. *The Olympics and the Cold War, 1948–1968: Sport as Battleground in the U.S.-Soviet Rivalry*. Jefferson, NC: McFarland, 2017.

Regli, Fulvio. "Women." *Track & Field News*, August 1952, 21.

"Reigning Sensations in European Track: Mrs. Blankers-Koen." *Amateur Athlete*, February 1949, 8.

Rein, Raanan. "Turning the Country into an 'Immense and Clamorous Stadium': Perón, the New Argentina, and the 1951 Pan-American Games." *International Journal of the History of Sport* 33, nos. 1–2 (2016): 29–43.

Rider, Toby C. *Cold War Games: Propaganda, the Olympics, and U.S. Foreign Policy.* Urbana: University of Illinois Press, 2016.

Rider, Toby C., and Sarah Teetzel. "The Strange Tale of Stella Walsh's Olympic Eligibility." In *Intersections and Intersectionalities in Olympic and Paralympic Studies: The Proceedings of the Twelfth International Symposium for Olympic Research*, edited by Janice Forsyth, Christine O'Bonsawin, and Michael Heine, 18–23. London, ON: International Centre for Olympic Studies, 2014.

Rider, Toby C., and Kevin B. Witherspoon, eds. *Defending the American Way of Life: Sport, Culture, and the Cold War.* Fayetteville: University of Arkansas Press, 2018.

Roberts, Randy, and Johnny Smith. *A Season in the Sun: The Rise of Mickey Mantle.* New York: Basic Books, 2018.

Robinson, Jo Ann Gibson. *Montgomery Bus Boycott: Women Who Started It.* Knoxville: University of Tennessee Press, 1987.

Rodis, Nicholas. "The State Department's Athletes Give a New Look to Foreign Policy." *Amateur Athlete*, August 1964, 18, 36.

Rogin, Gilbert. "Flamin' Mamie's Bouffant Belles." *Sports Illustrated*, April 20, 1964, 30.

Rosen, Karen. "Recalling: Alice Coachman." Team USA. https://www.teamusa.org/News/2012/January/01/London-Re-Calling-Home/London-ReCalling-Series-Alice-Coachman. Last modified January 1, 2012.

Rudolph, Wilma, with Bud Greenspan. *Wilma.* New York: Signet, 1977.

Russell, Thaddeus. "The Color of Discipline." *American Quarterly* 60, no. 1 (March 2008): 101–128.

Salisbury, Tracey M. "First to the Finish: The Tennessee State Tigerbelles, 1944–1994." Ph.D. diss., University of North Carolina at Greensboro, 2009.

Sanicky, Marilyn K. "Girls Age Group Track." *Amateur Athlete*, November 1961, 18.

Schulman, Bruce J. *The Seventies: The Great Shift in American Culture, Society, and Politics.* New York: Simon and Schuster, 2001.

Schulman, Bruce J., and Julian E. Zelizer. *Rightward Bound: Making America Conservative in the 1970s.* Cambridge, MA: Harvard University Press, 2008.

Schultz, Jaime. "Going the Distance: The Road to the 1984 Olympic Women's Marathon." *International Journal of the History of Sport* 32, no. 1 (January 2015): 72–88.

———. *Qualifying Times: Points of Change in U.S. Women's Sport.* Urbana: University of Illinois Press, 2014.

Schwenk, Melinda. "'Negro Stars' and the USIA's Portrait of Democracy." *Race, Gender & Class* 8, no. 4 (October 2001): 116–139.

"Scorecard." *Sports Illustrated*, February 13, 1961, 8.

Sims, Yvonne D. "Florence Griffith Joyner: Sexual Politician in a Unitard." In *A Locker Room of Her Own: Celebrity, Sexuality, and Female Athletes*, edited by David C. Ogden and Joel Nathan Rosen, 146–161. Oxford: University Press of Mississippi, 2013.

Skilton, Sydney. "Women in Olympics." *Amateur Athlete*, February 1957, 22.

Smith, Maureen M., and Matthew R. Holder. "Pioneers in the Pool: The Santa Clara Swim Club Mermaids of the 1950s and 1960s." In *San Francisco Bay Area Sports*, edited by Rita Liberti and Maureen M. Smith, 143–164. Fayetteville: University of Arkansas Press, 2017.

Smith, Yvonne. "Women of Color in Society and Sport." *Quest* 44 (1992): 228–250.

Snow, Mary. "The Girls at Pocna City." *Sports Illustrated*, July 4, 1955, 17.

Sober, Pincus. "U.S. Track and Field Teams Compete in Moscow, Warsaw, Budapest, Athens." *Amateur Athlete*, September 1958, 5.

Solinger, Rickie. *Wake Up Little Susie: Single Pregnancy and Race before Roe v. Wade*. New York: Routledge, 1992.

Spencer, Nancy E. "'America's Sweetheart' and 'Czech-Mate': A Discursive Analysis of the Evert-Navratilova Rivalry." *Journal of Sport & Social Issues* 27, no. 1 (February 2003): 18–37.

Starr, Mae Faggs. "Mae Faggs Starr." In *Better than the Best: Black Athletes Speak, 1920–2007*, edited by John C. Walter and Malina Iida. Seattle: University of Washington Press, 2010.

Starts, H. Jamison. "Supplies and Equipment Committee." In Bushnell, *Report of the United States Olympic Committee*.

"State Dept. Lauds U.S. Pan-Am and Olympic Participation." *Amateur Athlete*, February 1951, 8.

Temple, Ed, with B'Lou Carter. *Only the Pure in Heart Survive*. Nashville, TN: Broadman Press, 1980.

Terrell, Roy. "The High Meet the Mighty." *Sports Illustrated*, July 24, 1961, 13–17.

———. "Very Good, Very Tired and Winners All the Way." *Sports Illustrated*, July 31, 1961, 12.

Thomas, Damion. "Around the World: Problematizing the Harlem Globetrotters as Cold War Warriors." *Sport in Society* 14, no. 6 (2011): 778–791.

———. *Globetrotting: African American Athletes and Cold War Politics*. Urbana: University of Illinois Press, 2012.

———. "Let the Games Begin: Sport, U.S. Race Relations, and Cold War Politics." *International Journal of the History of Sport* 24, no. 2 (2007): 157–171.

Tomlinson, Alan, and Christopher Young, eds. *National Identity and Global Sports Events: Culture, Politics, and Spectacle in the Olympics and Football World Cup*. Albany: State University of New York Press, 2006.

Tricard, Louise Mead. *American Women's Track and Field: A History, 1895 through 1980*. Vol. 1. Jefferson, NC: McFarland, 1996.

Tulis, Matt. "Who Was Stella Walsh? The Story of the Intersex Olympian." *SB Nation*, June 27, 2013. http://www.sbnation.com/longform/2013/6/27/4466724/stella-walsh-profile-intersex-olympian.

Tygiel, Jules. *Baseball's Great Experiment: Jackie Robinson and His Legacy*. New York: Oxford University Press, 1983.

Tyus, Wyomia. "Wyomia Tyus." In *Better than the Best: Black Athletes Speak, 1920–2007*, edited by John C. Walter and Malina Iida. Seattle: University of Washington Press, 2010.

Tyus, Wyomia, with Elizabeth Terzakis. *Tigerbelle: The Wyomia Tyus Story*. Brooklyn, NY: Akashic Books, 2018, 57.

Underwood, John. "This Is the Way the Girls Go." *Sports Illustrated*, May 10, 1965, 35.

"U.S. Girls Set Relay Mark." *Amateur Athlete*, August 1952, 7.

"U.S. Track Athletes Hailed in Africa." *Amateur Athlete*, June 1956, 15.

"U.S. Track Squad Awaits Russia Meet." *Amateur Athlete*, August 1958, 5.

"U.S.-U.S.S.R. Track Meet at Moscow Tops List of International Events." *Amateur Athlete*, January 1961, 11.

Verbrugge, Martha. *Active Bodies: A History of Women's Physical Education in Twentieth- Century America*. New York: Oxford University Press, 2012.

Vertinsky, Patricia, and Gwendolyn Captain. "More Myth than History: American Culture and Representations of the Black Female's Athletic Ability." *Journal of Sport History* 25, no. 3 (Fall 1998): 532–561.

Von Eschen, Penny. *Race against Empire: Black Americans and Anticolonialism, 1937–1957*. Ithaca, NY: Cornell University Press, 1997.

———. *Satchmo Blows Up: Jazz Ambassadors Play the Cold War*. Cambridge, MA: Harvard University Press, 2009.

Walter, John C., and Malina Iida, eds. *Better than the Best: Black Athletes Speak, 1920–2007*. Seattle: University of Washington Press, 2010.

"Want a Trip to Finland?" *Amateur Athlete*, December 1951, 11.

Ware, Susan. *Game, Set, Match: Billie Jean King and the Revolution in Women's Sports*. Chapel Hill: University of North Carolina Press, 2011.

"What's Wrong with Wilma?" *Jet*, June 28, 1962, 53.

White, C. Todd. *Pre-Gay L.A.: A Social History of the Movement for Homosexual Rights*. Urbana: University of Illinois Press, 2009.

"Wilma Loses 1962 Track Debut, Praises Winner." *Jet*, February 8, 1962, 55.

"Wilma Rudolph Seeks Divorce, Gets Italian Award." *Jet*, February 14, 1963, 14.

"Wilma Rudolph Stars as Tennessee State Wins Indoor Track." *Amateur Athlete*, May 1960, 11.

"Wilma Wins Sullivan Award." *Amateur Athlete*, January 1962, 5.

Witherspoon, Kevin B. "America's Team: The US Women's National Basketball Team Confronts the Soviets, 1958–1969." In Rider and Witherspoon, *Defending the American Way of Life*, 99–112.

———. "Going 'to the Fountainhead': Black American Athletes as Cultural Ambassadors in Africa, 1970–1971." *International Journal of the History of Sport* 30, no. 13 (2013): 1508–1522.

———. "'An Outstanding Representative of America': Mal Whitfield and America's Black Sports Ambassadors in Africa." In Rider and Witherspoon, *Defending the American Way of Life*, 129–140.

BIBLIOGRAPHY

"The Women." *Sports Illustrated*, November 19, 1956, 59.

"Women Athletes Return: Alice Coachman Ends Track Competition." *Norfolk New Journal and Guide*, September 4, 1948, 19.

"Women's Results." *Track & Field News*, August 1948, 7.

"Women's Title Track Meet to Be Held at Shaker Heights." *Amateur Athlete*, August 1957, 15.

"Women's Track Meet in Mass." *Amateur Athlete*, January 1961, 35.

"Women Track and Field Tryouts for Pan-Am." *Amateur Athlete*, February 1955, 14.

"Words of the Week." *Jet*, August 10, 1961, 30.

"Words of the Week." *Jet*, December 14, 1961, 30.

Wynn, Linda T. "Diane Judith Nash (1938–): A Mission for Equality, Justice, and Social Change." In Freeman and Bond, *Tennessee Women*, 281–304.

"Youth Movement at San Mateo." *Amateur Athlete*, June 1961, 16.

Zimmerman, Jonathan. "Beyond Double Consciousness: Black Peace Corps Volunteers in Africa, 1961–1971." *Journal of American History* 82, no. 3 (1995): 999–1028.

INDEX

AAU women's track and field committee: and ideal image of American woman athlete, 55, 66, 86, 166; and meets, 19, 51, 54, 104, 133; and support for women's track and field, 23, 65–66, 70. *See also* American Athletic Union (AAU)

Abbott, Cleveland (Cleve), 14–15, 45, 84

Afro-American, 32, 61, 68, 95; on Alice Coachman, 16, 17, 19, 36, 43; on 1951 Pan-American Games, 48, 50–51; on 1952 Olympics, 70, 76, 77; on 1956 US women's Olympic track team, 96, 107, 110; on Wilma Rudolph, 133, 152, 157, 159, 161; on Wilma Rudolph's femininity, 144, 160

agency, of black American women track athletes, 6, 7, 97, 155; Mae Faggs, 9, 83, 97–100, 102; resistance to, 37, 71, 78; Wilma Rudolph, 132, 151, 160, 164. *See also* entitlement, of black American women track athletes

Aguilar, Hugo, 93

Albany Herald, 41, 62

Albany State College, 22, 41

Ali, Muhammad, 172

"Alice Coachman Day," 37

All-American Girls' Baseball League, 171

Amateur Athlete, 56, 71, 104, 126, 157; editorials on women's track and field, 52, 53, 65, 70, 86; on 1952 Olympics, 71, 75; promotion of TSU Tigerbelles, 115, 121, 124, 126, 133; promotion of white women track athletes, 56, 166, 167

American Association for Health, Physical Education, and Recreation, Women's Advisory Board, 167

American Athletic Union (AAU), 8, 18; and black American women athletes, 13, 23, 87, 89, 103; and men's National Championships, 21; and US track and field duals and tours, 120–121, 152, 162; and women's track and field, 19, 23, 25, 90, 118–121, 153, 165–167. *See also* AAU women's track and field committee; National AAU Championships, women's

American Sports Specialist program, 157–158

American Way, 104, 128, 182n6; advertisement of, at Olympic Games, 28, 65; black women track athletes as representatives, 29, 47, 68, 74, 80; 1952 US women's, 400-meter relay team as representatives, 47, 68, 74, 80; Wilma Rudolph as representative, 128, 144, 163; TSU Tigerbelles as representatives, 86, 87, 102, 104, 116

Andersen, Roxy, 65–66, 70, 86, 104, 166

Anderson, Karen, 103–104

Armitage, Heather, 46, 81, 113
Associated Negro Press (ANP), 27, 93
Associated Press, 41, 142
Atlanta Constitution, 40
Atlanta Daily World, 22, 53, 95; on Alice
    Coachman, 36, 37, 41–42; on Mildred
    McDaniel, 106–107; on Wilma Rudolph,
    144, 146, 150
Australian women's track and field, 71–72,
    74–75, 105

Backus, Bob, 91
Bagrjanceva, Elizaveta, 72
Bair, RaNae, 168
Barrett, Edward W., 49
Beckett, Vinton, 32, 33
Belmonte, Laura, 28, 67, 118
Bingham, Lyman J., 54
Birmingham Black Barons, 64
black citizenship: Cold War and, 77, 82, 87;
    gendered view, 22, 27, 61–62, 78, 147, 160–
    161; male athletes as symbols, 4–5, 77–78,
    94, 172; relationship with black sport,
    22, 36, 40–45, 62, 172; Wilma Rudolph as
    symbol, 134, 146; state-sanctioned con-
    structions, 67; women as symbols, 82, 89;
    women track athletes as symbols, 43–45,
    62, 82–84, 106–107. *See also* civil rights
    movement; race men; race women
black middle class: expectations for women,
    14, 127–129, 134, 161; expectations for
    women track athletes, 61–62, 106, 123,
    155; gendered expectations for Alice
    Coachman, 17, 32; gendered expectations
    for Wilma Rudolph, 131, 145, 147, 161
Black Power, 172
Blankers-Koen, Fanny, 35, 71; image, 29–32,
    44, 51, 52, 105
Boeckman, Dolores, 23
Brown, Dr. Aaron, 41–42
Brown, Earlene, 105, 121, 126, 133; image,
    116, 123–127, 197n34
Brown, Vivian, 1–3, 149, 150, 153
Brown v. Board of Education, 87, 117
Brundage, Avery, 18, 25–26, 28, 49–50, 54

Cahn, Susan K., 171, 190n37

Campbell, Milt, 79
Carlos, John, 172–173
Carroll, Diahann, 141
Chicago American Giants, 64
Chicago Catholic Youth Organization
    (CYO), 58, 69, 89
Chicago Comets, 89
Chicago Defender, 27, 78, 121, 123, 138; on
    Alice Coachman, 36, 41, 42; on Mae Faggs,
    97, 100; on femininity of women athletes,
    27, 96; on Barbara Jones, 92, 94–95; on
    Jean Patton, 60–62; on Wilma Rudolph,
    144, 161
Chicago Tribune, 110
Chudina, Aleksandra, 72, 93
civil rights movement: Cold War and, 77, 82,
    86, 103; respectability politics, 87, 107,
    145; role of women, 82, 89, 94, 107, 147.
    See also race men; race women
Coachman, Alice, 3, 12–15, 86; National
    AAU Championships, 16, 22–23; 1948
    Olympic Games, 26, 28–29, 32–36, 105;
    Olympic homecoming celebrations,
    36, 39–42, 62, 106; as representative of
    black womanhood, 15, 17, 27, 36–37, 95;
    self-conception, 37–39; as touchstone for
    black American women's track, 45, 48, 52,
    68, 173; in US-Canada duals, 12, 18–21,
    24, 56; White House visit, 43–45, 50
Cold War: cultural anxieties in US society
    during, 52, 70, 186n99, 187n128; gender
    and race in US society during, 69, 71, 75,
    79–80, 88, 190n31; influence on civil rights
    movement, 7, 77, 82, 86, 103. *See also* pro-
    paganda: Cold War; sporting Cold War
Connolly, Harold, 125
Connolly, Olga Fikotová, 125–27
Cooper, Brittney, 4, 7
Cowans, Russ, 27
Cowperthwaite(-Phillips), Nancy, 12, 19, 56
Cox, Aimee Meredith, 99
Craig, Maxine, 14, 78, 128, 134, 147, 161
Cripps, Winsome, 46, 75
Crooks, Mabel, 107
Crowder, Shirley, 133
Crowther, Bertha, 33
Culbreath, Josh, 92

INDEX

Cummings, Thomas, 62
Cuthbert, Betty, 81, 105–106, 112, 113

Daily Graphic, 104
Dandridge, Dorothy, 141
Daniels, Billie Pat, 153, 155, 167
Daniels, Isabelle, 108, 125; *Amateur Athlete* cover, 115–116; National AAU Championships, 91, 100; 1955 Pan-American Games, 92–93; 1956 Olympics, 80–81, 95–96, 105, 111, 113; 1958 US-Soviet Union dual, 120, 122; 1959 Pan-American Games, 132
Danzig, Allison, 31, 35, 72, 74
Davis, Margaret, 90, 91
Davis, W. S., 62
Decker, Mary, 171
democracy, symbols of: black male athletes as, 67, 88, 118, 159; black women athletes as, due to Cold War, 6, 87, 116–117, 123; black women athletes as, due to gendering, 24, 106, 125, 127; Mae Faggs as, 103–104; Wilma Rudolph as, 141–147, 153, 156–159, 162, 169; and sport, 18, 42, 47, 49–50, 79
Dicks, Janet, 69
Dillard, Harrison, 36, 43–44, 77–78, 79, 159
Doby, Larry, 88
dos Santos, Wanda, 59
double burden, 87, 103, 157, 174
Double V campaign, 13, 44
Drake Relays, 152
Dredge, Doreen, 33
Dudziak, Mary, 77, 86
Dulles, John Foster, 125
Dumbadze, Nina, 72
Dunham, Katherine, 67
Dwyer, Dolores, 58, 60, 69

Ebony, 146
Edwards, Harry, 172
El Gráfico, 58
Ellison, Jeanne, 169
Ellison, Margaret, 168–169, 170
entitlement, of black American women track athletes, 83, 97, 99, 108–109, 155. *See also* agency, of black American women track athletes
Evert, Chris, 171

Ewell, Barney, 43

Faggs, Mae, 3, 69, 114, 125, 155; entitlement, 98–99, 108–109, 114; as goodwill ambassador, 103–104; and National AAU Championships, 68, 100–101; 1948 Olympics, 26, 28; 1952 Olympics, 45, 46–47, 71, 73–77, 80; 1955 Pan-American Games, 90–93; 1956 Olympics, 81–82, 95–96, 105, 113; as TSU Tigerbelle, 83, 90, 97, 100–102
Fawcett, Farrah, 171
Feldstein, Ruth, 153
"feminine bargain," 171
femininity, 177n11; anxieties about racialized, 31, 44, 119, 122, 125–127, 190–191n37; black women track athletes' performance of, 15, 61, 89, 106, 115–119, 124–127; Alice Coachman's performance of, 17, 36–37; Wilma Rudolph's performance of, 134, 140–147, 159, 168, 171; TSU Tigerbelles performance of, 83–87, 96, 107; and whiteness, 29–32, 86, 125–127, 168–171. *See also* Temple Way
Ferris, Daniel J., 157; race and men's track and field, 21, 178n36; women's track and field, 19, 23–26
Flamin' Mamie's Bouffant Belles, 168–169
Fleetwood, Nicole, 11
Fonda, Jane, 171
Fort Valley State College, 69, 74

Garrett, Lula, 61, 144, 160
Geary, Kay, 12
Gibson, Althea, 191n37, 193n98
Gilmore, Glenda, 7
Good Neighbor Policy, 49
Gordon, Annie, 98
Gráfico, El, 58
Gray, James H., 41, 62

Hainsworth, Harry, 27
Hall, Evelyne, 53, 54–55, 59, 166
Hardy, Catherine, 45; national championships and meets, 68–69; 1952 Olympics, 46–47, 71, 73–76, 80
Harlem Globetrotters, 67
Harris, Elmore, 20

Harrison, Claude, 120, 148, 152
Hartsfield, William B., 37, 107
Heine, Jutta, 136
Helsinki Olympic Games (1952), 46–47, 64–65, 71–76, 79–80
heteronormativity, American: and citizenship, 6, 117–118, 128, 131, 174; performance of, by black Americans, 61–62, 123, 147; performance of, by black women track athletes, 107, 119, 125, 127, 155
Holmes, Jean, 160
Horne, Lena, 141, 146
HUAC (House Un-American Activities Committee), 77
Hudson, Martha, 100, 122, 133, 137, 138
Hyman, Dorothy, 136

individualism, black women athletes as representatives of, 142, 147, 153, 156
International Amateur Athletic Federation, 165
International Olympic Committee (IOC), 18, 136, 165
Itkina, Mariya, 1–2

Jackson, Marion E., 41, 42, 95, 107, 146, 150
Jackson, Marjorie, 46, 52–53, 71–72, 75, 92
Jackson, Nell, 37, 52, 60, 61; 1948 Olympics, 26, 28; 1951 Pan-American Games, 47, 56–59; White House visit, 43–44
James, Sidney L., 169
James E. Sullivan Award, 158–159, 167
"Jean Patton Day" 63–64
Jet, 144, 145, 151, 161
Johnson, Lyndon B., 142
Johnson, Rafer, 88, 118, 159
Jones, Barbara, 3; Amateur Athlete cover, 115–116; 1952 Olympics, 45, 46–47, 69, 73–77, 80; 1955 Pan-American Games, 82, 91–95; 1960 Olympics, 133, 137–138; US-USSR duals, 120, 132
Jones, Lou, 92
Joyner, Florence Griffith, 174
Joyner-Kersee, Jackie, 174
juvenile delinquency, 52, 70

Kazsubski, Frances, 86, 90, 102–103, 133, 166

Kennedy, John F., 45, 143
King, Billie Jean, 171
King, Martin Luther, Jr., 40, 61, 87, 158
Krepkina, Vera, 120

Lacy, Sam: on black male track athletes, 77–78; on Alice Coachman, 16, 17; on Wilma Rudolph, 152, 159–60; on US women's Olympic track and field, 68, 95
Ladies Home Journal, 142
Landry, Mabel, 56, 69, 92, 93
Larney, Marjorie, 69
Latimer, Elihu, 61–62
Lawler, Evelyn, 47, 52, 56–57, 59–60, 61
Liberti, Rita, 124, 141, 197n34
Life, 39–40
Lipsyte, Robert, 141
Little Rock Central High School, 117
London Olympic Games (1948), 18, 28–35
Los Angeles Coliseum Relays, 51–54, 75
Los Angeles Invitational, 148–149, 160

Madame Tussauds, 139, 164
Major League Baseball, 13, 77, 88
Mantle, Mickey, 88
masculinity: blackness and, 67, 77–78, 88; Cold War and, 70, 77, 79; whiteness and, 44, 88, 124, 125
Mason-Dixon Games, 150
Mathias, Bob, 44
Matthews, Margaret, 126–127; Amateur Athlete cover, 115–116; Atlanta celebration, 106–107; 1956 Olympics, 81, 96, 105, 110; 1958 US-USSR dual, 120, 122
Mayor Daley Youth Foundation, 163; track and field team, 156
McDaniel, Mildred, 3, 125; Atlanta celebration, 106–107; 1955 Pan-American Games, 82, 92–93, 95; 1956 Olympics, 105–106
McGuire, Edith, 2, 153, 167, 172
McNabb, Mary, 69
Melbourne Olympic Games (1956), 104–106, 108–114, 123, 125
Meyer, Catherine, 19, 24–26, 52, 53, 55, 70
Millheiser, Eleanor, 12, 19
Millrose Games, 148, 149

Monsanto, Patricia, 100
Montgomery Bus Boycott, 89
Moreau, Janet, 46–47, 58, 69, 73–76, 80
Morris, Earl, 93
Morrow, Bobby, 88, 105
Moses, Al, 78
motherhood, race and, 29–30, 128–131, 152, 163
Mulder, Marie, 169–170
Murray, James, 149
Musel, Robert, 121

Nash, Diane, 145
Nashville Black Cubs, 64
Nashville Student Movement, 145
Nashville Vols, 64
National AAU Championships, women's, 85; 1940s, 16, 19, 21–22, 52; 1950 Outdoor, 55; 1951 Indoor, 74; 1952 Outdoor, 69; 1953 Indoor and Outdoor, 97; 1955 Indoor, 89–90; 1955 Outdoor, 100–103; 1956 Outdoor, 95–96, 108; 1957 Outdoor, 126; 1958 Outdoor, 115; 1959 Outdoor, 132; 1960s, 150, 152, 165–167
National Association for the Advancement of Colored People (NAACP), 77, 146
National Institutes on Girls' Sports, 167
National Negro Press Association, 27
New York Amsterdam News, 39, 76, 94; Wilma Rudolph, 144, 146, 148, 149
New York Athletic Club, 149, 159
New Yorker, 30
New York Pioneers, 21
New York Times, 20, 105, 124, 125; on black American women track athletes at the Pan-American Games, 58, 59, 91, 93; on Fanny Blankers-Koen, 31, 51, 52; on 1948 US women's Olympic track and field team, 23, 26, 31; on 1952 US women's Olympic track and field team, 69, 73, 74; on Wilma Rudolph's athletic performances, 133, 140, 149, 150, 153–154; on Wilma Rudolph's femininity, 141, 142, 150, 153, 155; on US-USSR duals, 120, 121, 162; on white women track athletes, 35, 71, 72, 165
Norford, Thomasina, 144
Norton, Ray, 144

O'Brien, Parry, 124
Olympic Movement, 28, 47, 64
Olympic Project for Human Rights, 172
O'Neal, Lacey, 153
Ostermeyer, Micheline, 33
Owens, Horace, 51, 52

Pan-American Games: 1951, Buenos Aires, 47–51, 54, 56–59; 1955, Mexico City, 82, 83, 87, 90–95; 1959, Chicago, 132
Panter-Downes, Mollie, 30
Paris World Peace Conference (1949), 77
Parks, Rosa, 82, 89
paternalism, toward black American women track athletes, 84, 97–100, 118, 129, 161
Patterson, Audrey "Mickey," 22–24, 26–28; 1948 Olympics, 30–32, 36, 180n60; White House visit, 43–44
Patterson, Floyd, 88
Patton, Jean, 3, 47, 65, 68, 78, 86; Los Angeles Coliseum Relays, 52–54, 75; Nashville celebration, 63–64, 106; 1951 Pan-American Games, 56–57, 58–60; United Nations, 60–62
Patton, Mel, 44
Perón, Eva, 57
Perón, Juan, 57
Petersen, Marga, 46
Philadelphia Tribune, 38, 61, 78, 94, 95, 110; quotes Ed Temple, 85, 120, 132; on Wilma Rudolph, 134, 144, 148, 151, 152, 161
Phipps, Carmen, 32
Pickett, Tidye, 17
Pieper, Lindsay Parks, 122, 171
Pittsburgh Courier, 36, 44, 53
Police Athletic League (PAL), 26, 58, 68–69
Pollards, Ernestine, 133, 137
Popova, Galina, 1
Press, Tamara, 121
propaganda: black American women track athletes, 87, 90, 103, 116–117, 127, 167; Cold War, 28, 66, 67, 118, 185n80; Wilma Rudolph, 136, 138, 153–154, 156, 158, 162; sport, 47 49, 64, 67, 87, 93; white American women track athletes, 119, 125
Purifoy, Lillie, 19

race men, black athletes as, 22, 36, 62, 93
race women, black athletes as, 22, 82, 93–95, 99, 106–107
Reed, Emma, 26, 28, 32, 43, 44
Remigino, Lindy, 79
Richard, Rod, 91
Richards, Bob, 79
Rider, Toby C., 49
Rinehart, Janis, 169
Robeson, Paul, 77
Robichaux, Joe, 89, 104
Robichaux, Josephine, 104
Robinson, Bernice, 28, 32
Robinson, Jackie, 13, 77, 88
Rogers, Neomia, 133
Rogin, Gilbert, 168–169
Romaschkova, Nina, 72
Rome Olympic Games (1960), 124, 127, 134–138, 144, 155
Roth, Edwin, 33
Rudolph, Wilma: as American Sports Specialist, 157–158; attitude about athletic experience, 108–109, 114, 154, 160, 163–164; burdens of fame, 139–140, 148, 150–151, 161; image of all-Americanness, 116, 127, 142–143, 152–153, 158–159, 162–163; image of black athletic womanhood, 45, 80, 134, 144–147; image of femininity, 124, 141–142, 160, 197n34; influence on ideology of women's sport, 165–174; National AAU championships, 132–133, 166; national track meets, 148–150; 1956 Olympics, 81, 83, 96, 105, 108–113; 1960 Olympics, 134–138; 1961 international track meets, 152–157; 1962 US-USSR dual, 1–4, 162–163; pregnancy and motherhood, 127–131, 152
Russell, Thaddeus, 61

Sánchez, Julia, 58
San Mateo Girls' Athletic Association, 167
Santee, Wes, 88
Schultz, Jaime, 55
Shchelkanova, Tatyana, 3, 154
Sheehan, Joseph, 20, 162
Shipley, Helen, 165–167
Smith, James, 40–41
Smith, Janell, 167, 168, 169–170
Smith, Maureen M., 124, 141, 197n34
Smith, Tommie, 172–173
Sober, Pincus, 148
Southern Christian Leadership Conference, 40, 87
Soviet Union: criticism of the United States, 82, 87, 103, 116, 158; Olympics, 64, 73; women track and field athletes, 70, 72–73, 118, 120–122, 154. See also US–Soviet Union (USA-USSR) dual track and field meets
sporting Cold War: black American male athletes, 77–78, 118; black American women athletes and Pan-American Games, 51, 87, 91, 93; black American women athletes and US-USSR duals, 1, 116–123; black American women track athletes and Olympics, 47, 65–70, 76, 80; ideology, 46–47, 49–50, 73, 77–78, 82; Wilma Rudolph, 152–158, 162
Sports Illustrated, 100, 105, 156, 168, 169; Wilma Rudolph's appeal and image, 1, 140, 141, 142, 162; Wilma Rudolph's athletic performances, 149, 151, 153, 154
State Department, U.S.: black athletes as cultural ambassadors, 67, 87–89, 103–104, 118, 157–158; involvement in American sport, 49, 54, 117
Stewart, Ollie, 32
Stockholm Olympic Games (1928), women's 800-meter race, 92, 165
Stokes, Louise, 17
Strickland (de la Hunty), Shirley, 30, 72
Student Non-Violent Coordinating Committee, 40
Sulphur Dell Park, 63–64

Talley, Gladys, 52
Temple, Edward S. (Ed), 189n9; and Mae Faggs, 97, 99–100; 1956 US women's Olympic track and field team, 82, 96; 1958 US-USSR dual, 118–122; 1960 US women's Olympic track and field team, 138, 151; 1964 US-USSR dual, 168; and Wilma

INDEX

Rudolph, 108, 127, 129–132, 134–135, 146; and TSU administration, 101–102; and TSU Tigerbelles, 45, 83–85, 89, 155

Temple Way, 83; image, 87, 102; performance, 86, 94, 103, 127, 172; rules and restrictions, 84–85, 123

Tennessean, 53

Tennessee State University (TSU), 62–63, 83, 99, 129; athletic department, 97–98, 101–102

Terrell, Roy, 157

Terry, Jo Ann, 157

Texas Track Club, 168–169

Thomas, Damion, 67, 118

Till, Emmett, 88, 110

Track & Field News, 71, 72

Truman, Harry S., 43–45, 50

Truman Doctrine, 50

TSU Tigerbelles: expectations, 45, 83, 85–86, 97; as National AAU Championships, 90, 97, 100–102, 132; and Olympics, 26, 81–82, 107, 138; performance of femininity by, 115–116, 123–125; US-USSR duals, 120–122, 153

Turner, Ella Mae, 100

Tuskegee Institute, 14–15, 99, 102, 105

Tuskegee Relays, 14, 52, 98

Tuskegee Tigerettes: expectations of, 15, 45, 83–84, 125; and Los Angeles Coliseum Relays, 52–53; and National AAU Championships, 19, 55, 56; and Olympics, 26–27, 105

Tyler, Dorothy, 32–33, 35

Tyus, Wyomia, 10, 84–85, 100, 170, 172

United Nations, 18, 60–62

United States Information Association (USIA), 28, 66–67, 103, 104, 142

United States Olympic Committee (USOC): and black women track athletes at Olympics, 25–26, 35–36, 68; and black women track athletes at Pan-American Games, 48, 54–55, 59, 89–91; ideology about black women track athletes, 13, 44, 50–51, 60, 87; ideology about women's track and field, 28–29, 57, 70–71, 86, 167; women's track and field committee, 54–55, 65, 86,

166; and women's track and field teams at Olympics, 24–26, 65, 73, 155

University of California–Los Angeles (UCLA), 159, 163

US-Canada dual track and field meets, 12, 18–19, 24

US–Soviet Union (USA-USSR) dual track and field meets: 1958 Moscow, 117–124, 127; 1959 Chicago, 132; 1961 Moscow, 152–154; 1962 Palo Alto, 1–3, 162–163; 1963 US women's team, 170; 1964 US women's team, 168

US Women's Olympic track and field, 17; 1948 team, 27–29; 1948 tryouts, 24–27; 1952 team, 69, 71, 73–75, 78; 1952 trials, 68–69; 1956 team, 81–82, 96, 105, 107, 112–113; 1956 trials, 96, 108, 123–124; 1960 team, 133–134, 137–138, 155; 1960 trials, 133; 1964 trials, 168

Verbrugge, Martha, 15

Voice of America, 103

Von Eschen, Penny, 67

Walker, Mabel, 26–28, 37, 43, 44

Walsh, Stella, 12, 22–23, 101, 177n12; rivalry with Alice Coachman, 12, 16–17

Walter, Paula, 169

Ward, William, 144–145, 151–152, 161

West, Ben, 145

White, Willye: agentic experiences and attitude, 100, 102, 108, 110–112, 114; identity, 155–156; in international track meets, 2, 126, 153, 155, 156; in Olympics, 96, 105, 112–113, 133, 155

white racial anxieties, 41, 44, 88, 117

Whitfield, Mal, 43, 79, 159; as goodwill ambassador, 88, 118; as race man, 36, 58, 62, 78

Wilkie, Louis G., 90, 91

Wilkins, Roy, 146

Williams, Lucinda, 96, 100, 132; *Amateur Athlete* cover, 115–116; in 1958 US-USSR dual, 120–122; in 1960 Olympics, 133, 137–138

Williams, Mary Lou, 67

229

INDEX

Williamson, Audrey, 30, 31
Wilma Rudolph: Olympic Champion (film), 142
Witherspoon, Kevin, 119
Women in the United States (leaflet), 66

Yancey, Joe, 21

Yang, CK, 159
Young, Fay, 78, 96, 97, 102, 123
Young, Lillian, 19, 28

Zátopková, Dana, 72–73
Zybina, Galina, 121

CAT M. ARIAIL is a lecturer in the Department of History at Middle Tennessee State University.

SPORT AND SOCIETY

A Sporting Time: New York City and the Rise of Modern Athletics, 1820–70
   Melvin L. Adelman
Sandlot Seasons: Sport in Black Pittsburgh   *Rob Ruck*
West Ham United: The Making of a Football Club   *Charles Korr*
Beyond the Ring: The Role of Boxing in American Society   *Jeffrey T. Sammons*
John L. Sullivan and His America   *Michael T. Isenberg*
Television and National Sport: The United States and Britain   *Joan M. Chandler*
The Creation of American Team Sports: Baseball and Cricket, 1838–72
   George B. Kirsch
City Games: The Evolution of American Urban Society and the Rise of Sports
   Steven A. Riess
The Brawn Drain: Foreign Student-Athletes in American Universities   *John Bale*
The Business of Professional Sports   *Edited by Paul D. Staudohar and James A. Mangan*
Fritz Pollard: Pioneer in Racial Advancement   *John M. Carroll*
A View from the Bench: The Story of an Ordinary Player on a Big-Time Football Team
   (*formerly* Go Big Red! The Story of a Nebraska Football Player)   *George Mills*
Sport and Exercise Science: Essays in the History of Sports Medicine
   Edited by Jack W. Berryman and Roberta J. Park
Minor League Baseball and Local Economic Development   *Arthur T. Johnson*
Harry Hooper: An American Baseball Life   *Paul J. Zingg*
Cowgirls of the Rodeo: Pioneer Professional Athletes   *Mary Lou LeCompte*
Sandow the Magnificent: Eugen Sandow and the Beginnings of Bodybuilding
   David Chapman
Big-Time Football at Harvard, 1905: The Diary of Coach Bill Reid
   Edited by Ronald A. Smith
Leftist Theories of Sport: A Critique and Reconstruction   *William J. Morgan*
Babe: The Life and Legend of Babe Didrikson Zaharias   *Susan E. Cayleff*
Stagg's University: The Rise, Decline, and Fall of Big-Time Football at Chicago
   Robin Lester
Muhammad Ali, the People's Champ   *Edited by Elliott J. Gorn*
People of Prowess: Sport, Leisure, and Labor in Early Anglo-America   *Nancy L. Struna*
The New American Sport History: Recent Approaches and Perspectives
   Edited by S. W. Pope
Making the Team: The Cultural Work of Baseball Fiction   *Timothy Morris*
Making the American Team: Sport, Culture, and the Olympic Experience
   Mark Dyreson
Viva Baseball! Latin Major Leaguers and Their Special Hunger   *Samuel O. Regalado*
Touching Base: Professional Baseball and American Culture in the Progressive Era
   (rev. ed.)   *Steven A. Riess*
Red Grange and the Rise of Modern Football   *John M. Carroll*
Golf and the American Country Club   *Richard J. Moss*
Extra Innings: Writing on Baseball   *Richard Peterson*
Global Games   *Maarten Van Bottenburg*
The Sporting World of the Modern South   *Edited by Patrick B. Miller*

Female Gladiators: Gender, Law, and Contact Sport in America   *Sarah K. Fields*

The End of Baseball As We Knew It: The Players Union, 1960–81   *Charles P. Korr*

Rocky Marciano: The Rock of His Times   *Russell Sullivan*

Saying It's So: A Cultural History of the Black Sox Scandal   *Daniel A. Nathan*

The Nazi Olympics: Sport, Politics, and Appeasement in the 1930s
   Edited by Arnd Krüger and William Murray

The Unlevel Playing Field: A Documentary History of the African American Experience
   in Sport   *David K. Wiggins and Patrick B. Miller*

Sports in Zion: Mormon Recreation, 1890–1940   *Richard Ian Kimball*

Sweet William: The Life of Billy Conn   *Andrew O'Toole*

Sports in Chicago   *Edited by Elliot J. Gorn*

The Chicago Sports Reader   *Edited by Steven A. Riess and Gerald R. Gems*

College Football and American Culture in the Cold War Era   *Kurt Edward Kemper*

The End of Amateurism in American Track and Field   *Joseph M. Turrini*

Benching Jim Crow: The Rise and Fall of the Color Line in Southern College Sports,
   1890–1980   *Charles H. Martin*

Pay for Play: A History of Big-Time College Athletic Reform   *Ronald A. Smith*

Globetrotting: African American Athletes and Cold War Politics   *Damion L. Thomas*

Cheating the Spread: Gamblers, Point Shavers, and Game Fixers in College Football
   and Basketball   *Albert J. Figone*

The Sons of Westwood: John Wooden, UCLA, and the Dynasty That Changed
   College Basketball   *John Matthew Smith*

Qualifying Times: Points of Change in U.S. Women's Sport   *Jaime Schultz*

NFL Football: A History of America's New National Pastime   *Richard C. Crepeau*

Marvin Miller, Baseball Revolutionary   *Robert F. Burk*

I Wore Babe Ruth's Hat: Field Notes from a Life in Sports   *David W. Zang*

Changing the Playbook: How Power, Profit, and Politics Transformed College
   Sports   *Howard P. Chudacoff*

Team Chemistry: The History of Drugs and Alcohol in Major League Baseball
   Nathan Michael Corzine

Wounded Lions: Joe Paterno, Jerry Sandusky, and the Crises in Penn State
   Athletics   *Ronald A. Smith*

Sex Testing: Gender Policing in Women's Sports   *Lindsay Parks Pieper*

Cold War Games: Propaganda, the Olympics, and U.S. Foreign Policy   *Toby C. Rider*

Game Faces: Sport Celebrity and the Laws of Reputation   *Sarah K. Fields*

The Rise and Fall of Olympic Amateurism   *Matthew P. Llewellyn and John Gleaves*

Bloomer Girls: Women Baseball Pioneers   *Debra A. Shattuck*

I Fight for a Living: Boxing and the Battle for Black Manhood, 1880–1915   *Louis Moore*

The Revolt of the Black Athlete: 50th Anniversary Edition   *Harry Edwards*

Pigskin Nation: How the NFL Remade American Politics   *Jesse Berrett*

Hockey: A Global History   *Stephen Hardy and Andrew C. Holman*

Baseball: A History of America's Game   *Benjamin G. Rader*

Kansas City vs. Oakland: The Bitter Sports Rivalry That Defined an Era
   Matthew C. Ehrlich

The Gold in the Rings: The People and Events That Transformed the Olympic
   Games   *Stephen R. Wenn and Robert K. Barney*

Before March Madness: The Wars for the Soul of College Basketball
  Kurt Edward Kemper
The Sport Marriage: Women Who Make It Work   *Steven M. Ortiz*
NFL Football: A History of America's New National Pastime, NFL Centennial
  Edition   *Richard C. Crepeau*
Passing the Baton: Black Women Track Stars and American Identity   *Cat M. Ariail*

REPRINT EDITIONS
The Nazi Olympics   *Richard D. Mandell*
Sports in the Western World (2d ed.)   *William J. Baker*
Jesse Owens: An American Life   *William J. Baker*

The University of Illinois Press
is a founding member of the
Association of University Presses.

———————————————

University of Illinois Press
1325 South Oak Street
Champaign, IL 61820-6903
www.press.uillinois.edu